# Developing courses for students

**Other Paul Chapman Publishing books by Derek Rowntree:**
Educational Technology in Curriculum Development
*(second edition)*
1—85396—040—3

# Developing Courses for Students

Derek Rowntree
*Professor of Educational Development*
*The Open University*

P·C·P
Paul Chapman
Publishing Ltd

Copyright © 1981 Derek Rowntree

First published 1981 by McGraw-Hill Book
Company (UK) Ltd

This edition published 1985 by Harper & Row Ltd

Reprinted by
Paul Chapman Publishing Ltd
144 Liverpool Road
London N1 1LA

**British Library Cataloguing in Publication Data**

Rowntree, Derek
  Developing courses for students.
  1. Education — Curricula
  I. Title
  371.3     LB17

  ISBN 1—85396—120—5

Printed and bound by Athenæum Press Ltd,
Gateshead, Tyne & Wear

C D E F  8 7 6 5

# Contents

# Dedication

This book is dedicated to the development of courses that are both more demanding and more rewarding than the one in which the student quoted below seems to believe himself to be engaged:

'Oh, I didn't think about this problem. I just bashed the numbers out. I went straight through it without looking back at anything. I wasn't really interested but, well, you've got to do this stuff. In this sort of problem you've just got to get through to the answer. I find it pretty dull doing it this way so I don't spend long on it.

I've got these notes, from the lectures. These ones aren't too bad, but you often miss things, and can't make head or tail of them afterwards. You don't need to read the books—provided you get it all down you can't go wrong. It's getting it all down that's the problem. But here it was O.K. You just have to more or less get the right formula and bung the figures in.

Provided you get it right you're O.K., you'll get enough marks. It's the safest way really, to pass the course. For the exam I'm banking on recognizing the same sort of problems—then you can just trot it out. Easy. If it's something you've never done before you don't stand a chance. Bit hit-and-miss. Scary, really.

I only need a pass 'cos I've got this job lined up, or at least I hope I have. I never thought I'd come to see things like that, you know, I sort of expected it to be different to school, more interesting, even exciting, but you soon have to get down to it. If you work hard enough you'll get by. Some of the others seem to read the books and discuss it and things, but it's not really on, discussing it over coffee, is it? I bet they'll fail.'

(from Gibbs *et al.*, 1980a)

# Preface

I have written this book principally for teachers in post-secondary education, who are producing courses in colleges, polytechnics and universities. As it happens, much of its content will be relevant also to teachers in the later years of secondary school. My intention is not to give a theoretical discourse on further and higher education nor is it to summarize the research findings on such education. That has already been well done elsewhere (Beard *et al.*, 1978; Beard, 1979; Bligh, 1975). Rather my intention is to lay before you and discuss a number of approaches to, and issues in, course development. I will be dealing with the strategy of course development rather than the tactics, that is, discussing such issues as when to use lectures rather than, say, self-teaching materials, as opposed to advising how to give better lectures (or produce self-teaching materials). The tactical issues also are well covered elsewhere, e.g., Brown, 1978; Harris, 1979; Lewis and Jones, 1980; UTMU, 1976; Rowntree and Connors, 1, Yorke, 1981.

This is in no sense a step-by-step 'how to do it' handbook, but I hope that it will spark off flashes of illumination—striking different dark areas in different readers—which may encourage and enable you to look anew at course development. I will be discussing many techniques and approaches. Not all will appeal to every reader, and those that do may become extensively modified in being put to the reader's use. This is to be expected. In short, my intention is not to urge *the* one best way of course development (there is none) but to help you reappraise what might be the best way(s) for you.

As you will see from the contents list, I have isolated eight main areas in which course developers need to make decisions:

- Courses and constraints
- Developers
- Students
- Course content (including objectives)
- Structure and sequence
- Teaching methods and media
- Student assessment
- Course evaluation

Now I am *not* suggesting that these are the only areas in which decisions are made during course development. For example, what about the decision as to whether the course should be mounted at all? Nor am I suggesting that decisions should be taken about the areas in the order I have listed them. One may well form quite definite ideas about, say, how students are to be assessed, before deciding on the detailed content of the course.

Indeed, we could commence the development of a course by having ideas, and making tentative decisions, about any of the eight areas. But, wherever we start, we need to visit each of the other areas quite early in our deliberations. It will be impossible to get far in thinking about any single area (e.g., course structure and sequence) without raising questions or making assumptions about other areas (e.g., content or assessment). Furthermore, we should expect our deliberations to be *cyclical*. We should always be looking back to areas considered earlier in order to reassess our tentative decisions in the light of our more recent considerations of another area. Also, different course developers are likely to choose different areas to begin thinking about and, thereafter, take different routes through the remaining areas of consideration and decision.

That being so, I would not like you to feel obliged to read through the chapters in the order in which they are printed in this book. Perhaps Chapter 1 is a sensible place to start because it sets the context for course development. But later chapters can be read in any order you wish. If assessment seems to you the key issue, that is where you will want to begin, and going on from there perhaps to content or to methods and media, or whatever is your choice. To allow such flexibility I have tried to ensure that no chapter depends on ideas developed in any other. This means that, occasionally, ideas have been repeated in more than one chapter. Alternatively, where I have referred to ideas developed in other chapters, you should find no trouble in tracking them down, if necessary, with the help of the index.

## Acknowledgements

This book owes more than any other I have written to the discussions I have had with my colleagues in the Open University, and especially in the Institute of Educational Technology, over the last ten years. Many of the examples I quote are drawn from their work. In particular, my approach in certain chapters has been appreciably influenced by the thinking and writing that

Clive Lawless, Roger Harrison, and I did together a couple of years ago while collaborating on an Open University course about the production of learning materials. I was aware of Clive Lawless's influence chiefly in Chapters 2 and 4, and of Roger Harrison's in Chapters 2 and 5. Also, my colleagues Brian Lewis and David Hawkridge will find some of their thinking reflected in Chapters 2 and 6, respectively; and I am grateful for the comments of my colleague Alistair Morgan which influenced me in Chapter 1 and elsewhere. As always, despite my recognition of contributory ideas and influences, for the manner in which they have been brought together, assimilated to my own reflections upon experience, and articulated as an individual overview of course development, I bear all the responsibility.

Derek Rowntree

# 1. Courses, developers, and students

## What is a course?

Courses come in all shapes and sizes. The term 'course' can apply to three or four related lessons or sessions or to a whole degree programme lasting several years. Essentially, we are talking about a sequence of structured learning with a time interval between each session and the next. It may occupy the student part time or full time for half a term, a whole term or two, or two semesters, or two years (part time), and so on.

Perhaps a course stands on its own, e.g., a six-day course bringing nurses up to date on, say, the treatment of mentally disturbed patients. Or it may be part of a programme of studies aiming towards a formal qualification, e.g., a service course in statistics for engineers. At the Open University, the standard course represents one-sixth of a degree (one-eighth of an honours degree) and is meant to provide about 12 hours of work per week for the 32 weeks of the academic year. There are also 'half courses' supposedly demanding half that amount of student work over the same time period. And, in the continuing education area we have 'short courses' in such subjects as *The Handicapped Person in the Community* or *Governing Schools* or *Energy in the Home*, that may demand a total of only, say, 40 hours of study. As I write these words, I am teaching a summer course at Concordia University, Montreal, consisting of nine three-hour sessions spread over four and a half weeks. At other times of the year the 'same' course, while occupying the same total class time, is spread over 13 weeks.

You will know what counts as a course in your own institution. Maybe, like the Open University, you will have courses of various lengths. The ideas I discuss in this book will be relevant whatever the length. Indeed, you may think that many of them are relevant also to the design of a single lesson or session *within* a course.

## On-campus versus distance courses

The ideas we discuss should be equally relevant whether you are thinking of a 'distance education' course, or of a course 'on campus'. By distance education I mean a system in which the student does the bulk of his learning from pre-prepared teaching

**1**

materials and has very little face-to-face contact with tutors. He may or may not have occasional contact with other students. The pre-prepared teaching materials can vary all the way from standard textbooks, plus a study guide written by his 'distance teacher', through to integrated multimedia packages of the kind made famous by the Open University.

With on-campus courses we usually think of lectures, seminars and tutorials, practicals, assigned reading, and so on. Theoretically, this implies regular contact with a teacher, and certainly with other students. But, especially in large classes, students often report feelings of anonymity and lack of regular personal feedback that might seem more redolent of distance education. They do, however, have the advantage of being able, in principle at least, to learn from one another.

Paradoxically, some on-campus courses have incorporated some elements of distance education in such a way as to *increase* the amount of personal attention students receive. There will be more about this when we discuss the Keller Plan and similar schemes later.

However, even now, you must be considering, even if it has not already been decided for you, whether your course is to be chiefly interactive (between tutors and students, or students and students) or whether it is to be largely self-instructional. And, if the latter, whether the self-instruction is to take place on or off campus. The discussion of course development in this book takes all these possibilities into account.

### What will be taught?

What will our course be teaching? I have found it useful to distinguish between courses that put their emphasis on *subject-matter knowledge* and those that emphasize the *methodology* of an academic discipline (or profession) or of some specific task for which the student is being prepared. All courses are to some extent mixed, but it is usually possible to recognize a bias in one of these directions.

KNOWLEDGE-ORIENTED COURSES

I would regard as knowledge-oriented any course in which the aim is to get the student to learn and apply the subject-matter included in the course. This subject-matter must be mastered by the student, and it must be learned for its own sake, not as a vehicle for learning something else.

Most pure science courses come into this category. For example, physics students will be required to study heat, light, sound, properties of matter, quantum theory, nuclear physics, and so on. Such subject-matter makes up the basic core of the discipline. No-one can begin to be any kind of physicist until he has acquired a grounding in this subject-matter knowledge. Doubtless a similar list of necessary topics could also be produced for courses in economics, law, medicine, and so on.

In a well-defined field like physics, where professionals have been producing knowledge for many years, there is abundant subject-matter to be learned. The student cannot sensibly be encouraged to ignore the work of his predecessors. As Isaac Newton pointed out, progress in science can be achieved only by standing on their shoulders.

On the other hand, there are dangers. Paul Black (1969) noted that more than 40 per cent of questions in final examinations for university degrees in physics could be answered from memorization alone. There is no reason to believe that the percentage would be any less today.

Unfortunately, the struggle to teach and learn the ever-expanding body of subject-matter often leaves little time for thinking about it. The following comments (Abercrombie, 1969) concern students who were academically competent enough to gain entry to a highly selective medical school:

> It was found that students who . . . were well grounded in the facts of biology, physics and chemistry, did not necessarily use scientific ways of thinking to solve problems presented in a slightly new way. They might be able, for instance, to recite all the lines of evidence for the theory of evolution but yet be unable to use this material to defend the theory in argument with an anti-evolutionist. They might know what the functions of a certain organ is believed to be but did not always know why, nor did they clearly understand on what kind of evidence a belief of that sort was based. When asked to describe what they saw in dissecting an animal or in looking through a microscope, they often did not distinguish sufficiently sharply between what was there and what they had been taught 'ought' to be there. It seemed that scientific ways of thinking did not automatically result from learning the facts of science.

I hope you will not assume that I am opposed to knowledge-oriented courses. The learning of subject-matter does not

**3**

necessarily imply brainless memorization. Though even the fashionable distaste for memorization may be overdone. Like many students I often curse the time I spend looking up facts that I feel might well be in my memory had I ever acquired the habit of memorization. But I suppose I should be thankful that I even remember the existence and relevance of the facts whose detail I have forgotten!

The Abercrombie quotation indicates how subject-matter might be approached other than through memorization. Thus the subject-matter (in this case, of science courses) might be learned through solving problems presented in a slightly new way; through arguing opposing interpretations; through considering how beliefs are explained and justified; through paying attention to knowledge of the world as well as to that of books; and so on.

In other words, the quality of a knowledge-oriented course must depend on the nature of the content and whether it encourages worthwhile forms of learning. Too often there is a drift from worthwhile and demanding subject-matter towards subject-matter that is easily assessable: memorizable facts, definitions and principles, together with standardized, algorithmic recipes for processing new data. Lars Dahlgren (1978) reports how less than 50 per cent of a group of economics undergraduates were able to give an interviewer satisfactory explanations of such concepts as 'opportunity cost' or of how average and marginal costs of production would differ with increasing, decreasing, or constant returns to scale. But 89 per cent of those students gave satisfactory answers to seemingly more sophisticated questions on such issues in the course examination. This they did by more or less blind application of memorized procedures, without any attempt at analysis.

One of the two major problems with courses oriented towards subject-matter is that they are liable to contain just far too much of it. Dahlgren suggests that, as a result, 'students probably have to abandon their ambitions to understand what they read about and instead direct their efforts to passing the examinations'. And the second of the two major problems is the fact that we continue to set examinations that measure quantity rather than quality. That is, we too often reward a student's superficial acquaintance with a lot of subject-matter rather than his deeper understanding of a more limited range. Dahlgren believes that if we really wished to develop students' thinking, and so made understanding the main criteria of progress in higher (or any) education, the content of many courses would have to be reduced by something like 50 or 75 per cent.

METHODOLOGICAL COURSES

Let me turn, by contrast, to what I have called *methodology*-oriented courses. In these, the emphasis is on acquiring *procedures or skills*—intellectual, physical, or social. Knowledge will be necessarily involved, but the aim of the course will not primarily be to have the student learn that knowledge. Rather, the subject-matter—and different teachers may choose different items for this purpose—may be used simply as material on which to practise developing skills, e.g., of literary criticism. Or it may be used, e.g., in learning to drive a car or to interview patients, as an interim guide to the student until the procedures or skills become automatic and he can forget the verbal representation. In short, the student learns to be a *performer* in the subject, rather than a spectator or a commentator on the knowledge achieved by others. It seems to me that methodology-oriented courses are of two types: *task*-oriented and *discipline*-oriented.

*Task*-oriented courses (or sections within courses) train the student to carry out some clearly defined activity. Purely task-oriented courses are mostly confined to the technician/craftsman area of education, e.g., television repairs, plumbing, bricklaying. In such areas it is possible to identify a series of quite specific tasks and procedures which the student must be able to carry out in fairly predictable situations. He is not expected to be able to generalize his training into radically new situations. Nor is he expected to innovate within his trade by introducing new knowledge or practices.

Such training is common in further education but in higher education it occurs only as a component of a wider, more ambitious course. For example, both geographers and civil engineers are commonly trained in the techniques of surveying. Medical students, too, must learn a large number of clearly defined tasks, e.g., taking a blood pressure. Biologists may well be expected to learn statistics as a set of techniques to be chosen from and applied according to a more or less standard routine.

In any task-oriented course, or section within a course, subject-matter will be strictly limited. What knowledge there is will be 'how to do it' knowledge. Only what is essential to the anticipated performance will be taught. It may even be assumed that too

**5**

much knowledge would be confusing. It might hinder the student in applying what is really quite a limited methodology. I have already quoted Dahlgren's work in suggesting that some knowledge-oriented courses in higher education may, in-advertently, encourage the student in looking for algorithmic, recipe-like ways of using the subject-matter. Thus he may become an uncritical technician.

In a *discipline-oriented* course, however, the student is learning a methodology that should be adaptable to a wide variety of circumstances. These cannot be pre-specified in any sort of detail. The intellectual processes that the student is acquiring will need to be deployed in new ways and perhaps themselves be extended and improved in doing so.

We might take a history course as an example of such discipline-orientation. The aim would be to have the student acquire some of the techniques of the professional historian: how to gather and assess evidence, how to draw valid conclusions, how to present an argument. As Jerome Bruner (1964) said, 'to get a student . . . to consider matters as a historian does', or more generally, 'to participate in the process that makes possible the establishment of knowledge'. We assume, you see, that the purpose of the course is to enable the student to practise the discipline for himself (at least in some measure) rather than simply be an admirer of the works of the professionals.

Such a course, built on teaching the skills and thought-processes of the professionals, is not to be seen as a special kind of task-oriented course. The 'task' of the historian, philosopher, economist, etc., can never be sufficiently clear-cut to be broken down into subtasks and obvious chains of procedure like that of a television repairer or a plumber. Indeed, we must recognize that there is no one accepted 'best' way of 'doing' history, or philosophizing, or being an economist. The student may encounter a variety of models to try out and combine as best fits his personal style and the problem in hand. Whether what he emerges with is to count as acceptable history-making or philosophizing will depend not just on what he does—the pro-cedures he adopts—but on how he justifies those procedures. A Marxist historian and a 'free-enterprise' historian might examine, say, the industrial revolution in Britain and disagree as to whether the people's standard of living was rising or falling (*Economic History Review*, 1963); yet the contradictory conclusions would not lead us to suggest that one at least was a poor historian. Each might have a proper justification for his procedures and hence the conclusion that emerged.

What of the subject-matter in a discipline-oriented course? Generally speaking it can be regarded as a vehicle, a means of practising the more crucial methodological abilities. The subject-matter is *not* studied for its own sake. Which particular slice of history is studied may be almost immaterial. Historians are well known for dodging a difficult discussion by saying 'I'm afraid it's not my period'! One does not have to be full of insight about every poem and novel ever written to be a competent literary critic. Nor does one need to have been on a guided tour of all the world's philosophers in order to philosophize oneself. To a very large extent, the subject-matter can be determined by the interests of the teacher and the students. The chief criterion is whether or not it allows for the development of a satisfactory range of methodological insights and skills.

MIXED COURSES

I do not want to suggest that all courses fall neatly into one or another of the above categories. The distinctions are not always clear-cut and practically all courses are *mixed*. For me, the categories are interesting chiefly as a device for identifying and comparing the balance or blending of the components to be found within a particular course. It will be this blend that gives it its characteristic 'flavour'. In fact the flavour may be similar in all courses in that particular discipline or subject-area. Thus, while pure science courses may be *predominantly* knowledge-oriented, they will have a number of task-like components, and there is likely to be some obvious discipline-orientation. Similarly, while arts courses may be generally discipline-oriented they often contain task-oriented and knowledge-oriented components. Two types of course, in particular, may straddle the categories set out above. These are the *issue-* or *problem*-based course and the *interdisciplinary* course (which may or may not be problem-centred).

*Issue-based courses* Courses that are issue-based or problem-centred are becoming increasingly popular. Instead of teaching the students a body of knowledge which is prescribed by the traditions of the discipline or subject, the teaching centres on some issue or problem. This will be one that can be seen as relevant or significant by students. The teaching will aim to

7

provide students with the conceptual and methodological tools for resolving the issue or arriving at a reasonable solution of the problem. For example, in an Open University course on materials technology, one problem is 'what materials could usefully be considered for the manufacture of car bodies?' This provides the focus for consideration of strength of materials, materials processing, manufacturing methods, and so on. The student is helped in comparing steel, aluminium, and reinforced glass fibre; and he can discuss sensibly, in general terms, the relative merits of each for the manufacture of car bodies.

What is to be said in favour of issue- or problem-based courses? Sometimes an issue or problem is adopted to make the subject-matter 'relevant', 'interesting', 'motivating'. An issue-based course that was justified in these terms would probably be recognizably knowledge-oriented. Some issue-based courses, however, reject the aim of trying to teach students all they might ever need to know—which the proliferation of knowledge is making ever more futile—and try instead to teach students procedures whereby they may identify and solve real problems themselves. Here, the discipline-orientation would seem to predominate. The ultimate in this approach is perhaps the project-based course, in which the student is pursuing his own issue or problem. The teacher's role here is to provide methodological advice and ensure that the student acquires a worthwhile set of insights while pursuing his enquiry.

In such courses, it may not matter too much what issue or problem is chosen. For instance, in the materials technology course mentioned above it might have made little difference whether the student considered car bodies or refrigerators. Either might have given him equivalent knowledge of materials and manufacturing processes or equal facility in investigating and choosing among materials.

While issue- or problem-based courses have considerable potential, they are not without snags and pitfalls for the unwary or the over enthusiastic. For instance, the chosen issue or problem might turn out to be one that allows only a distorted or incomplete grasp of the subject or discipline. Also, an undiluted diet of such courses might leave the student without a coherent perspective on the parent disciplines.

*Interdisciplinary courses* These also are becoming increasingly common as the boundaries between subjects are being eroded, producing such new studies as: ecology, bionics, psycholinguistics, behavioural science, oceanography industrial archaeology, period studies in the humanities, and so on. Essentially, the inter-disciplinary course brings more than one discipline to bear on a topic or period or issue. Thus an issue-based course can also be interdisciplinary.

For example, a course on *Health and Environment* might bring together, say, the disciplines of social medicine, architecture, and economics to illuminate the cause-and-effect relationships involved. A course on *The Age of Revolutions* might look at the nineteenth century through the eyes not only of historians but also of literary critics, philosophers, musicologists, art historians, and political commentators.

Another common approach is to begin a course with what we might call a *multi*disciplinary section. Here the contributing disciplines are introduced separately with no attempt being made to interrelate them. This is then followed by an interdisciplinary part in which the disciplines are brought together to examine a common problem. Hopefully, the disciplines will interact in such a way as to enhance one another's insights. As an example, here is a brief outline of the contents of an Open University Course on *Oceanography*.

> Some 70 per cent of the Earth's surface is covered by oceans, and oceanography is a science which is growing rapidly. It is multi-disciplinary and the course initially studies each branch of oceanography—physical, chemical, biological and geological—as a basis to an interdisciplinary approach in the later units.
>
> There are seven main parts to the course:
>
> 1. An introduction to the oceans: Man and the oceans, the shape and geology of the ocean basins, the ocean water environment.
> 2. Physical oceanography: the physical properties and movement of sea water.
> 3. Chemical oceanography: the chemical composition and variation of sea water, and interaction with the atmosphere and sediment.
> 4. Biological oceanography: the nature and distribution of marine organisms.
> 5. Geological oceanography: components, sources, and dis-tribution of marine sediments.
> 6. Inter-disciplinary studies of aspects of oceanography, including ocean basin, evolution, cyclical changes, upwelling systems.
> 7. Man and the exploitation of the oceans, and the scientific, political, economic and social implications.

**9**

Interdisciplinary courses, like issue-based courses, are commonly justified in one or other of two ways. They may be offered as relevant, 'real-life' ways of 'putting across the content': or they may be held to introduce students to the 'integrated, multifaceted thought-processes' required of people pursuing enquiries in many new subject areas. Perhaps the former intention would tend to result in a knowledge-oriented course while the latter would suggest a discipline(s)-orientation.

The success of the latter kind of interdisciplinary course (where, in effect, the methodology for a new integrated discipline is being developed) surely depends on whether the integration is real. Are the separate disciplines really brought to bear on the same subject in such a way that they 'learn' from one another and produce an approach that is somehow greater than the sum of the parts? Or are they wheeled on to the stage one at a time (in 'multidisciplinary' fashion) and allowed to operate almost as if no one of them had ever heard of the other interested disciplines? Sad to say, allegedly interdisciplinary courses often do take this latter form. Perhaps the student is being left to make the inter-disciplinary fusion in his own mind. But it is more likely that what he will notice is the need to pick up several separately wrapped parcels of subject-matter, perhaps with some methodological trimmings, which will probably be tested separately in the end-of-course examination. If that examination, or whatever other kind of assessment is used, takes the form of an interdisciplinary exercise, then the desired effect may be demonstrated even if the prior teaching has been multi-, rather than interdisciplinary. All the same, it can hardly be considered fair to assess (and grade) on the basis of the student's powers of 'interdisciplinary fusion' without his first having been given practice, feedback, and an opportunity to improve.

I do not expect you to agree entirely with my ways of distinguishing between courses. I am sure, however, that you will be well aware of differences within your own institution, perhaps within your own department, and that you will know what kinds of course will be both practicable and acceptable to staff and students.

## Constraints

Just as you are aware of what will be accepted as a course in your institution, so too you will be conscious of many other *constraints*. By 'constraints' I mean factors that may prevent you from

**10**

mounting exactly the course you would prefer. It is as well to recognize such limiting factors from the outset. For instance, only so many staff—and of certain backgrounds and specialities—will be available to work on the course. And they will have only a certain amount of time available: to plan the course and to select or prepare teaching materials, to meet students, to assess the students' work, and so on.

Students too will have only so much time to devote to the course. Other courses may be making demands on them also; other aspects of their lives certainly will. The ability of students on entry to the course will also act as a constraint. What existing level of knowledge and skills and relevant attitudes can you expect? What level of motivation? What will be students' expectations as to what constitutes a 'respectable' course, in terms of workload, teaching methods, assessment, and so on? Indeed you may be constrained by whether or not you can get any students at all. Perhaps you will have to carry out some kind of market research within your institution or the wider community. This is called 'needs assessment' in some parts of the world. Will students be forthcoming for the kind of course you have in mind? After all, it could be that other institutions, or departments, are already mounting courses that fully satisfy the existing and potential needs. How many students are you likely to have; and what will be the staff-student ratio?

Facilities and money also clearly impose constraints. Extra money can sometimes obtain one of the missing facilities but not necessarily. For an on-campus course, do you have adequate library and laboratory provision? Are the lecture rooms, seminar rooms, and study spaces large enough and furnished appropriately for the kinds of teaching and learning you might wish to create? With distance education are your students easily accessible by telephone, mail, or other means? Can they be expected to have access to tape recorders? Would there be enough of them in any one area that they might get together in self-help groups? What variety of teaching methods and media may be used?

Other people's expectations may also constitute a constraint. Teachers of other courses (especially subsequent courses) may have strong ideas about what ought to be included in yours. So too may external validating bodies (e.g., TEC, BEC, and CNAA in the UK), potential employers, professional institutions like the British Psychological Society or the British Institute of Engineers, and the students themselves.

The pessimists among us will accept the constraints as given and do their best to work within them. The optimists will challenge them and aim to remove as many as possible. In truth, the constraints may be powerful enough to prevent the course taking place at all. On the other hand, many constraints turn out to be imaginary. We may say 'The Dean wouldn't approve', but no-one has asked him. When someone does he may become highly supportive. Then again, many real constraints can be overcome—the extra facilities, staffing, money, etc., can be found (at the expense of something else) if the 'powers-that-be' are *persuaded* that the course you propose will bring commensurate credit to the institution and adequately benefit its students or augment their number. Such persuasion usually depends not only on meeting with the goals of those who wield the power but also upon a well-developed curriculum plan that clearly has been rigorously thought through. As much as anything else, this book is intended to help in the creation of a well-developed curriculum.

Naturally, such a curriculum is one that shows signs of having *been* developed rather than simply of having happened or been roughed out at short notice on the back of an envelope one wet lunch time in the bar. Hopefully, the plan may leave abundant room for development to continue once the students have started upon the course. But anticipating such developments and how they might be facilitated can be an important part of the plan. They may not happen unless they are considered in advance. This is not to imply that course development is, or can be expected to become, a totally rational process. Intuition, inspiration, and social interchange has an undeniable and potentially vitalizing role to play. But that role can be made most of when it is anticipated and allowed for in the design of the course.

## The developers

We have mentioned courses and their development, but who are we to suppose might be doing the developing? Clearly this is a prime role of the teacher. But, as I will be suggesting, other people—including the students—may be seen as course developers also.

Will you be developing your course alone or will you be working with colleagues? More and more, the *team* concept is being adopted in post-secondary education. Here the course is planned and taught by a group of people who share the various duties among themselves and meet regularly once the course is running in order to evaluate and improve it. If your course is in any way meant to satisfy external criteria, e.g., those of a vocational or professional bodies, your planning team may also include, or at least take advice from, a group of external experts. Such planning team members or advisers may help ensure the 'relevance' of your course, if such relevance is appropriate.

### Course teams

In the Open University, all courses are developed by course teams. The joys and sorrows of working in them have been widely reported on (Mason, 1976; Newey, 1975; Riley, 1975; TAAD, 1979). Such a team may consist of several (3 to 20+) academics—experts in the relevant subject matter—together with media specialists (especially BBC radio and television producers), an editor, a graphic designer, a course coordinator (one of whose main tasks is to liaise between the team and other areas within the University upon whose services the team must draw), and an educational technologist who acts as an adviser on pedagogical issues. Apart from these central members, the team may also draw in contributions from respected colleagues in educational (or other) institutions elsewhere. In this context, course developers are clearly of many kinds.

By and large, it is probably fair to say that the people in the teams produce courses of better quality than they would if working alone. This is due in large part to the stimulus of discussion and the need to satisfy one's peers. While some members find the regular group evaluation of one another's work to be somewhat stressful (at least, at first), most end up acclaiming its benefits. Several heads, if not always better than one, can at least be relied upon to be more diverse. Having produced ideas and draft materials for a course, it can be difficult to see how they might be developed further and improved. A few minutes' discussion with course team colleagues, however, soon convinces one that there are several other ways the ideas or materials could (should!) be furthered. Even if one ends up rejecting all the actual suggestions (or at most, adapting some of them), the very excitement of responding to constructive criticism can be sufficient to galvanize one into developing fresh perspectives of one's own.

On the other hand, a great deal of time and energy can be lost in academic gamesmanship if the dynamics of the group are not supportive and trust-inspiring. In such cases, teamwork can

**13**

reduce itself to the lowest common denominator of each member trying to maximize his influence on how other members tackle their sections while minimizing the influence they can exert on how he tackles his.

A team approach is virtually essential when the course being developed is multidisciplinary, as so many new courses are nowadays. Renaissance men (and women) being rather few and far between, it becomes necessary for specialists from different backgrounds (even from different departments or institutions) to find a way of pooling their expertise. However, I must agree with my colleague Judith Riley (1975) when she says:

> . . . team preparation of courses is very time-consuming and I would not recommend it even for such situations, unless it is reinforced by a strong commitment to team work, probably best expressed by giving teams their own budgets and a formal place in the administrative structure. Some lecturers will never enjoy working in a group and should probably not be forced to join course teams; nor can the majority of staff be expected to work well in the exposed and demanding situations which course teams create, unless they are professionally prepared for it and unless promotions reward their co-operation.

Teams of one kind or another, usually looser than those of the Open University are now quite common in colleges, polytechnics, and universities. For reports of how they can work see, for instance, Crick (1978), Coffey (1980), Nuffield (1975) and Stringer (1980).

The minimal 'team' consists of one person, the teacher responsible for teaching the course and/or for preparing any necessary self-instructional materials (see TAAD, 1980). He may additionally have one or more 'critical friends' to whom he knows he can turn, *when he wishes*, for wise and dispassionate comment.

WHO IS IN THE 'TEAM'?

Even the sole developer is likely to have a secretary/typist working with him. And what about an illustrator or graphic designer? And will he need to call upon a technician to prepare specimens or set up demonstrations? Furthermore, if the course is to include specially written self-instructional materials or study guides, there may be several authors. Perhaps also there will be colleagues from other colleges or universities who can be asked to produce materials or comment on drafts. If people other than the course initiators will be acting as tutors or assessors, perhaps they too

**14**

should be invited to join the team. Even if you distinguish between 'central' members and 'service' members, all are likely to work better if they know who else is involved and what role everyone is to play. How is the 'chairman' or leader of the team to be decided upon? What qualities will he or she need?

## WHO MAKES WHICH DECISIONS?

Who is to make decisions (e.g., about whether or not particular ideas or materials are acceptable)? There seem to be three possibilities:
1. The 'course team' makes all decisions by consensus after discussing the issues involved.
2. A 'chairman' makes decisions on behalf of the team.
3. Each member makes decisions about his or her 'own' area of the course in the light of course team discussion.

Some types of decision can be made by one method, some by another. But, to minimize disharmony later, an early discussion of the issue is recommended.

## HOW IS THE WORK TO BE SHARED?

Again, try to reach early agreement on just what work the course will involve and share it out as equitably as possible. Try not to overlook tasks like writing study guides, preparing evaluation questionnaires, marking assessment tests, commenting on one another's draft materials, and so on. Unless early decisions are made about who will do everything that needs doing, someone is likely to end up doing more than his or her fair share or vital tasks may be left unperformed. The team may or may not have rewards and sanctions with which to 'encourage' its members.

## WHAT IS THE SCHEDULE?

Agree on a production timetable so that everyone knows when his or her contribution is expected. (This is particularly vital if one author needs to see another's plans before he can get started.) Ensure that there is sufficient time for critical reading of one another's plans (or draft materials), for obtaining comments from external experts, and so on. Have contingency plans in case course planning and/or production should slip behind schedule. (What might be jettisoned?)

## HOW TO COMMUNICATE WITHIN THE TEAM

The members of your team may be familiar with one another,

possibly from the same department, probably from within the same institution; but they may not be well acquainted. You may even have members from more than one college or university. So what can be done to ensure all are on much the same wavelength, i.e., tuned in to one another's assumptions, perspectives, terminology, intentions, etc.? How are they to get to trust and accept one another? There are at least two ways of helping communications:

*Meetings* How often can/should the team get together? With what purpose? Some of your meetings may be strictly business occasions (e.g., brainstorming sessions or discussions of schedules or the first draft of a member's plans or course materials). Some may be professional (e.g., a seminar, perhaps with outsiders invited, on a topic relating to the course). Some may be purely social (e.g., parties, lunches, visits to theatres or concerts). Some meetings may be a mixture. All, however, should contribute to getting the course developed or the team members better acquainted.

*Documentation* Groups and committees everywhere are accused of producing too much paperwork. (The birth of every new Open University course must mean the death elsewhere of some sizeable forest!) Nevertheless, if more than a couple of people are involved in producing a course, they would be well advised not to stint on paper. Every important decision (e.g., about schedules, or intended content, or allocation of tasks) should be written down and circulated to all members. Just as the team need to discuss and agree on overall structure for the course as a whole, so individuals or groups should be expected to circulate their colleagues with a 'specification' of the section of the course they are to be responsible for. The following list suggests what such a specification might be expected to contain. This list assumes some use of self-instructional materials but most of its items would be relevant whether they were to be used or not:

● Proposed title of section.
● Dates by which certain key activities are to be completed (e.g., distribution of first draft materials for comments from colleagues).
● Names of any external experts, other than course team colleagues, who have agreed to read plans and materials.

● Relationship to rest of course (e.g., prerequisite skills/knowledge assumed of student).
● Aims and objectives.
● Outline syllabus (main theories, concepts, methodology, data, etc., to be covered).
● Teaching media to be used (e.g., textbook plus notes, cassette tape, tuition, etc.).
● Chief types of student activity (e.g., reading, listening, project work, etc.).
● Total estimated study time.
● Type of assessment required (e.g., objective tests, 'own answer' tests, practicals, projects, etc.).
● Possible problems (e.g., costs, student weaknesses, inaccessible source materials, over-abundance of content, etc.).

The course team should also receive a copy of each draft of each member's materials. Even if it has been agreed that not everyone will produce detailed comments on each draft, *all* should see any materials that might influence them in how they would want to plan their own. In fact, those members who are going to produce detailed comments on a draft might well receive *two* copies. They could then give their annotated copy back to the author (perhaps with a covering note of general comments) and keep one copy as an *aide memoire*.

## The students

So far in our discussion, the intended beneficiaries of all this activity—the students—have been somewhat taken for granted. What do we know of them? What do we need to know? What difference might it make to the way we develop a course? What assumptions shall we be making about what students want or need from the course and how they will approach their learning?

To begin with, we can use the racing metaphor to distinguish between the 'courses for horses' and 'horses for courses' approaches to course development. In the former, the emphasis is on suiting the (race-) course to the horse, or, in this case, student. In the latter, it is on selecting the horses (students) who can best cope with the given course. That is, you may be developing a course that will be able to adapt itself freely to whatever variety of students chooses to embark upon it. Or, on the other hand, you may feel constrained to design a course that is fairly inflexible in its demands (e.g., in order to satisfy the requirements of potential

**17**

employees or of teachers of subsequent courses) and then *select* only those students who can be expected to cope with its demands (e.g., by virtue of having attained certain specific prerequisite learnings).

In practice, most courses compromise. No matter how open and adaptive teachers might want to be, most feel that there are certain 'core' demands a given course must make on *all* students. On the other hand, however stringent other teachers may be in selecting students thought capable of benefiting from the course 'as it must be given', they usually find that individual differences among students must be catered for. Thus they may need to provide remedial teaching in areas where—despite the insistence on prerequisites—certain students turn out to have weaknesses; again, they may need to provide alternative teaching for students with different learning styles or to find ways of making more palatable the learning of any material that, while necessary, appears for some students to be tedious.

### Finding out about students

Whatever one's position on the 'courses for horses–horses for courses' continuum, knowledge about one's students is necessary. Much of this knowledge can be gathered only once one has begun to meet (or at least correspond) with them. But some will be needed in the very early stages of course planning, before the students have even officially enrolled.

What sort of information might be desirable in advance? Well, it would be useful to know why your students will be enrolling in the course at all. What will they hope to get out of it? Why will they choose it rather than others? Even if, in effect, they have no choice, they may nevertheless have certain expectations you may wish to ponder on. As Norman MacKenzie *et al.* (1970) point out:

> There are those who want to be entertained, there are those who want an easy pass, there are those who want to cover as much educationally relevant material as possible, there are those who want to think deeply, and there are those who want to browse and explore.

In passing, it is worth remarking, however, that students' expectations and orientations can be changed (for good or ill) by the learning environment our course creates for them. Such a change is described by one student (quoted in Beaty, 1978):

'I never came here looking for the grade . . . I came here because I wanted to do the course, it was the interest and knowledge not really the degree. But the minute you come here, people are talking about things like 2is and 2iis and immediately there is pressure.'

Again, you will need to know what sort of learners to expect. How old will they be? How 'intelligent'? How accomplished in 'study techniques'? How conversant with the language and concepts of your subject? What views of the subject-matter do they already possess?

Furthermore, you may be curious about students' interests and prior experiences, as a guide to your course planning. Their interests may suggest possible leads into the subject-matter, or analogies, examples, and case studies through which to develop it. Their prior experiences—even if not as vital as they would be if you wished to stipulate certain prerequisite experience—may likewise suggest ways of enriching the course content; they may also suggest ways in which the students can be usefully enabled to learn *from one another* on account of their variety of prior experience.

How is such knowledge to be acquired? If you are lucky, you may already have taught your potential students, or students you *believe* to be very similar, on a previous course. In this case, you may feel you 'know' your students fairly well already. If not, you may be able to talk with other teachers who have taught them recently, or at least to read reports written by such teachers on those students.

QUESTIONNAIRES AND DISCUSSION
Such prior knowledge can be very vivid. One often uses it, consciously or otherwise, in planning a course for people assumed to be like some small group one already knows well. However, one's impressions are often partial and, having perhaps been gathered in a different context, may be insufficiently precise on points of detail. Thus, whether or not you can learn from your own or colleagues' previous experience of the students, you may believe it worthwhile to initiate new discussions with them now that you have a new course to talk about. If you are teaching 'at a distance' and potential students cannot easily be brought together in one place, you may try to 'talk' with them by questionnaire. And even if your students are on campus, or can be brought together somewhere, a questionnaire may serve both

**19**

as an agenda for the discussion and as a means of recording information that might otherwise never be elicited or might escape your notice if brought up in discussion. A questionnaire can also incorporate a simple *pre-test* to find out what potential students already know about your subject.

As an example, Fig. 1.1 shows a questionnaire designed by my colleague Roger Harrison for use with a group of potential students expressing interest in a course on Diet and Nutrition. As always with questionnaire design, he would now wish to acknowledge certain weaknesses. For example, too many 'technical' questions, like questions 9–14, might scare off some potential students, especially if they got the impression that the implied knowledge was being demanded as a condition of entry to the course. Such issues, together with answers to questions that might have been asked, but were not, will arise in subsequent discussion with those potential students who were asked to complete the questionnaire. Some such discussion is always valuable, even if it has to be conducted by telephone. However, it is as well to guard against irrelevant or misleading questions, and to provide some further opportunity for recognizing important questions that ought to be included, by trying out questionnaires in draft form on just two or three prospective students before sending it out to the full group taking part in your 'market research'.

Despite its shortcomings, such a questionnaire, when followed up with discussion, may indicate, for example, that your students will be: young adults, 70 per cent female, with some domestic culinary experience, who want to plan better meals and who have little knowledge of the basic concepts of the course and are rather varied in their ability to handle arithmetic and, especially, statistical ideas. Alternatively, the prospective students may be predominantly men with a vocational interest in nutrition, little experience of planning and preparing meals, etc. Even within either of these possible groups, you could find that individuals hold very divergent notions about the subject-matter of the course. Whatever one learns of one's students, and especially of the diversity among them, can help breathe the realities of life into course planning.

### Can students influence content?

Between them the students may also have come up with a set of questions they would like to see addressed within the course. This

**Questionnaire** (Put a tick in the box alongside each answer you choose)

1.   **What is your sex?**
     (a)   Male
     (b)   Female

2.   **How old are you?**
     (a)   Less than 20
     (b)   20-25
     (c)   25-30
     (d)   30-40
     (e)   40-50
     (f)   Over 50

3.   **Why do you want to take this course?**
     (a)   Because you think it will be interesting
     (b)   Because you want to be able to plan better meals for yourself or your family
     (c)   Because you want to be able to help or supervise other people who plan meals but without wanting some professional qualification
     (d)   Because you want to get some sort of professional qualification in dietetics
     (e)   Because you have been told to by your employer or a teacher
     (f)   Because it completes your timetable of courses for a qualification not primarily in dietetics
     (g)   Some other reason (please specify)

4.   **What is the most important reason for wanting people to eat a reasonably balanced diet?**
     (a)   To make sure they get enough to eat
     (b)   To make sure they get the right sort of food
     (c)   To keep them healthy
     (d)   To make sure that the food is appetising
     (e)   To ensure variety in meals
     (f)   To make sure their bodies get enough of each of their requirements
     (g)   To avoid waste of food and unnecessary expense

5.   **Do you think your own present diet is adequately balanced?**
     (a)   Yes
     (b)   No
     (c)   Don't know

6.   **Do you think it is important to be able to judge how well a diet is balanced?**
     (a)   Yes
     (b)   No
     (c)   Don't know

Fig. 1.1   Questionnaire to potential students

**21**

7. **Have you ever planned and prepared a meal for others?**
   - (a) Yes, regularly
   - (b) Yes, occasionally
   - (c) No — only part of a meal
   - (d) No — only helped others to do so
   - (e) No — only watched others do so
   - (f) No — never

8. **Which of the following have you studied in the last three years? (Tick as many as apply)**
   - (a) Cookery
   - (b) Elementary biology
   - (c) Elementary physics and/or chemistry
   - (d) Basic arithmetic
   - (e) Elementary statistics

   (Write in any examinations you have passed in any of these subjects and the year you passed them.)

9. **How many different classes of nutrient are found in food?**
   - (a) 1   (b) 2   (c) 3
   - (d) 4   (e) 5   (f) 6
   - (g) 7   (h) More than 7

Here is a list of terms used in connection with nutrition.
(Put the appropriate letters in the boxes below.)

| | | | | | |
|---|---|---|---|---|---|
| A | Ascorbic Acid | G | Fibre | M | Obesity |
| B | Beri-beri | H | Iron | N | Pellagra |
| C | Brassica | I | Kwashiorkor | O | Protein |
| D | Carbohydrate | J | Methionine | P | Scurvy |
| E | Energy | K | Mineral | Q | Tryptophan |
| F | Fat | L | Nicotonic acid | R | Vitamin |
| | | | | S | Water |

## Questions 10-14

10. **Which of the above constitute major classes of nutrient?**

11. **Which of the above are names of diseases caused by a deficiency of some ingredient in food?**

12. **Which of the above are major sources of energy?**

13. **Which of the above, apart from 'vitamin' itself, are either vitamins, sources of vitamins, or are associated with vitamin deficiency?**

14. **Which of the above, apart from 'protein' itself, would you associate directly with protein or protein deficiency?**

raises the issue of how far you can countenance the idea of students helping decide the *content* of the course. This will need to be borne in mind also in subsequent stages of course development, but the earlier we start thinking about it, the better. How far can we allow the course to adapt to different students' expectations?

Different answers will arise with different courses and different teachers, and maybe with different kinds of students. Much will depend on where the particular course is seen to lie along a spectrum from *education* through *training* to *indoctrination*. The indoctrination end of the spectrum would be characterized by the learner being manipulated to achieve someone else's expectations of him, unwittingly, and unaware that he might be learning to do otherwise. Few teachers would openly identify with this process. Entering the 'training' band of the spectrum, we find that the student *knows* he is preparing to meet other people's expectations of him, but he broadly concurs with this and, provided his personal 'style' is to some degree taken into account, is content to shape himself to the normal demands of whatever trade or profession he is aspiring to. Towards the educational end of the spectrum, facilitation predominates: the student's individual needs and purposes and rational autonomy are respected and he is being helped to enhance and fulfil expectations of his own. Another way of viewing this spectrum is to say that, at the educational end, the student is treated as the 'client' for a service, while towards the other end he is treated as the 'product' of a service.

In practice, of course, the distinctions are not clear-cut. Most educational systems contain some undertones of training, if not of indoctrination. Obvious perhaps when we think of doctors and lawyers; slightly less obvious when we consider how curricula in, say, chemistry or engineering are influenced by the supposed expectations of the professional institutions in those fields, regardless of whether all students intend to enter them; and minimally obvious but no less true when we think of thousands of students being similarly groomed for standardized school-leaving exams. Yet, conversely, many training institutions bend over backwards to individualize what they have to offer and enable different students in different ways to get more than the required basics out of the course. It is not uncommon to find industrial trainers using facilitative concepts like 'personal growth', 'inter-personal awareness', and 'positive self-image'.

Mostly, teachers and students move to and fro over the middle ground between education and training, with occasional drifts towards indoctrination, often inadvertently and unintentionally through the messages of some 'hidden curriculum' (Snyder, 1971). Humanistic ideals pull the participants one way; the pressures for standardized qualifications and credentials pull them the other. But rarely, if ever, does the content of a course emanate solely from the desires of students or solely from those of others. Choice of content is a complex 'transaction' in which all parties concerned reach tacit agreement as to what is to count as valid educational knowledge. Through persuading and influencing one another, through bribery and coercion, through trust and mutual responsiveness, teachers and students negotiate an acceptable compromise between what 'the system' requires, what the student wants to learn about, and what the teacher feels capable of teaching.

A fascinating account of how such negotiation works out, even in a 'training' milieu like a medical school, is provided by Everett Hughes *et al.* (1958). They describe how the students, as a group in intensive contact with one another, reach general consensus that they will concentrate their academic efforts on those parts of the curriculum that seem to them relevant to their futures as general practitioners. Thus, for example, they pay most attention to common and curable diseases, they take short cuts in laboratory work knowing that they will not do such work as doctors, and in the final years they put their efforts into clinical activities, examining and taking histories from patients, rather than into swotting for the formal examinations. The assessment system appears flexible enough to validate such emphasis by not penalizing deviance from what might appear to be the institution's formally stated objectives. The authors stress the social nature of the transaction:

> . . . student culture provides the students with the social support that allows them, in individual instances and as a group, independently to assess faculty statements and demands so that they can significantly reinterpret faculty emphasis and, in a meaningful sense, *make what they will of their education.* [My italics]

HOW REAL IS STUDENT CHOICE?

Some may say that in colleges and universities as they are at present, students who are allowed to choose one activity rather than another, or one course rather than another, are implicitly electing to pursue one set of purposes rather than another. However, the true emphasis of a course is often obscure or liable to

**24**

misinterpretation: witness the many students who come to subjects like psychology or sociology only to find them less relevant to their 'interest in people' than they had anticipated. In any case, students may well choose not the courses and activities that are going to stretch and challenge them and allow for maximum personal growth, but those that promise to be least demanding and least likely to end in loss of face.

Once embarked upon a course, it can be only too easy for the teacher to find himself manipulating students towards his, or 'the system's' purposes, rather than facilitating them in developing purposes of their own. The teacher with a syllabus 'to cover' at all costs is particularly prone. Hence the importance of considering how far students' purposes might be accommodated early on, before 'the syllabus' has come to take on a life of its own in one's mind.

Essentially, to be open to a diversity of student purposes, one needs some over-arching aims for the course. These, which may themselves be agreed in discussion with the students, indicate what all students are expected to get out of it. The purposes proposed by individual students can then be assessed in terms of the extent to which they will contribute (albeit in different ways) to each student's attainment of those more general aims. Aims and purposes negotiated in this way can ensure that the student's activities are motivated by the meanings he attaches to them, while at the same time leading him towards knowledge and abilities that the teacher also considers important. In Chapter 2 I consider how students' perceptions might be used in deciding the content of a course.

TOWARDS INDEPENDENT LEARNING

Even with the pre-packaged, teaching-at-a-distance correspondence courses of the Open University, certain course teams are now attempting to give the student some latitude in how he interprets the course. For example, while each student is expected to return essays or reports for assessment at particular points in the course, the topic need not be one that hundreds or even thousands of other students are all tackling at the same time. Rather, he may be invited to agree with his correspondence tutor a topic of his own devising that allows him to explore whichever aspects of the course appeal most to him. Some courses go even further by building in a substantial project component, accounting for perhaps half of the student's time or more on the course. In such a project, he is free, with guidance from his tutor, to apply the methodology he is learning from the more structured sequences of the course to a problem he formulates for himself. This he researches using whatever resources are available locally. In a course on architecture and design, for instance, the student can spend about one-fifth of his time in studying a locally accessible building or artefact of his own choice, backing this up with work on primary documentary material and relevant secondary sources. This kind of project, demanding that the student define his own goals and select his own resources, is to be distinguished from those 'projects' in other courses that require the student to use local resources but stipulate the topic on which he is to collect data, e.g., pollution levels or children's attitudes, and give him a 'recipe' to follow. One technology course (T401) consists *entirely* of a student-initiated project.

Such courses have also been pioneered on campus in, for instance, the School of Independent Learning at Lancaster University and, covering an entire degree programme, by the University Without Walls in the USA, and by the University of Roskilde (Denmark). That the student should learn to plan his own education can be said to be one of the teacher's prime aims in such courses. Roger Harrison (not my Open University colleague, this time) and Richard Hopkins (1967) illustrated this dramatically in their training of Peace Corps volunteers (described further on page 123). Since they wanted to wean recruits away from dependence on experts and enable them to cope in highly fraught situations on their own, what they looked for in their students, right from the start, was nothing less than the willingness to plan and assess their own training.

Having students learn to plan their own education may not be one of your aims for your course. If it is, or even if you merely want students to exercise some choice as if from within a menu, you may well find you have to teach them *how* to do it. Not all will have the maturity, certainly at first, to cope with the consequent responsibilities and complexities, even at university level. Liam Hudson (1970) distinguishes between two-types of students: 'the sylbs', who are syllabus-bound, and the 'sylfs', who are syllabus-free. Some like to be told what to study; others like plenty of choice in the matter. William Perry (1970), whose descriptions of the intellectual and ethical development of students during their four years at Harvard echoes Piaget's observations of young children, notes a progression of much consequence here. He illustrates, with extensive interview transcripts, how a student often begins with the expectation that knowledge consists of right answers, one per problem, and his teacher will tell him what they are. Later on he may recognize that teachers appear to be presenting several right answers to the same question, but he assumes this is a teaching technique to help him find the real right answer for himself. It is some time before he conceives of knowledge as relativistic and dependent on context, and comes to see that several answers can be right, not because 'everyone's entitled to his opinion' but because they can be justified in particular frames of reference. Only those students who are well on the way towards this relativistic viewpoint are likely to commit themselves to purposes of their own.

These last few paragraphs may alarm some teachers. This vision of students as course developers may seem totally alien. Such teachers may see their own role as being to determine and convey all necessary content and the students' role as being 'simply' to learn it.

## *Teachers' views of students*
Indeed it is as well to remember, especially if we are cooperating with other teachers, as in a course team, that teachers differ in their professional world-views—their pedagogic paradigms. Such differing 'pedagogic paradigms' are compounded out of the various beliefs teachers hold about education, knowledge, students, and the processes by which they are assumed to learn. As so often, I tend to think of a continuum. One extreme is characterized by the teacher whose first loyalty is to a public corpus of pre-existing knowledge (which he knows every student ought to acquire) and whose concern is to 'get it across' to a succession of students who learn, as far as their limited capacity and motivation will allow, by absorbing and reproducing the products of other people's (experts') experience. Many teachers who would not publicly, or even consciously, subscribe to such notions, nevertheless act *as though* they do in their teaching and, especially perhaps, in the ways in which they assess students' learning.

The other extreme is characterized by teachers who eschew generalizations about what every student ought to learn and who, believing people to have unlimited capacity for growth unless 'discouraged', give their first loyalty to individual students, encouraging them to develop their own motivation and pursue

**27**

their own purposes in enjoying, and getting better at, the *process* of making their own meanings and creating new knowledge out of their own ideas and experiences.

Put bluntly, where one extreme sees students as passively responding to received knowledge, the other concedes them an active role in making knowledge, at the very least by filtering what we tell them through their own experience and forming their own conclusions. Few teachers are likely to dig in at either extreme of the continuum. Most of us tend, *in general*, to edge towards one rather than the other. But each of us is likely to vary his position according to the particular aspect of education in question; according to the subject we are teaching (or even from topic to topic within it); according to how we see a particular group of students; and so on. (See also Chapter 3 on our diverse metaphors for teaching and learning.)

### Students' learning styles and strategies

In truth, too little is yet known of the ways in which individual students learn, although it is a growth-area in research (see HE, 1979). What we do know is that students differ. William Perry's work (mentioned earlier) is significant in this respect. How can we cope, in the same group, with students who may be operating on three (or more) different levels of intellectual development? Again, how can we accommodate Hudson's sylbs and sylfs within the same course?

The work of Gordon Pask (1976) and his associates has sharpened our awareness of another difference: between 'serialist' and 'holist' learning. Students using a serialist strategy work through a topic step-by-step in linear sequence. Their focus is narrow and they prefer to learn each item thoroughly before going on to the next. In recalling what they have learned they will usually follow their original sequence. Students adopting a holist strategy, on the other hand, try to roam freely over the topic, examining it from many viewpoints, looking for analogies and examples, and building up a general picture before attempting to learn details.

Though some learning tasks favour the serialist strategy and some the holist, both are usually needed for full understanding. Where the serialist learner may sometimes suffer from not being able to see the wood for the trees, the holist may sometimes find himself over-generalizing or missing important distinctions. Pask's work on these strategies and the thought processes that underlie them are discussed by J. S. Daniels in Entwistle and Hounsell, 1975.

A student may sometimes seem more or less wedded to one strategy or another, as an expression of a more general learning *style*, itself perhaps related to some dimension of personality. Or he may be flexible enough to switch from one strategy to another according to the nature of the task in hand. It would certainly be dangerous to assume (e.g., see Laurillard, 1979) that our students possess learning styles that are inherent, unalterable, and inflexible. Rather, as teachers, we should be asking whether the learning environment we create—especially in the kinds of course content we favour, the assessment demands we make on students, and the guidance we give on approaches to study—are such as to encourage or discourage a student in expanding his repertoire.

Ference Marton and his colleagues at Gothenburg University have helped throw interesting light on the way in which students may adapt their approaches according to how they perceive a certain task and what they hope to get out of it. (See Dahlgren and Marton, 1978; Marton, 1975; Marton and Säljö, 1976). As a result of interviews with students on completion of a learning task, they were able to distinguish between what they called 'surface-level' and 'deep-level' approaches. The surface-level approach is passive and shallow, with the student looking for isolated facts or ideas that he can learn by rote on the assumption that these are what he will be questioned on. Students using a deep-level approach, however, are those who attempt to penetrate the surface of the material, looking for an underlying theme or message, trying to evaluate an author's (or speaker's) arguments in terms of their own previous experience of related matters.

Here is a student (quoted in Laurillard, 1979) describing his surface-level approach to a certain task:

> 'The main thing is to be able to explain it in the exam. I just try to reason it out, and explain how it works. If you can explain how it works it makes it easier to remember. I read it through once, then again, and over again until I felt I knew their explanations. I'm still not too happy about it, but I take their word for it. I didn't think about anything else. I was just trying to learn it parrot fashion.'

And here is a student describing his deep-level approach to a different task:

> 'I have to use this for my project. I want to do as much of the steps as I can to understand what's going on—it seems a bit daft just to

**29**

copy it out. Changing the notation helps to understand it. I have to check it with another book because it misses out some steps. . . . First I read the introduction to see what they had to say about it, why it gives a reasonable approximation, and what it neglects, because you have to realise the limitations of the method. I worked through in steps within sections. . . . Some bits I had to concentrate on—had to put in values and then you can see that one step does follow from another. I am trying to understand it. It's not like learning for an exam.'

Perhaps some students do habitually apply a deep-level approach and others a surface-level approach. But, in the research reported by Diana Laurillard (1979), two-thirds of her sample of students used different approaches on different occasions. Thus, the two quotations above could well have come from the *same* student, deciding that the intrinsic interest of his project calls for a deeper approach than the extrinsic demands of a perhaps superficial examination. (Why has the student quoted in the dedication at the front of this book adopted his chosen approach?)

At present, I suspect that many of the tasks we set students, and the assessment procedures we use, do conspire to let them slog through, even to the end of a degree course, with surface-level approaches only. For instance, see Black (1969) for a study of physics final-examination papers in UK universities; apparently more than 40 per cent of the questions could have been answered from memorization alone. Surely one of the central aims of post-secondary education should be to deepen students' approaches to learning?

So our 'student body' can never, in fact, be regarded as one monolithic mass whose every member can be expected to react to our course offerings in a uniform manner. They will differ among themselves in their styles and orientations to learning: some will be at a higher stage of intellectual development than others; some will be more independent and willing to take initiative; some will be collaborative with other students, some will be competitive, and some will simply want to be left alone to get on with it; some will be interested chiefly in mastering the subject, others more in getting good grades; and so on. Furthermore, any individual student is likely to have a different range of strategies to draw on for any given learning task.

One thing, in particular, we should remember is that few of our students will necessarily learn like we learn. New teachers, fresh from several postgraduate years spent in the heady company of *la crème de la crème*, often appear to have forgotten, if they ever had occasion to notice, the difficulties faced by their less successful contemporaries. Unless we take this into account, students may justifiably criticize (Ramsden, 1979):

> '. . . the lack of empathy that some of the staff have about the ability levels of the students relative to their subject. . . . In some of the areas we're talked at at a very high level. So you can't attach anything that you've been told to something you already know, which of course is a very important point in learning . . . they've gone so far into their own area that they've forgotten that we know nothing, essentially, compared with them.'

Students being so diverse, we can never expect 100 per cent success with anything we offer them. To achieve the maximum learning among the maximum number, we'll need to offer a *variety* of things and make possible a variety of approaches. This will be discussed at greater length later.

We may also think it not entirely a waste of time to discuss the diversity of learning style with the students themselves. Even if we do not put pressure on them to change their learning styles, the knowledge that there is more than one approach to learning may cause many of them to start making beneficial experiments anyway.

## Is your course really necessary?

One final point before we go any further with course planning. As part of our preliminary market research we should have asked— even if no-one else was thoughtful enough to ask for us—whether, by any chance, a course such as we might be proposing exists already elsewhere. And, if so, is it adequately catering for the existing and potential demand? If such a course does exist and is adequately catering for the demand, we may as well turn our energies to another project. If such a course exists but is *not* adequately meeting the demand, we can continue with our proposal. But, in defiance of the 'not-invented-here' syndrome— which so often hinders valuable cross-fertilization of ideas between educational institutions—we may ask whether such courses have any worthwhile features we might incorporate into our own.

Henry Brickell (1969) offers a useful approach to appraising other people's innovations. We can derive from it twelve key questions to be asked about any new materials or methods we are thinking of adopting:

**31**

| | |
|---|---|
| 1. How suitable? | Are its objectives, methods, and outcomes appropriate to our students? |
| 2. How effective? | Does it achieve satisfactory results? |
| 3. How big? | How much time, staff, and resources does it need? How many subjects? What range of students? |
| 4. How complete? | Does it need extra supporting material? |
| 5. How complex? | Is it difficult for teachers and students to work with? |
| 6. How flexible? | Is there room for innovation and adaptation by teachers and students? |
| 7. How different? | Is is sufficiently distinct from other approaches in outcome, method, cost, or whatever? |
| 8. How repeatable? | Are there any special factors (e.g., unusual teachers or local resources) to hinder repetition elsewhere? |
| 9. How compatible? | Would it interfere or fit in with the rest of the existing system? |
| 10. How ready? | Can it be started this week/term/year, etc.? |
| 11. How 'samplable'? | Could we give it a trial run and abandon it if unsuccessful? Or would the decision have to be all-or-nothing (e.g., a computer system)? |
| 12. How expensive? | What are the initial costs, installation costs, and running costs? |

It is not often that educational institutions ask such questions about one another's courses. The 'not-invented-here' syndrome has usually served to discourage interest. However, the increasing costs of course development, especially when the design and creation of new learning resources is involved, is likely to make colleges more curious about one another's productions. Already, for example, many UK colleges, polytechnics, and universities are using course materials produced by the Open University and by the National Extension College. Furthermore, the Council for Educational Technology is now sponsoring trial collaboration between colleges in the production of learning materials. If one college can produce just a segment of a course in the knowledge that, in exchange, it will be provided with the complementary segments by other colleges, many courses that would be too daunting for any one college to consider producing alone might thus become possible for all—or at least for all who felt able to share in a common course design. In the remainder of this book, however, I am assuming that you are developing your course, alone or with colleagues, for use in your own institution only.

Chapter 2 deals with the content of a course; but please remember that there is no necessity for you to make that the next chapter you read. Having read this first chapter, you should feel free to read the remaining chapters in whatever order suits you.

# 2. The content of your course

## Introduction

By the 'content' of a course I mean the *ideas* and the *relationships* between them that will be dealt with in that course. What topics are to be included? What examples? Counter-examples? Definitions? Rules? Theories? Principles? Generalizations? What ideas belong in the course? What *skills* and *abilities* might the student develop in relation to these ideas? What *attitudes* might we wish to encourage? How do we decide?

It may be that you see no problems. Perhaps the content of your course (the syllabus) has already been decided by someone else: a head of department or an outside body. You might then feel it is not your job to question the content, but merely to 'get it across' to the best of your ability. This might seem a quite inflexible position, having to teach to someone else's syllabus. Even then, however, this chapter should demonstrate that questioning (probing, analysing, criticizing) the stipulated content might in fact help you find your best way of 'getting it across'.

The more likely situation is that you have at least some scope for deciding content yourself, or cooperatively with colleagues. The course you are planning may even be a completely new venture, giving you a free hand in deciding content. Even if your course is to be a 're-make' of an existing course, its previous content should not be taken for granted. Use the re-make as an opportunity to re-examine the content as well as the form.

Inevitably, as I suggested in Chapter 1, thinking about content will bring other questions to mind also. What about the best sequence for the content? Which teaching methods shall I use? How shall I assess my students? In considering content, one should be open to such questions, and even be deciding on possible answers. But we look more closely at those decisions in other chapters. Here, we are considering what content is to go into the course. How are we to decide?

There are *many* ways one can set about generating (and sequencing) course content. Those that suit one teacher/subject/situation/student group will be inappropriate to another. A few years ago I would not have been so ready to recognize this. Rather, I would have (e.g., in Rowntree, 1974) put great emphasis on *objectives* as the ideal place to begin—if only teachers could have been persuaded of that truth! Since then, my approach has softened. Partly, this is because I have been forced to appreciate the difficulty many teachers have with the 'objectives-first' approach. Partly, and more disturbingly, because I have come to realize that *my own* course planning does not necessarily begin with objectives!

This certainly does not mean I am renouncing objectives. I still believe they are extremely valuable in course development. Asking oneself what students should be able to *do* by the end of the course that they could not do (or not do so well) at the beginning can be highly illuminating. Many teachers (and I am one) would claim their teaching has been far better since they were introduced to objectives. (Even when they are not consciously using objectives.) And, of course, many teachers must learn to work with objectives anyway, because they are demanded by others, e.g., colleagues, heads of department, external validation bodies. I certainly believe that objectives must be considered *at some stage* of course planning. If they are not themselves used as the means of arriving at course content, then they can provide a powerful tool for analysing and elaborating content arrived at by other means.

By what other means? Well, there is a distinction I would like to make between what might be called informal or *intuitive* approaches and systematic or *analytical* approaches. The use of objectives would be an example of the latter. Broadly speaking, the intuitive approaches are those that give us most help in thinking up possible content in the first place. The analytical techniques, on the other hand, tend to be most useful once we have generated a few ideas and are ready to see how they hang together and can be extended. In reality, of course, we are thinking both intuitively and analytically at all stages of course planning. Sometimes one predominates, however, and sometimes the other.

## Intuitive approaches to content

Intuitive approaches are relatively informal, unstructured, non-systematic. Nevertheless, they may be highly productive. Here is a list of such approaches, not in any particular order:

- Sitting and reviewing one's own knowledge of the proposed subject.
- Asking other teachers and subject-matter experts.
- Analysing similar courses elsewhere.

● Reading textbooks aimed at students working at about the same level as ours will be.

● Reading more advanced books and scholarly articles on the subject.

● Reviewing films, radio and television tapes, newspaper and popular journal articles, etc., relating to the proposed subject.

● Asking prospective students what topics they would like to see the course include.

● Discussing with students their existing conceptions of, and attitudes to, the key concepts of the subject-matter.

● Choosing books (or other source materials) around which the course will be organized.

● Thinking of essential activities that students need to engage in as part of the course.

● Considering how student attainment on the course might most sensibly be assessed.

● Studying an examination syllabus, the question papers, and examiners' reports from previous years, and so on.

Maybe you can add more examples of your own. But a dozen is perhaps enough to be going on with, and quite sufficient to demonstrate that teachers who choose not to start with objectives need not be entirely bereft of ideas. A few words of comment follow to expand on the outlines above.

### Reviewing the subject

Sometimes one starts by reflecting on one's own knowledge of the proposed subject. A useful procedure here is 'brainstorming', in which you simply let possible content ideas flow through your mind and write them down without stopping to evaluate or organize them. Ideally, one should do it without selecting or censoring, letting the thoughts tumble out, in whatever order they will: major themes, trivialities, potential digressions, linking themes, and so on. Nevertheless, ideas do tend to arrive in bunches, and one leads to another in such a way that structures and sequences begin to suggest themselves.

Perhaps the most fertile way of storming one's brain is to do so in company with three or four colleagues who are doing likewise. I am always being pleasantly reminded that a small group of people can generate more ideas when thinking together than they can when thinking on their own. Clearly, the more familiar you and your colleagues are with the subject-matter and the more comfortable you are with one another, the more abundant the ideas.

The problem then becomes to select from among the many ideas produced and to identify underlying structures or themes. You may perhaps decide that some of the ideas produced are irrelevant; some are subsumed under others that have been mentioned; some are alternative ways of expressing others; and so on. So you can begin pruning and combining and, at the same time, filling in any necessary connecting ideas that have not been thought of previously. We all have our different ways of handling this more critical phase of the operation. Perhaps the most flexible is to have a good supply of small cards on each of which you can pencil a topic or an idea, and move them around on a table top until you have established all the essential relationships and filled in all the yawning gaps in your content.

Whether or not you have been able to get other people involved in the brainstorming, you may still find it valuable to talk with other teachers or subject-matter experts individually. This will be particularly valuable if you are planning a course (e.g., an interdisciplinary course) in which you cannot claim to be an expert in all areas. However, it is wise to consult more than one authority. All disciplines contain factions and 'schools of thought'. If your course is to play fair by its students it will need to be balanced. It should avoid idiosyncratic biases and should explore, or at least point out, the full range of viewpoints acceptable within the subject area.

The same cautions apply in analysing courses similar to yours elsewhere; in reading student textbooks and more advanced materials; in reviewing films, tapes, newspaper and magazine articles, etc. Consult several if you are going to consult any. This will enable you to identify the boundaries of consensus and dissent within the subject-area. It will also lessen your chances of accepting and passing on errors of fact or interpretation, or lapses of judgement, while at the same time provoking your own creativity through (one hopes) the conflicting diversity of ideas and approaches you encounter in other people's work. Needless to say, your library staff can be enormously helpful in discovering thought-provoking material, especially in sources that you might not otherwise think to consult, e.g., television and radio programmes, newspaper articles, and 'semipopular' journals like *Scientific American, New Society, National Geographic, History Today*, and so on.

### Considering student activity

The intuitive approaches so far mentioned involve the teacher in considering the subject-matter pronouncements of teachers and experts. The remaining ones direct his thoughts towards the students and what they might want or could gladly involve themselves in.

The obvious approach here is to ask prospective students what topics they would like to see tackled in the course. For instance, I once asked a group of students intending to take an introductory psychology course to write down a few questions they hoped the course might help provide answers to. ('Don't rack your brains for questions. If none spring to mind, we'll be happy to assume you have no strong expectations as yet.') Here are a few of the questions they produced:

● How can we best use psychology in bringing up children?
● Why are some people violent?
● How can one overcome stress?
● Are there inherent intellectual differences between races/sexes?
● What is the effect of early environment on children's mental development?
● How can boring jobs be made more interesting and worthwhile?
● Does advertising misuse psychology?
● Why do people who are quite reasonable on their own become antisocial when they are part of a crowd (mob)?
● What do dreams mean?
● How can a person increase his creativity?

Many of the recognized branches of psychology are touched upon in the students' questions. This may please the kind of psychology teacher who wishes to present a knowledge-oriented course, giving respectable coverage to each branch. He may, however, be vexed to see that some of the questions lean into sociology or philosophy. He may or may not be perturbed to notice that many of the questions have an 'instrumental' flavour; that is, psychology is sometimes being seen not as interesting in itself but as a means of solving real-world problems. Perhaps this arose because students were asked to pose questions rather than list topics. The more discipline-oriented teacher, however, may be happier to base his content on such questions, especially if he is able to take a problem-centred approach. At the very least, however, even if a course cannot be based around students' questions, a teacher should find it helpful to know the kinds of issue he might touch on for illustrative purposes with some hopes of their being found relevant and interesting by students.

A related approach is to discuss with students their existing conceptions of and attitudes to the subject-matter of the course. Some of my colleagues (see Gibbs *et al.*, 1980b) have recently done this in connection with (as it happens) psychology. The 29 students concerned were not asked the plain question 'What is psychology?' for fear of getting 'blank stares in reply, or clichéd definitions picked up from book titles or TV'. Instead, they were asked 'If Esso garages were to invite a psychologist in to improve the efficiency of petrol-pump attendants, what sort of things would the psychologist do?' The ensuing interviews revealed that few of the students had more than one or two conceptions of a psychologist's role and, while in total they identified nine distinct and valid conceptions, not one of those incorporated the objective, systematic, experimental, scientific aspects that would normally be given prominence in most courses on psychology. A course for these students could thus be sensibly based on the recognition not that they are ignorant and need a simple introduction to the basics, but that, between them, they already have many quite valid notions, yet seem totally unaware of some of the major dimensions of the subject. Similarly, one teacher on another Open University course has used students' answers to the question 'Is Britain capitalist?' to help him decide how to introduce and handle the concept of capitalism.

Sometimes, to move on to the next approach, course content will come to mind as a set or sequence of *materials* on which a worthwhile course can be centred. Usually this will involve books, as in the 'Great Books' courses (e.g., the study of Plato's *Republic*, Aristotle's *Politics*, Locke's *Essay*, etc.) offered at some US colleges. More recently, colleges have taken a television series (e.g., a BBC series like Robert Kee's *Ireland: a Television History* or, from Thames TV, David Bellamy's *Botanic Man*) as the core of a course.

In subject-areas where it is possible to identify seminal works that, between them, constitute a coherent field, a course can justifiably be built around them. They can be treated as primary sources to be studied intensively and elucidated. Many literature courses are of this kind. However, where the works concerned are 'secondary sources', e.g., works of criticism or commentary, like the

**39**

television material mentioned above, the teacher may need to give considerable thought to how far he should let the material dictate the content of the course, and how much additional content will be needed, anyway, to round out its inevitable limitations.

Rather than thinking first of things students might read (or view), one's ideas for course content often come in the shape of things they might (indeed must) *do*. Thus, a course sometimes defines itself in one's mind as a set of essential activities. Practising, enjoying, and getting better at these activities is what the course will be *about*. For instance, a practical drama course may be conceived in terms of the students practising mime, movement, role-playing, improvization, and so on. Similarly, a philosophy course may be conceived in terms of students taking part (under guidance) in philosophical discussions. Such a course would, no doubt, differ from one based on the idea of students writing essays about books about philosophers' books. My colleague, Nick Farnes (1976) describes a course, conceived in terms of essential activities, to 'help the student to structure his learning without our specifying its content'. Thus he expects the student to be formulating questions he wishes to pursue, organizing them into manageable learning tasks, surveying likely learning resources, refining and developing his questions, organizing and storing the information he uncovers, evaluating the evidence, reporting on the implications, and so on.

Another colleague, Phillipe Duchastel (1976) describes a university art course in which 'art' is 'taken as the collection of processes which involve the experiencing of environment. These certainly include the sensory processes (touching, hearing, etc.), but go beyond them as well to involve cognitive processes such as imaging, stereotyping, boundary shifting, etc.' Hence, the reading material in the course is presented not as subject-matter to be learned but as a stimulus to creative and reflective activity. For example, students may record an improvized or scored 'performance' of sounds produced by 'found objects'; make self-portraits using a distorting mirror; modify their home surroundings using provided materials such as tarred string; report their observations on a walk in which the route is determined by chance (e.g., flipping a coin at each corner); and so on. Such activities served to define the contents of the course for a course team that had little time for objectives.

My remaining two intuitive approaches to content can be disposed of fairly rapidly. Both are fairly well known to teachers.

The first of them is to ask oneself how student attainment on the course might sensibly be assessed. In a way, this is like asking 'what would you like students to be able to *do* (or do better) as a result of the course?' but without needing to mention the bogey-word 'objectives'. Many teachers will find that the ploy of imagining an ideal form of assessment, even if it cannot be put into effect, gives them new ideas as to the content (and form) of the course. Thus, if students would ideally be assessed by having them criticize previously unseen sources, then criticism of such sources must form part of the content of the course. If students should be able to deploy their subject matter knowledge in relationship with other people—medical students with patients, for instance—then human encounters must also be built into the course.

The final method I mentioned is also part of the stock-in-trade of the professional teacher. Serious students have always attempted to 'read the entrails'—looking for cues as to what will be expected of them—by poring over syllabuses, attempting previous years' examination papers, and studying examiners' reports where they exist. What comes as a surprise to many of them is that their teacher may have to do the same if he is teaching to a syllabus or objectives or assessment strategy designed even partly by someone else. If you should be in this situation for some part or all of your course, the ensuing pages, in which we explore the more analytical approaches, should help you amplify, reorder, criticize and shape-up the content ideas you arrive at by this last, or any of the previously mentioned approaches.

At this point, poised between the intuitive and analytical, I find myself wondering whether listing all these 'approaches' is not a pretentious over-technologizing of what really is a matter of common sense and inspiration. After all, we have probably often said of the content and structure of a course that 'it just came to me' (in the bath or out of it)? How often is one conscious of having needed a 'tool-kit' such as I am displaying in this chapter? On the other hand, I am aware that inspiration favours the well-prepared mind. Maybe course development ideas would not come to me so easily had I not made myself familiar with such approaches to the point where I am scarcely conscious of using them. And there certainly are times when ideas simply do not come or when I, or a course team I am working with, get bogged down in a very limited approach to content. At such times, a conscious review of techniques can open up new possibilities. I am also, I hope, honest enough to admit that the ideas that 'just come to me' usually need to be worked on subsequently! Anyway, I am sufficiently convinced to carry on presenting techniques to you. I am sure that at least some of them will be both new and useful to you.

## Analytical approaches

By analytical approaches, I mean nothing very grand: simply ways of examining, extending, and organizing ideas that one has arrived at intuitively. As perhaps hinted earlier, this is the role in which I now personally tend to use objectives. Traditional course developers may already be scandalized that I have managed to get so far through this book without yet expounding the virtues of objectives. So, let us make them the first analytical approach to be looked at, and then go on to *competence analysis* and *content analysis*.

### Analysis by objectives

Perhaps the major boost to deliberate course development in the last couple of decades has come from the realization that an early attempt to decide one's objectives can lead to better teaching and learning. Objectives are supposed to state as clearly and un-ambiguously as possible what students should be able to *do* (or do better) as a result of working through their course.

The use of objectives is grounded in an assumption that the purpose of education is to help people change. They are to become different from what they were, developing their existing qualities and abilities, and acquiring new ones. They are to change the ways they think, act, and feel. They are to become more knowledgeable, more skilful, more confident, more rational, more insightful, more autonomous, and so on.

FROM AIMS TO OBJECTIVES
Such a change-orientation may be hinted at in the published aims of a course. But such aims are often expressed in terms of what the *course* will do, e.g., 'we hope to stimulate your interest in and understanding of Environmental Control and Public Health and enable you to become, for example, an "informed observer" in any public inquiry concerning the environment.' This is helpful, but still leaves in doubt what the *student* will be expected to do (as a result of the stimulus and in order to count as an 'informed observer').

**42**

So how do objectives differ from aims? Both are statements of educational intent. But, as previously noticed, aims are sometimes expressed in terms of what the teacher is planning to do to the student: to stimulate, introduce, show, discuss, compare, etc. Objectives state specifically what the student will be able to do *as a result*.

Also, even when expressed in terms of intended student attainment, aims are a more general statement, e.g., the student will learn to 'understand', 'appreciate', 'realize the significance of', 'achieve a working knowledge', and so on. Objectives, however, should be more specific, as if in answer to the questions: 'But what do you mean by "understand", "appreciate", etc? How might the student *demonstrate* his understanding, appreciation, knowledge, etc.?' Thus objectives need to be phrased in terms of verbs like 'explain', 'calculate', 'describe', 'list', 'analyse', and so on, all of which imply more explicit and demonstrable activity. We can say that aims and objectives lie towards (though not at) opposite ends of a general–particular or abstract–concrete continuum.

For example, one of the broad general aims of a nutrition course might be to 'introduce the student to healthy eating habits'. Further consideration might produce the rather more specific aims that 'the student should know about the components of food, appreciate the importance of balance in a diet, and be aware of the difficulty of getting people to change their diets'. These aims could then be translated into objectives as follows: 'The student should be able to *list* the components of food and *describe* the function of each in the body; *calculate* (using appropriate dietary tables) whether a given diet is or is not balanced; *explain* the possible consequences of diets that are out of balance in various ways; *judge* how best to persuade a given group of people to reconsider their diets', and so on. Again, one of the broad general aims espoused by a college might be 'to open out the student's imagination and sympathies'. A teacher of English literature might translate this broad aim into one slightly more particular: 'to foster an appreciation of twentieth-century literature', and for a certain course he might further specify 'some novels of D. H. Lawrence'. At some subsequent stage he might then decide an appreciation of the novels might be demonstrated in the attainment of such objectives as the student being able to:

● Identify with Lawrence's characters.

**43**

● Relate Lawrence's viewpoints to his own experience.
● Analyse the literary elements that have provoked his involvement.
● Describe an incident from his own experience as if seen by Lawrence.
● Assume the persona of Lawrence in replying to hostile contemporary criticism.
● Make and justify a personal statement as to Lawrence's 'meanings'.
● Seek out and read more of Lawrence's writings than are set for assignments.

Some such objectives could be suggested by the teacher in advance of meeting his class, perhaps because of his experience with similar classes in the past. Others would arise out of the uniqueness of the people in this particular class, yet still be seen to relate to the over-arching but more general aims. The teacher could move even further towards the particular, concrete end of the continuum by asking himself how would he assess attainment of the objectives. He might consider possible test questions, e.g., 'What would you have done if you'd been Mrs Morel in such-and-such a situation' (not actually described by Lawrence); or 'Reply as Lawrence to this review of your latest book in *The Times*', or 'Why does Lawrence end the novel with that particular paragraph?' etc. He might also specify further by mentioning situations in which the individual's responses to Lawrence might be observed, e.g., in conversations, dramatic improvizations, students' writings on other topics, and so on.

WHAT USE ARE OBJECTIVES?
As suggested, objectives can be a valuable guide in designing worthwhile assessment (and evaluation) activities. This is further dealt with in Chapters 5 and 6. Also, as I show in this chapter and in Chapters 3 and 4, objectives can help you in deciding on the content of your course, on its structure and sequence, and on the way you will use the available teaching methods and media.

In addition, objectives are a means of *communicating* (or negotiating) the educational intentions of a course. If you are teaching to an externally imposed syllabus, they may help you identify what is to be achieved. If you are developing your own syllabus, they may enable you to discuss your intentions with colleagues and with students.

Broadly phrased aims usually sound too worthy to quarrel with. Yet when they are translated into objectives, the illusion of consensus is often shattered, enabling colleagues to enter into a productive debate about just what is worth learning and teaching. Such communication is clearly essential in any team-teaching situation. It is also essential where students pass from one teacher to another as they progress through a series of courses or course modules. Otherwise, some objectives may be tackled by more than one teacher and, worse still, others may be skipped by every teacher on the assumption that someone else is tackling them.

Objectives may also be well worth communicating to the students. They may tell the student what you want him to get out of the course. Ideally, students should be encouraged to formulate and communicate to you their own objectives as well as or, in some courses, instead of, accepting those of the teacher.

In some courses, especially with a highly technical subject-matter, it may be pointless to try communicating the objectives in advance because they will need to be couched in such specialist language that students will not be able to understand them until they have achieved them! Even so, it may be possible, and well worth the imaginative effort, to give the student some idea of the objectives by describing the kind of problem he will be able to deal with after he has achieved them. If students are left to guess your intentions, they are likely to play safe and act *as though* the objectives were to memorize your every word of wisdom and/or to attain the pass mark in an examination.

However, as already admitted, not all teachers take readily to spelling out objectives. Some find the very idea alien to the traditions of their discipline. Others are daunted by the practicalities of generating objectives, and knowing at what level of specificity to stop. Objections to objectives are explored at length by Macdonald-Ross (1973) and Rowntree (1974). The latter book deals also with use of objectives as do many others, e.g., Baume and Jones (1974), Beard (1979), and Bligh *et al.* (1975). If you are not at present an adherent of objectives, it is hoped that you will at least suspend any disbelief for the remainder of this section while I say something about where objectives come from and the different kinds that arise.

TYPES OF OBJECTIVE

Objectives ultimately have their source in the perceptions of teachers, students, parents, employers, and all who believe they have a stake in education. They come from the views we all have about the present and future needs of people living in society and about the skills and insights that have been developed through various arts, crafts, and sciences. Our beliefs about what is worth learning may, as we have seen, find expression in broad curriculum aims. In turn, these may, as we have seen, be used to generate and/or justify a particular set of educational objectives. These will be more specific and serve to indicate what we might look for in the enhanced capacity for thought, action, and feeling among students who have benefited from a curriculum developed with reference to those over-arching aims.

How are we to distinguish between different kinds of objective? Is it worth the effort? I believe that some discrimination in this area is worth attempting: many critics of the use of objectives make points that would be devastating if all objectives were of the kind they castigate; but often they seem not to have noticed the several other kinds that would evade their censure.

Almost any framework for distinguishing among types of objective could be helpful, in so far as it might lead to our surveying the possibilities more systematically. Several frameworks are available to us. One common distinction is in terms of level: that is, some objectives demand more of the student than others (e.g., using a foreign phrase appropriately in a conversation is a higher level objective than merely being able to recall the phrase). Indeed, we can distinguish, as I do later, between an objective that can be totally attained and one that could never be fully attained to his own satisfaction even by the most eminent scholar or practitioner in his field.

Another distinction, exemplified in the taxonomies of Benjamin Bloom and his colleagues and followers (see page 182), is between cognitive, affective, and psychomotor objectives—that is, between what we might otherwise call thinking, feeling, or action objectives (remembering, of course, that many objectives will be mixed). One distinction I find very useful is between objectives involving, primarily, knowledge or attitudes or skills. (Again, mixtures are possible within a single objective.) Unfortunately, to my mind, those three are sometimes identified one-to-one with the three just mentioned (cognitive, affective, and psychomotor). To do so obscures the fact that, for instance, skills can be cognitive or affective as well as psychomotor; knowledge can be knowledge of one's own or another person's feelings or of how to perform bodily movements; and so on. But I discuss the distinction between knowledge, attitudes, and skills at greater length in Chapter 5 in connection with student assessment. In the present chapter (though I distinguish, later on, between course objectives and lesson objectives), I pursue just one three-fold classification which I have personally found very fruitful. This distinction is between life-skills, methodological objectives, and content objectives.

Life-skill objectives relate to abilities and qualities a student might acquire which, even though attained in an academic context through work on a subject or discipline, contribute ultimately to his humanity and rationality rather than merely to his academic interests—which, indeed, he may not pursue once his formal education is completed. For instance, Neil Postman and Charles Weingartner (1971) propose an 'inquiry' curriculum in which the teacher looks for such life-skill changes as the following among his students:

● The frequency with which they ask questions.
● The increase in the relevance and cogency of their questions.
● The frequency and conviction of their challenges to assertions made by other students or teachers or textbooks.
● The relevance and clarity of the standards on which they base their challenges.
● Their willingness to modify or otherwise change their position when data warrant such change.
● Their willingness to suspend judgements when they have insufficient data.
● The increase in their skill in observing, classifying, generalizing, etc.
● The increase in their tolerance for diverse answers.
● Their ability to apply generalizations, attitudes, and information to novel situations.

As indicated earlier, many educators distinguish between objectives that are essential *cognitive* (involving thought processes) and those that are essentially *affective* (involving the feelings). Many objectives are mixed, however. Most of those above may be chiefly cognitive, but an affective element is present in at least two, as is indicated by use of words like 'conviction', 'willingness', 'tolerance', and 'attitude'.

This same mixing of cognitive and affective life-skills is seen in the 'self-actualization' objectives suggested by Carl Rogers (1961):

● The person comes to see himself differently.

**47**

- He accepts himself and his feelings more fully.
- He becomes more self-confident and self-directing.
- He becomes more the person he would like to be
- He becomes more flexible, less rigid in his perceptions.
- He adopts more realistic goals for himself.
- He becomes more acceptant of others.
- He becomes more open to the evidence, both of what is going on outside of himself and what is going on inside himself.

In the two sets of life-skill objectives quoted above, we see frequent use of the words 'increase' and 'more'. That is, the student is expected to enhance his power to do this or that. What would be adequate attainment for one student would not be considered so for another or even for the same student at different stages of his career. Such objectives are relativistic, needing to be specified still further with regard to the present and possible future states of particular individual students.

None of us will ever fully attain objectives such as those listed above and this is worth noting. While some objectives allow for mastery—100 per cent attainment—others imply *infinite improve ability*. I have never seen this distinction made clear in debates about the usefulness of objectives and I suspect its absence is responsible for much unnecessary controversy. Much of the criticism centres on objectives that are masterable and therefore relatively trivial, ignoring the challenge posed by attempts to identify, and then pursue, those more transcendental objectives that are infinitely improvable.

In embracing such life-skill objectives as 'critical thinking' or 'problem solving', one can do so prior to specifying any particular subject matter. They are content-free. But philosophers (see Hirst, 1968 and Hirst and Peters, 1970) very properly point out that one does not develop abilities like 'critical thinking' or 'problem-solving' or 'collaborative enquiry' except in relation to some specific area of subject-content or body of knowledge. Furthermore, different areas of subject-matter or bodies of knowledge can be expected to demand *different kinds* of critical thinking and problem-solving and collaborative enquiry. Thus, the motorcycle mechanic and the lawyer might be expected to acquire these skills in different ways. So might the historian and the biologist. Hirst and Peters talked of distinct 'forms of knowledge', Philip Phenix (1964) of distinct 'realms of meaning', exemplified in but not restricted to the various curriculum 'subjects', which all demand

48

specialized 'modes of enquiry' and 'ways of knowing'. Jerome Bruner (1964) suggests that our chief purpose in teaching a subject or discipline should not be to get the student to commit specific content to mind:

> Rather, it is to teach him to participate in the process that makes possible the establishment of knowledge. We teach a subject not to produce little living libraries on the subject, rather to get a student to think mathematically for himself, to consider matters as a historian does, to embody the process of knowledge-getting. Knowing is a process, not a product.

This brings us to what I have called *methodological* objectives (Rowntree, 1974). By this I mean whatever cognitive, affective, and psychomotor *processes* the student engages in and develops that can reasonably be held to be peculiar to the subject-matter he is investigating: the differing methods of framing problems, the differing forms of investigation, the differing kinds of response to experience, the differing criteria for proof and truth, the differing modes of explanation and justification. I am talking here not of the concepts peculiar to various subject-matter areas but of the ways of generating and manipulating such concepts, ways that are distinctive of that subject-matter and not to be easily categorized as special applications of generally useful (life-skill) abilities.

Such a distinction between methodological objectives and life-skill objectives should theoretically be possible when the student is investigating part of some established discipline like astronomy or dentistry or economics. It should also be possible when the subject is one of his own devising, like 'an analysis of television advertising' or 'designing a car for handicapped people' or 'civilian life during the Second World War'. In these inter-disciplinary projects, of course, the student would need to borrow from the methodologies of several contributory disciplines as well as generate new ones out of his own style of enquiry. Thus, the student who wants to investigate the effects of the Second World War on the civilian population might need to draw on the methodologies of history, statistics, sociology, economics, social survey, art history, political science, literary criticism, and philosophy, among others.

You may well find, however, that the distinction between life-skill and methodological objectives is more easily made in theory than when looking at examples. Here, for instance, are some objectives proposed by Alan Bishop (1971). Are they life-skills or methodological objectives and, if the latter, for which subject area(s)?.

1. Model construction and exploration:
   (a) To search for, and find, similarities occurring in a variety of situations.
   (b) To isolate and define the variables underlying these similarities.
   (c) To determine and define the relationships that exist between the variables.
   (d) To establish the necessary validity of statements of these relationships.
   (e) To search for the axioms from which this model can be logically derived.
2. Model application:
   (a) To recognize that a given situation is one in which a certain model is applicable.
   (b) To make assumptions about the variables defined in the model.
   (c) To manipulate the model in order to solve the problem.
   (d) To verify that the chosen model is the best analogue of the given situation.
   (e) To use the model for making new predictions.

Actually these were proposed as mathematics objectives but they seem to have a relevance for enquiry in almost any disciplinary area. They also seem applicable to 'everyday' problems like 'Why won't the damn car start?' or 'Isn't it time I considered a new career?' Perhaps, then, they are life-skills of very wide application? Practitioners of different disciplines may have more in common than they think. Richard Whitfield (1971, page 25) goes so far as to suggest that 'our higher mental processes are surely more basically the result of cognitive processes acting upon content, which has been appropriately structured to bring out the essential principles, truth criteria, and generalizations, than a function of the content itself'.

As if to recognize this, some writers lump life-skill and methodological objectives together under the label *process* objectives (Cole, 1972). But that leaves us with a third category of objectives, relating to the knowledge—the concepts and principles—that these processes produce and act upon. These I have called *content* objectives. By this I mean the student's ability to recognize and expound the concepts, generalizations, and principles that make up the substance and structure of his subject area. The nutrition objectives mentioned earlier were of this type. So, too, are the following, from an Open University course in educational psychology (Cashdan, 1971, page 10):

1. To define learning 'set' and give your own examples of learning sets.
2. To define learning styles and strategies: to distinguish and give examples of Bruner's two main learning strategies.
3. To summarize Watkin's work on field-dependence/independence.
4. To summarize Kagan's work on reflection/impulsivity.
5. To discuss the main cognitive and personality correlates of 3 and 4.
6. To criticize and evaluate 3 and 4, both theoretically and in terms of children's actual performance (e.g., in school).
7. To suggest (and evaluate) links between 2, 3, 4, and 5.
8. To justify experimental method in educational psychology and to explain reliability, validity, and correlation.
9. To interpret the results of simple correlational studies.

These also contain references to life-skill or methodological abilities—to summarize, to criticize, to evaluate, to justify, and to interpret.

So, apart from life-skills and methodological objectives, worthwhile objectives can also be derived by asking what concepts and unifying principles are relevant to a given subject and how we can assess the depth and extent of our student's understanding of them. The student investigating civilian life during the Second World War, for example, may emerge able to describe, and suggest cause-and-effect relationships among such topics as: social organization and adaptation; public disruption and personal loss; health, nutrition and living standards; employment, industrial relations and pressures for social reform; communication; morale; and so on. The content objectives he thus achieves will integrate concepts peculiar to this particular subject-area (e.g., evacuation, rationing, conscientious objection), with whatever more general concepts (e.g., socialization, norms, the price mechanism) he finds worth borrowing, along with the methodologies, from the many related disciplines.

This classification into life-skills, methodological objectives, and content objectives is rough and ready, but it does seem to relate to many public pronouncements about aims and objectives. Thus, for example, John Dixon (1972), in his influential reflections on an Anglo-American conference on the teaching of English, outlines three widely held models in the teaching of literature— the personal growth model, the skills model, and the cultural heritage model—which seem closely related to my three categories of objective. Brian Lewis (1973) writes of the student learning to recognize and recall, to explain and to justify in each of three different problem-solving domains:

1. The domain of individual *problems* which arise within the discipline being taught, and which are characteristic of that discipline (content?).
2. The domain of *problem-solving* procedures which are used to solve the problems of 1 (methodologies).
3. The domain of *higher-order problem-solving procedures* which are implied in the use of 2, and which can be applied to seemingly-different problems in seemingly-different disciplines (life-skills?).

The same trio seem to occur again when Walter Elkan (1974) suggests that teachers of economics:

> ... really have to do three things. First, to teach people through the medium of economics to *reason*, to learn to be *critical*, to express themselves *lucidly* (life skills?) ... Second, I see our task as teaching students the very *basic notions* of economics, for example that there is a relationship between price and quantity demanded, the idea of choice and opportunity cost, the idea that consumption is ultimately determined by how much is produced (content-objectives?) ... Third ... some broad indication of *how* most of us would sub-divide and classify economics. ... Students should also have some idea of what is meant by the *techniques* that are most commonly used by economists, like cost-benefit analysis ... and national income accounting (methodological objectives?). [My italics throughout.]

Courses with a conscious emphasis on life-skill objectives are probably rare at college and university level. However, the study of many subjects (e.g., classics or philosophy, politics and economics, or history) has long been expected to provide a 'liberal' (i.e., humanizing) education. That is to say, the graduate was expected to emerge not necessarily as a professional classicist, philosopher, historian, etc., but as a wiser and more humane person. Here is an ex-Eton scholar talking of his one-time tutor, famous for his Latin verse:

'Stephen major', he once said to my brother, 'if you do not take more pains, how can you ever expect to write good longs and shorts? If you do not write good longs and shorts, how can you ever be a man of taste? If you are not a man of taste, how can you ever hope to be of use in the world?'

(From the *Life of Sir James Fitzjames Stephen, Bart*, by his brother, Leslie Stephen, pages 80–81.)

In other words, life-skill objectives can be attained through the pursuit of methodological or content objectives. It is even possible nowadays to teach (or at least teach about) science and engineering as 'liberal studies' (especially since the 'social responsibility of science' movement has injected ethical issues into the curriculum). Again, students of medicine and law are now confronted with issues (e.g., euthanasia and civil rights) which encourage a kind of thinking that can help them develop in their personal as well as professional lives.

COURSE OBJECTIVES VERSUS LESSON OBJECTIVES

I am often asked whether there is a difference between course objectives and the objectives of individual lessons (or units, modules, etc.): 'Aren't the objectives for a course just all the lesson objectives added together?' or 'Aren't the course objectives really just the general aims?' In certain courses, this may be so: the course has general aims and these can be realized through a number of separate, specific objectives, each of which can be identified with a separate lesson within the course.

However, there are at least two other forms of course objective that cannot be tied to individual lessons. Firstly, some course objectives may require the student to be able to review and draw upon the experience of the *whole* course (all the lessons). For example, from an introductory science course:

Suggest simple scientific explanations for given phenomena that are not described in the course but that are wholly or partially explicable in terms of ideas from the course.
*or*
Demonstrate your appreciation of the affective (emotional) and aesthetic aspects of science by being able to quote examples from the course of scientific discoveries or advances which you found (or which you imagine the protagonists found) particularly exciting or satisfying, or which to your mind exhibited a particular intellectual or conceptual beauty, and give reasons for your choice.

Secondly, some course objectives, especially (but not exclusively) of the affective and/or of the infinitely improveable variety, relate to the whole course because the student will be practising them and enhancing his 'performance' *throughout* the course. There will be no single lesson in which a 'breakthrough' to a new level of competence can be expected; or certainly not for every student. Take, for example, Carl Rogers' self-actualization objectives (page 48) or the mathematics objectives of Alan Bishop (page 50). Or, as a new example, consider this course objective which could by no means be mistaken for that of an individual lesson:

> Given a poem he has not seen before, the student will be able to write an account of his developing perceptions of it, assessing the extent to which these are controlled by the poet and by his own previous experiences. He will define the central theme and attitude of the poem and outline his own considered interpretation (whether psychological, philosophical, religious, sociological, political, or whatever) contrasting it with the interpretation of at least one colleague. His interpretation will be assessed according to how amply it is supported by reference to the imagery, diction, rhythm, etc of the poem and how well it manages to account for the poem as a whole. Students will need to consult with one another; they may consult any texts they wish; and they may take up to four hours to complete the exercise.

Close study of this course objective will confirm that objectives may reveal not just the intended outcomes of the course but may also contain many clues as to its content, teaching/learning methods, and likely forms of student assessment and course evaluation.

### Competence analysis

Here we arrive at decisions about what to put in our course by asking what do people competent in the subject-matter *do*? Now the answer we give depends upon what we mean by '*competent*'. Do we mean 'experts,' e.g., master craftsmen, internationally acclaimed professional scholars working at the frontiers of knowledge? Or do we mean people who have achieved an acceptable standard, e.g., getting what we regard as a 'good degree' in an average year? Or something in between the two? Let us now discuss what can be called master performance analysis.

54

MASTER PERFORMER ANALYSIS

This can be applied to any type of course but will probably be most fruitful when your intentions are discipline-oriented. The purpose of the analysis is to identify the skills and procedures employed by the expert (or, less ambitiously, by the recognizably competent performer) in the discipline as he sets about 'doing physics', or 'philosophizing', or 'being a biochemist'. If you are working on an issue-based or interdisciplinary course, like *Health and Environment* or *Understanding Society*, you may have difficulty identifying a model master performer. Is there such a person? Or is he a notional amalgam of the master performers in the various contributing disciplines? Especially if the subject is a new one, considerable imagination may be needed to decide what competence in it would look like.

At present, master performance analysis is a relatively unexplored technique. Carrying out a full master performance analysis would be an enormous task and has never, to my knowledge, been performed. However, there are many partial examples, like the one that follows, to give some fair idea as to what might be involved. Fig. 2.1 comes from an Open University course on Earth Sciences (geology, etc.) in which the student is encouraged 'to consider the way in which Earth Scientists set about planning and executing their investigations, how they communicate their results and conclusions to their colleagues, and how these colleagues come to accept or reject such work'. I do not have space to print the supporting discussions and examples, but the chart alone gives some indication of the factors that need to be taken into account.

In carrying out a master performance analysis, we might ask questions like these:

1. What sorts of problems do master performers interest themselves in?
2. How do they set about seeking solutions: what kind of conceptual frameworks do they operate within; what kinds of evidence do they seek; what criteria do they have for truth and proof?
3. How do they explain and justify their solutions: what styles of argument and criticism do they adopt?

Here is a rough sketch towards a master performance analysis in

**55**

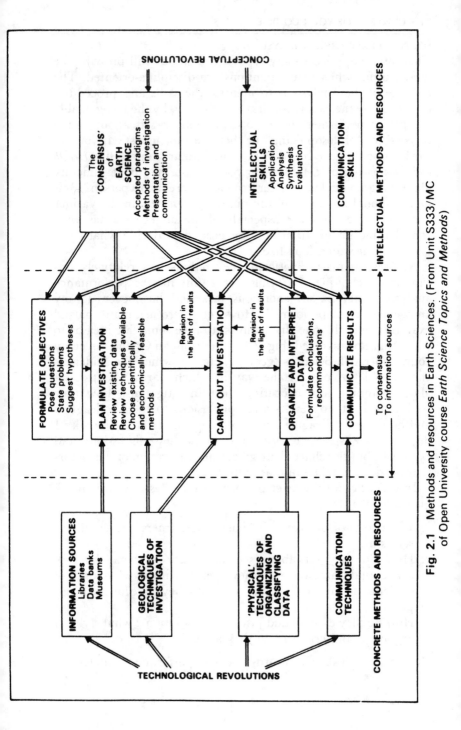

**Fig. 2.1** Methods and resources in Earth Sciences. (From Unit S333/MC of Open University course *Earth Science Topics and Methods*)

the field of history (drawn from units on History in the Open University's Arts Foundation Course, A100):

1. Depending on the level of communication the historian is aiming at (monograph, pop history, student essay, etc.) he should make efficient and critical use of all the sources available to him. For example, he should:
   (a) Distinguish between primary and secondary sources.
   (b) Identify primary sources appropriate to the various kinds of historical data he requires.
   (c) Assess the credibility of his sources.
   (d) Determine the usefulness of a source.
   (e) Distinguish between valid and invalid inference that might be made from a source.
   His work should, in this sense, be scientific.

2. Again, depending upon readership aimed at, the historian should communicate his information in a clear and efficient manner. At best his manner of presentation should conform to the highest canons of literary style, showing that history is art as well as science.

3. Depending on the subject of study, and bearing in mind that history is concerned both with change through time, and with explanation and interconnections, he should establish a reasonable balance between narrative, analysis and description.

4. He should seek always to be concrete and precise and to steer clear of the dangers involved in
   (a) periodization
   (b) relating art, etc., to historical context
   (c) historical semantics.

5. History should not be propaganda. Grosser subjective influence should always be eliminated. Yet historical writing often derives an extra quality from the special point of view of the author. Completely objective history is an impossibility.

Notice that the list above is not composed entirely of things the master historian does do. It also includes things that he *avoids* doing. Thus, the master performer avoids (a) periodization (chopping history into rigidly segmented periods each quite different from those on either side), (b) failing to take into account the historical context of works of art, and (c) semantic problems such as would arise if he used vague phrases like 'the people' or was careless with words like 'feudalism' that did not exist at the time he

**57**

was writing about; he also avoids undue subjectivity in his writing. In a book that has something of the flavour of master performance analysis about it, and in which he gathers the views of seven Oxbridge historians, Ralph Bennett (1974) suggests that the historian's chief protection against such dangers is 'common sense' (p. 5). This is echoed by Brian Pullan (p. 49) who talks of 'that impressive common sense on which all the best historical writing depends' and he fleshes out the portrait by mentioning (p. 50): 'a cultivated intuition for the way things really happen, a grasp of what the world was and is really like, a realistic sense of the past—these are the hallmarks of the good historian at any level'.

Such analyses of the performance of masters can be suggestive of worthwhile student activities. Obviously we cannot expect students to become masters during one course. But the master performance, once identified, can set an ultimate goal towards which we may direct our students' footsteps.

*A Caution*  As a lead into our discussion of the next analysis techniques, let me make a final point about master performer analysis. I have already said that, especially in a new subject or an interdisciplinary field, it may be difficult to find an actual master performer. A converse problem may also arise: in some fields there may be radically different masters at work. In other words, the same subject may be applied and practised in quite different, although equally respectable, ways.

My colleague Roger Harrison suggests, as an example, the teaching of statistics as a 'service course'. Suppose you are in a Mathematics department which is asked to put on a statistics course for the benefit of students in the Biology or Physics departments. No doubt the master performer to come to mind would be the mathematical statistician or possibly the statistical consultant. He would have a good working knowledge of the principal statistical techniques, and would also be well versed in the theory underlying them and the methods by which they were derived.

However, colleagues in the Biology or Physics departments may well say 'But that is not the kind of "master performer" we had in mind at all!' They may have in mind not specialist statisticians but specialists in other disciplines who use statistics as a *tool* in their studies. Such 'master performers' will have a good knowledge of when and how to use the standard techniques; but they will be relatively ignorant of the underlying theory; they will be unconcerned with derivations; and they will be unable to cope with novel situations except by calling on a specialist for advice.

A useful subtechnique within any kind of competence analysis is *critical incident analysis* (see Flanagan, 1954). This is the identification of key moments within the life of the expert that are particularly revealing about how he tackles his work, e.g., how does a school teacher cope with an unruly pupil? Clearly, our two kinds of statistician would have quite different 'critical incidents'.

Failure to acknowledge the differences between the two types of statistical master performer in designing the requested service course could easily lead to frustration and anxiety. The students would get very impatient with the mathematical details, which in their eyes would be unnecessary; while the teacher would deplore their shallow approach and see the students as inadequate because they failed to grasp 'fundamentals'.

In fact, if you were asked to arrange a 'service course' in statistics (or any other 'tool subject') for students who would be using it in routine, repetitive ways, in thinking about course content you might well use the next analysis technique—task analysis.

TASK ANALYSIS
The techniques of task analysis originated in military and industrial training (Seymour, 1968). They are particularly useful when planning how to teach people to carry out repetitive tasks in circumstances where there are clear-cut criteria as to whether or not the task has been adequately performed. 'Critical incident analysis' may be needed to help you decide which tasks are really important enough to be worth teaching. The procedure is, in essence, very simple. You keep company with someone who is carrying out the task and you note exactly what he does, when he does it, how he does it and what results he produces. You then analyse his activity very carefully, breaking it down into the set of fairly minute substeps which need to be followed in order to ensure success. This analysis should enable you to decide on a suitable sequence of instruction and practice.

Here is a framework, devised by my colleague Clive Lawless, for analysing and designing a task-based component in a course:

1. What is the task?
2. When should the task be carried out?
3. What tools, equipment, and materials are needed?
4. What are the objects on which the task is carried out?

5. How is the task carried out? What order is followed? How long does each step take? What safety precautions have to be observed? What are the most likely errors?
6. What are the criteria of successful performance? (How can the performer tell when he has carried out the task successfully?)
7. What is the use or application of the task?
8. How much practice must be built into the training?

(Most task analyses need to be carried out in much more detail but even at this simple level you may gain considerable guidance in designing effective instruction.)

Here is an example of task analysis, provided by Clive Lawless and Roger Harrison from a course for paramedical trainees:

*Checking a Patient's Blood Pressure*

| | |
|---|---|
| What is the task? | Ascertain systolic and diastolic blood pressures, compare values with checklist, and proceed to next stage of diagnosis. |
| When should task be carried out? | When diagnostic checklist requires. |
| What tools, equipment, and materials are needed? | Stethoscope and sphygmomanometer. |
| What are objects on which task is carried out? | Patients. |
| How is task carried out? Order? | Get patient to bare arm. Reassure and explain. Put band of sphygmomanometer around arm. Inflate until pulse disappears. Note systolic pressure. Release more air until pulse heard in stethoscope disappears again. Note diastolic reading. |
| How long? | 1–2 minutes. |
| Safety precautions? | Do not keep pressure on arm for too long. |
| Most likely errors? | Failure to locate pulse correctly. Sound in stethoscope masked by extraneous noise. Incorrect reading of scale. |
| What are criteria of successful performance? | Repeat reading, by self or instructor, gives same result. |
| What is use or application of completed task? | If blood-pressure is satisfactory, seek other causes for patient's symptoms; if unsatisfactory, investigate related causes; refer for other medical advice. |
| How much practice is needed? | Three practice determinations, then use as necessary in making diagnoses. |

For a rather different approach to task analysis, see how Daly and Dunn (1976) identified the steps to be followed by undergraduate mathematicians in solving integration problems of the following kind:

$$\text{Find } I = \int x \sqrt{(5 + 3x^2)} dx$$

1. Select $u$ as a function of $x$.
2. Differentiate $u$ with respect to $x$.
3. Write $du = \frac{du}{dx} dx$
4. Using 3, replace $\frac{du}{dx} dx$ in the integral by $du$ and express the original integral as an integral with respect to the new variable $u$.
5. If the new integral is simpler than the original, progress has been made. Perform the necessary integration, if this is possible: express the final answer in terms of $x$ and the problem is solved. If it is not possible to integrate the new integrand, a further change of variable is necessary and a return to 1 must be made. If the new integral is not simpler than the original, return to 1, discard the function of $x$ already chosen and make a new selection for $u$.

The two examples above are quite limited in scope. Each forms a component of a course rather than being a complete course in itself. Task analysis is not, however, restricted in this way. It is possible to consider a complete course on a task basis. Macdonald-Ross and Rees (1972) describe how task analysis was used in designing a service course on electricity for university biologists:

> ... surveys showed that biologists need two distinct but inter-connected sets of skills in the electrical field. They need a knowledge of electric circuit terminology and the electrical properties of networks involving some quite sophisticated electrical concepts; and they must be able to operate equipment such as CROs, transducers, stimulators and amplifiers. These needs form the basis of the program objectives. . . .
>
> The characteristics of the student population, the entry behaviour if you wish, were examined in great detail. We analysed the students' capabilities in handling practical electrical equipment, their grasp of basic physical concepts (especially electrical concepts), and we examined their mathematical ability, for so much electrical design

work and operation is dependent on mathematics. We expected that they would not be too good at handling equipment (we were right), but we were a little alarmed to find how deficient their mathematics were, or rather, their translation of mathematical concepts into the domain of electrical science. Imagine, service courses having service courses, which on their back do bite 'em!

*Algorithms* Just because you have identified a task as being necessary to your course, it does not follow that you must teach the student how to do it. For one thing he may be able to do it already (e.g., measuring blood pressure) as a result of previous courses. Again you may be able to save him the trouble of memorizing the steps in the task by giving him some kind of checklist that will remind him at the time when he needs to perform that task.

One very powerful form of checklist, for use when a number of decisions have to be taken while performing the task, is the *algorithm*. An algorithm contains within it the solutions to a variety of related problems. The user is led to the solution or outcome appropriate to his situation (bypassing all others) by answering a series of yes/no questions. Fig. 2.2 shows part of a medical algorithm concerned with diagnosing peripheral vascular disorders when patients exhibit skin colour changes in their limbs.

In order to compile an algorithm it is usually necessary to do a task analysis first. You may then use the algorithm to structure your teaching. Alternatively, if it would be convenient for your student to use the algorithm each time he performed the task, you might decide not to bother teaching him. Or at least, you might decide he did not need so much practice. He could let the algorithm guide him rather than his memory. This could be well worth considering if he were to be performing the task very infrequently. For, in such a case, he would be quite likely to forget the sequence by the time he needed to use it again.

Daly and Dunn believe that their task analysis for integration, mentioned earlier, cannot be converted into any kind of algorithm because the first step, selecting a 'sensible' value of $u$, demands subtle and complex judgement that cannot be routinized. Nevertheless, our medical algorithm in Fig. 2.2 demonstrates that considerable prior understanding of concepts may be required of users (e.g., what is 'claudication'?) and clinical judgement is by no means rendered superfluous (e.g., what is *extreme* pallor'?).

Constructing an algorithm can be as valuable an experience for the teacher as using it will be for the student, since it will lead him

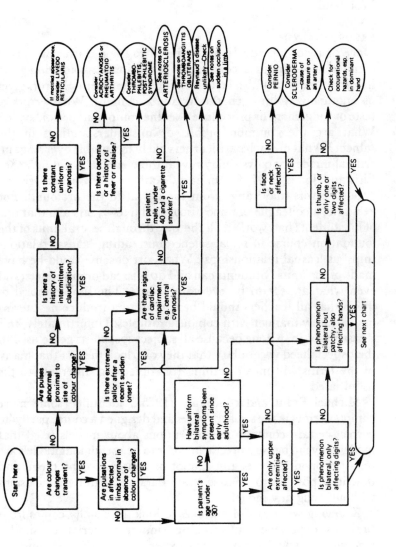

**Fig. 2.2** Part of an algorithm to assist medical diagnosis. (After B. N. Lewis and P. J. Woolfenden, 1969)

perhaps to a deeper knowledge both of the concepts and of the decision-processes involved in the task. For guidance in producing algorithms, see the self-instructional text by Lewis and Woolfenden (1969).

### ERROR ANALYSIS

Once or twice already I have referred to the negative aspects of competence—things a competent practitioner avoids doing (in his discipline or task). In fact, thinking about potential errors gives us another way into generating course content. What errors of taste or judgement or procedure does the competent person avoid? What are the common pitfalls or misunderstandings in the subject? What obstacles are learners likely to stumble over? Again, critical incident analysis may reveal these errors 'in action'. (See Fitts and Jones, 1947, for an early example of error analysis.)

Such errors may range from the trivial to the profound. For example, a colleague of mine discovered a few years ago that one of his students had worked all the way through several units of the foundation course in social science misreading 'causal relationships' as 'casual relationships'. What sort of sense could he have made of the units? Students can and do misread or misunderstand even what appear to be everyday words. The simple moral of this is that all teachers should be careful to introduce new terms in a leisurely manner with copious examples. Unfortunately, this is easier said than done because all subject specialists get so used to their specialized vocabulary that they overlook the fact that many of the terms will mean nothing (or something different) to the uninitiated.

Michael Eraut and colleagues (1975a) identified some more complex errors in the social sciences and designed a course partly 'to correct certain common misconceptions about models (e.g., that models have to be very precise in order to be useful; that models are imposed upon students and cannot be constructed by them, and that it is possible to analyse "raw data" and draw conclusions without using any models').

Knowing what sort of mistakes to look for usually comes from previous experience in teaching similar material to similar students. If you have no such experience, then you must be particularly alert for feedback when you first try out your ideas on a group of students. What kinds of misunderstandings actually occur? To illustrate the sort of way in which error analysis might work, let us take a simple example. Suppose a student who is

**64**

given a problem '$0.3 \times 0.3 = ?$' comes up with the answer 0.9. Assuming that it is not just a careless error, it is likely that the same student will also get similar problems wrong, e.g., '$0.2 \times 0.3 = 0.6$; $0.2 \times 0.4 = 0.8$'. It is more than just an isolated error. There is what my colleague Brian Lewis calls an *underlying dimension of confusion* which gives rise to a whole class of mistakes. It is even more complicated when you realize that $0.3 \times 0.4 = 0.12$.

This should remind us of another important need in teaching: it is often not enough that the student should be able to solve the problem: he should also be able to *explain* it. Particularly in higher education, this ability to explain a solution is what distinguishes the student who has understood the subject and can make effective use of it from the student who has merely learned by rote and will be at a loss when faced with a slightly novel situation. Part of giving an explanation probably involves showing that the answer is reasonable. We may need to ensure that students develop techniques for checking the reasonableness of their solutions.

The last example may have seemed rather trivial, though anyone who has tried to develop any kind of mathematical technique with arts-oriented undergraduates will no doubt recall one or two similar examples from his or her classes. Let us look now at two more examples of potential errors that my colleague, Clive Lawless, has spotted being identified and avoided in Open University courses.

The first example is from biology (Unit 18 of the Open University Science Foundation Course, S100). See how the writer tackles the potential error by drawing the student's attention to it:

> Thus for the organism, as for the single cell, one of the overriding factors governing behaviour is the existence of systems that maintain the constancy of its internal environment. Much of the internal economy of the organism seems devoted to this end. Those nineteenth-century philosophers who argued that life was governed by divine laws, distinct from those of chemistry and physics, would have claimed that this self-regulating property of homeostasis is evidence that the body was designed and that its properties could be understood only if we ascribed a purpose to them: 'the plant grows upwards in order to reach the sun'. Such arguments as to the purpose of particular actions are described as 'teleological' (noun, teleology), and scientific purists object to them on the grounds that it is both misleading and inaccurate to argue from purpose in this way.

'Purpose' and 'design' are words perhaps better applied only to human activities and only at the psychological or creative level, as they have a significance which is inappropriate to other situations. Nonetheless, although it is strictly speaking wrong to use teleological arguments in scientific discussions, and respectable scientific publications would not permit them, some biologists use them as a more dramatic form of statement. It is therefore important that you should recognize a teleological argument.

Which of the following statements are teleological, and which are not?
1   The stomach secretes the enzyme pepsin in order to digest proteins in the food.
2   The amount of glucose in the blood leaving the liver is controlled by the action of hormones on the liver cells.
3   The heart beat increases during exercise so that more blood can reach the muscles.
4   During sleep the metabolic rate is low and little energy is used up by the body.

---

1 and 3 are teleological: they can be rewritten as follows.
1   The stomach secretes the enzyme pepsin; this digests proteins in the food.
3   The increase in heart beat during exercise means that more blood reaches the muscles.

These are now statements of fact with no suggestion of motive.

---

How could you express the following statement in non-teleological form: 'The skin capillaries contract in order to reduce heat loss'?

---

'Heat loss is reduced when the skin capillaries contract' or 'contraction of the skin capillaries results in a reduction of heat loss'.

---

The temptation to use teleological descriptions is particularly strong when discussing the control processes that occur within the body, and coordination through the central nervous system in mammals and man. But there is no need to use teleology, though it may serve as convenient shorthand.

As you will have seen, the student is warned about the misuse of teleological statements in scientific discussions. Specifically, the student is counselled against writing as though various parts of the body act as they do because of some intention or purpose on their part. The teacher deals with this potential error by explaining, by giving an example, and by getting the student (through exercises) to recognize examples of teleological statements and to rewrite one in nonteleological form.

Our next example comes from an Open University course in the

History of Science (Unit 1 of Course AMST 283: *Science and Belief from Copernicus to Darwin*), though the error described could occur in any kind of history:

> Whiggishness in the history of science is really an attitude of mind which is preoccupied with the triumphant progress of science from its early days to the present, and which looks back upon past achievements through the spectacles of contemporary scientific attitudes. Now in a sense there is nothing wrong with this. Indeed, it may be said that once one has had some acquaintance with modern science it is impossible ever completely to dissociate oneself from it, and so the past is always studied in terms of the present. But it is rather a question of emphasis. The point about this approach which is so much decried by some modern historians of science is that it fails to take into account the *less successful* aspects of scientific progress and it concentrates only on those which led to the present state of affairs. Thus, for example, it largely ignores such strange pseudo-sciences as astrology and phrenology (a Victorian fashion for correlating psychological effects with the shape of one's head!). It never explores the blind alleys or the cul-de-sacs or the strange secondary paths of experience which led ultimately nowhere but which loomed largely in the minds of those who explored them. If one is writing a kind of scientific genealogy, showing how a certain doctrine of science today was derived from a similar one five years ago and that in turn from a yet earlier version, and so on back to an arbitrary starting-point, then one can well afford to ignore such false starts. But at the end of the day one will certainly have no real insight as to why the history turned out as it did. If one wishes to discover something of the underlying reasons for the developments in science, one must certainly take into account the 'bad' as well as the 'good' and the failures as well as the successes.

In this brief extract, the error is described as 'whiggishness': viewing the past selectively according to what has most influenced the present. It would be regarded by historians of science as a very serious 'underlying dimension of confusion', leading to a very partial and unbalanced view of the past. If you were determined to help students avoid this error, you might well decide to include examples of 'unsuccessful science' that were important in their day even though they led to nothing. Students would have to be warned against whiggishness themselves—a difficult self-discipline perhaps for students with a traditional science background.

So, error analysis can be a help in deciding what to put in the course. At the lowest level, it may simply alert you to the need to explain new words (or old words used differently) when they first occur and occasionally thereafter perhaps, or to warn against common misapprehensions. At a slightly higher level, you may decide to include practice and reminders at intervals throughout the course to maintain the student's error-free competence. It may even suggest the inclusion of whole sections (e.g., the 'unsuccessful science' examples mentioned above) to demonstrate error-free scholarship to the student.

### Concept analysis

One advantage of the various kinds of 'competence analysis' described above is that they can easily lead to fairly precise objectives. Or at least they seem useful to the kind of teacher who finds little difficulty in deciding on objectives. Hence they are directly suggestive of appropriate student exercises, relevant content and course sequence, assessment procedures, and so on. When we start talking about content-oriented courses, however, the objectives-first approach is less likely to appeal to the teachers.

Suppose one asks the content-oriented teacher what he wants his students to get out of the course. He is unlikely to reply with a list of precise, behavioural objectives. It is true that he may mention one or two general *aims* that could, with diligence, be converted into objectives. Again, he may be persuaded to suggest the kinds of *question* he would hope students should be capable of dealing with as a result of the course: they too might be generalizable into objectives. More likely, however, he would say something like 'I want students to appreciate/understand the subject'. Hence we have to ask 'What is the subject?' and 'What does appreciation/understanding consist of?'.

Rather than talking about objectives, then, the content-oriented teacher might well respond more sympathetically to the question: 'What *concepts* will students be dealing with in your course?' Even methodologically-oriented courses cannot get very far without some content of concepts (topics, ideas, principles). But the content-based course, since it places no great emphasis on methodological objectives and requires the content to be learned for its own sake, can justify that content only by discussion of the concepts involved. Hence, for both kinds of course, but especially for the content-oriented, there seems to be a need for *concept analysis*.

FORMING AND RELATING CONCEPTS

Students beginning a course at college or university will come to it with various sets of relevant concepts already in their minds. For example, economists may know about 'marginal cost', 'perfect competition', 'comparative advantage', etc.; students of literature will know about 'metaphor', 'rhythm', 'theme', etc.; ecologists about 'food chains', 'plant successions', 'adaptive advantages', etc. They may or may not also have some kind of grasp of methodological concepts like 'inductive', 'model', 'generaliza-tion', 'dichotomy', 'experimental design', 'frame of reference', and so on. They will certainly have a rich repertoire of commonsense concepts, e.g., 'equality', 'crime', 'health', 'patients', 'culture', etc. Many of these may be highly relevant to their studies, especially perhaps if they are students of the social sciences, arts or health sciences. Furthermore these sets of concepts will not be held separately, as individual entities, but will be related together in what we may call conceptual frameworks or structures.

You, however, will wish to alter the student's conceptual structure. At the very least you will wish to extend it. You will wish to introduce him to new concepts, and the only way of doing so is by hooking them onto what he already knows. This, in itself, may be a tricky undertaking. The student's grasp of some concepts he 'already knows' may turn out to be quite tenuous. As soon as you try to make one of those concepts bear the weight of a newly attached idea it may shake itself loose from his grasp, perhaps by developing overtones that conflict with other ideas he is still holding on to.

Furthermore you will often be setting out to alter the student's conceptual framework by *challenging* it. Perhaps you will assume quite explicitly that his existing concepts (even if he has studied your subject before) are held at too superficial a level. You may be telling him that you are helping him transcend, say, a common-sense way of looking at the world and to take on a new specialist viewpoint.

One way or the other, your course will be calling upon the student to restructure his ideas. This may be a painful process. He will have spent many years building up his conceptual frameworks and, like most of us, may be reluctant to, or rather incapable of, sloughing it off overnight in favour of a new perspective. Here is a student (quoted in Goodyear, 1976, page 27) describing the enormity of the task that beginning students often feel they are faced with:

'Implicit in the Foundation Year and the Social Science courses are a lot of background knowledge and reading and understanding of certain basic things and certainly of long words and simple things like that. . . . I met a lot of people who were working class. . . . who were really struggling, everything was unfamiliar. It wasn't just having to learn to swim, it was having to learn what water was, and what a swimming pool is, and what people do in it'.

In teaching concepts, we are teaching *meanings*, not words. Beginning students, especially in the social sciences, often complain about jargon, saying all we are doing is teaching them a fancy vocabulary for perfectly everyday ideas. However, we may well be using familiar words but attaching new meanings to them. For example, the student of mechanics will learn to attribute a specialist meaning to words like 'force' and 'work', quite different from the meaning he will attach to those words in his everyday conversations. In certain cases, the everyday meaning of a word will interfere with a student's ability to appreciate how it is being used to identify a new concept. Thus, students of statistics may learn that a 'significant' result in a sample is one that is unlikely to have arisen by chance; but they may also carry on assuming (erroneously) that the 'significance' of the result means (as the everyday usage would imply) that it is also big or important.

It has been said that every teacher is a teacher of English (or whatever is the language of instruction). And, clearly, all students are students of language, whether they are acquiring new meanings to go with new words or whether they are having to extend their usage of words that are already in their vocabulary.

One of the minor crisis points in learning a 'real' language (e.g., French or Chinese) is when one realizes that there is more to it than encoding and decoding. That is, it dawns on one that something more is needed than word-by-word translations of an English thought or, conversely, than asking oneself 'Now, what would this foreigner have said if he'd been able to write it in English!' It may come as something of a shock to realize that what he was thinking could not have been put into English at all because there are no English equivalents for the *ideas* he was expressing. A good, much quoted example is the fact that the certain Eskimo groups have fifteen (or is it more?) different words for snow, whereas we stop discriminating between types of snow after 'snow', 'sleet', or 'slush'. The truth is, snow is simply so important a factor in the Eskimos' battle for survival that they think about it more extensively than we do—making far sharper discrimination.

So too with students of the language (and the underlying concepts) of sociology, law, medicine, and so on. Very often they are being asked, in learning new concepts, to take on board new ways of looking at the world. Thus, the student being introduced to the 'labelling theory of deviance'—e.g., that 'crime' is created by certain groups in different societies attaching the label to various particular kinds of behaviour and not to others—may see it, at first, as either trivial or else immoral. Only by being persuaded to enter into the spirit of that approach, and contrast it with theories of crime based on genetics or views about human wickedness, and link it to concepts like 'situational ethics' and 'self-fulfilling prophecy', might he come to accept that this is 'a' (not necessarily 'the') useful way of looking at the world.

But such shifts of conceptual framework do not come easily. As I suggested earlier, we may resist the pressures to abandon our comfortable and habitual ways of looking at things. Here is one student likening the change to a sudden shock rather than a flowering of illumination (Goodyear, 1976, page 17):

> 'I think there is a culture shock. I remember experiencing this in the second year. . . . suddenly you've got new eyes for looking at the world, and the old times that people keep on about, that you've known for many years and it's a rhythm that they keep up, you suddenly realise that perhaps they're not so acceptable as they were. And where you thought education was going to be a flowering, you suddenly find that you've got new eyes and you see things very much more sharply and you don't accept what you see as easily as you did.'

In my own recent experience, I can acknowledge how reluctant I was to surrender behavioural objectives as the key to course development. As my experience deepened, and the weight of the countervailing evidence accumulated, I was put to more and more desperate measures to hang on to a principle that had hitherto served me well. First, I softened the definition of objectives (dispensing with the need for them to be expressed in strictly behavioural terms). Then I accepted that they might emerge from thinking about the curriculum, rather than preceding such thinking. I suggested next that they might arise and be recognized during the teaching rather than that they must precede it. Despite having conceded so much ground I was still reluctant to abandon objectives altogether. I was hanging on to the tattered remnants of the original concept because I had nothing coherent to put in its place. It was only when someone asked me 'But do you use objectives in planning your books?' that I was able to leap from the old viewpoint into a new one, that was more descriptive of what I actually do. It takes some courage to abandon an old viewpoint, even if obviously defective, when the new one has not yet become clearly articulated. Similarly, in teaching students, we may often find them highly resistant to a new conceptual structure until we can find a way of using it to give them some recognizably valid insight that they can see they would not otherwise have enjoyed.

These insights may need to be produced differently for different students. We shall be dealing with different conceptual structures. The student who has recently been 'mugged' will view 'crime' differently from the student who has recently been socialized by vacation-work colleagues into the niceties of 'fiddling' or 'reasonable perks'. The medical student whose father and mother are doctors may have a very different concept of 'the patient' than one who has just spent three months in a hospital bed after a motorcycle accident. We need to be alive to the variety of connotations that can attach to the concepts we are dealing in. At the very least, I suggest the need for some kind of concept analysis.

ANALYSING A CONCEPT

How do we set about the business of analysing concepts? Here are some basic techniques of analysis we might use (based on the ideas of John Wilson, 1974).

*Isolating the concept*   The first step is to sort out the concepts from all other material that might go into our course, e.g., from facts, examples, and exercises. Thus, for instance, if we wish to explore with our students a question like 'Has racial prejudice increased in Britain since the last war?' we must recognize that we are not dealing with just a question of fact but with a question of concept. Clearly there are concepts like 'increase' and 'Britain' and 'last year' involved, but their meanings will be fairly easy to agree on. The concept that really needs analysing is 'racial prejudice'. This could have many meanings, and whether it has increased, decreased, or stayed about the same depends on what meaning we adopt in trying to measure it.

Isolating the concept is not a trivial step. Many students may be slow to recognize that, say, 'progress' or 'culture' or 'learning' can have more meanings than they personally attribute to them. Likewise, we teachers may be slow to recognize their lack of recognition. So deliberate concept-hunting is recommended.

As soon as you flush out one concept you may find others lurking behind it. Thus, if your students were to learn about behaviourist learning theory, they might encounter concepts like:

    Adaptation
    Conditioning
    Habituation
    Learning
    Extinction

Along with each of these key concepts, we might notice ancillary concepts which enlarge it or qualify it. Thus, concepts ancillary to 'habituation' include 'fatigue' and 'vigilance'; the concept 'conditioning' brings with it 'respondent' and 'operant'.

*Defining the concept*  We should be able to give a definition such as might be found in a dictionary or textbook, e.g., 'learning' might be defined as 'a relatively permanent change in a behavioural tendency or knowledge resulting from reinforced practice'. But both we and the student know this is unsatisfactory. More is needed to elucidate the concept and put it into context. We need to know how it is used and what its boundaries are.

*Listing model examples*  Hence the next step in analysis is to identify some clear-cut examples. Thus we might say that a model example of 'learning' is a dog acquiring the ability to shake hands with its master who has been rewarding it with biscuits. We would then take other model examples and ask whether they share all the same characteristics as the first example. Which are essential characteristics; which are merely incidental? (For instance, examples of 'learning' may or may not involve conscious deliberation on the part of the learner, but all must involve a changed response to stimuli.) Thus we narrow our definition of the concept by eliminating incidental characteristics found in examples of it.

*Listing counter-examples*  This is really the opposite approach to listing model examples. We say 'Whatever we mean by X, this certainly isn't an example of it'. Suppose one of our concepts were 'learning'. We might mention our tendency to blink when something approaches our eyes at speed, or a bird's ability to build a nest. These, we would say, are not learned but instinctive. Considering why we make the distinction leads us into a discussion of the mechanisms involved in acquiring different kinds of behaviour.

*Examining related examples*  Once we start analysing a concept, we find ourselves confronted with related concepts. I mentioned 'ancillary concepts' earlier, 'habituation', for example, bringing with it the concepts of 'fatigue' and 'vigilance'. Looking at 'learning' brought us up against 'instinctive' behaviour. It is difficult to grasp any one concept without seeing how it fits into some surrounding network of concepts. Thus, getting clear about the meaning of 'instinctive behaviour' may help us make clear the criteria for talking of 'learned behaviour'.

*Identifying borderline examples*  Here we look for cases that are possibly, but not certainly, examples of the concept. Take, for instance, the tendency of newborn ducklings to follow the first moving and quacking object they meet. Usually this object will be their mother; but it is possible to have them follow a human being or even a mobile tape recorder instead. Is the resulting behaviour (due to 'imprinting'—another related concept) the result of learning or of instinct? Perhaps both are involved? Whatever the answer, asking the question helps us firm up our criteria for using the concept 'learning'.

Here we are examining *odd* or peculiar examples. We might ask, using 'learning' still, what people mean when they talk of a nation or an industrial organization learning. And how can machines, computers for example, be said to learn? We may end up deciding that such usage is meant jokingly or metaphorically. Nevertheless, if we do decide that this is not quite what we mean by 'learning' it should enable us to recognize true examples more confidently.

*Inventing examples*  Sometimes we can test our concept by inventing imaginary cases. Perhaps we need to go beyond our everyday experience to look for limiting criteria, perhaps into a science fiction world. It is not uncommon to find textbook writers saying 'Let us look at this situation as it might be seen by a visitor from Mars' or 'Consider how this might have been dealt with by Robinson Crusoe alone on his desert island'.

**74**

Thus, with 'learning' for example, we might ask whether our concept would apply to a person who was abducted by creatures from another world and given their superior knowledge, instantaneously, by means of an injection or some mysterious drug. His knowledge and ability would be greatly enhanced, but would it have been through learning? Conversely, suppose a modern man were able to return to, say, Roman times and tell a Roman philosopher about the principles of flight. Could this Roman really be said to learn the principles if the materials did not exist in his time to allow them to be put into practice? As you see, one may sometimes become rather fanciful in the pursuit of one's concepts.

*Comparing social contexts*   With some concepts it is important to recognize that people from different places and times, or even from different subcultures here and now, might not agree with our examples and nonexamples. 'Democracy' is the case most commonly cited here: clearly, the concept of democracy embodied in the German Democratic Republic (and the other 'people's democracies' of the Warsaw Pact countries) is very different from that of the British parliamentary system, and both concepts of democracy are different from that of Athens in the fifth century BC.

Similarly a concept like 'murder' (or 'culpable homicide') is highly dependent on the social context. At one time in this country, killing someone in a properly organized duel would not have been considered murder. But the concept would then have included a killing that we would now recognize as having been performed while the killer was 'out of his mind' and therefore not culpable. Today, intentional killing is permissible (and not counted as murder) if it is sanctioned, in advance, by a 'higher authority', e.g., because our country is at war with that of the person we killed. Complications arise when a subculture within a country regard themselves as being at war with the dominant culture or with other subcultures. Thus, in Northern Ireland, the killings perpetrated by the Irish Revolutionary Army and by the Ulster Defence Association are regarded by the great majority of the population as murder but as legitimate 'acts of war' by those armed groups who see themselves as soldiers on active combat.

*Exploring personal contexts*   Just as concepts take on different meanings in different times and places, so too in different

**75**

individuals. Therefore, we must give some heed to the 'pheno-menology' of a concept. What does it mean, personally, to different individuals? How do individuals differ in the connotations they attach to a concept?

Many concepts have for each of us both a public and a private dimension. It is the public dimension we share with other people, and that enables us to communicate with them (to a greater or less extent) in terms of that concept. Thus, for example, you and I will probably be sufficiently agreed about the concept of 'dog' that we would agree whether or not a particular animal qualified for the label. At the same time, our different experiences, values, anxieties, knowledge, etc., will have ensured that the concept has acquired private nuances and connotations in which you and I will differ. For example, we may differ in our view of the man:dog relationship; of the respective merits of various breeds; of the economic and social aspects of the pet-food industry; of the health hazards of dogs in public places. Hence, communication may be impeded because, although we seem to be talking about the same thing, we are attaching different thoughts and feelings to it.

With many concepts, especially in the arts and social sciences, teachers and students can find themselves talking at cross purposes because of interference from unacknowledged private connota-tions. I mentioned earlier the students who differ in their private concepts of 'crime' and 'the patient'. It is important that we at least recognize that students will differ from us (and among themselves) in the meanings they attach to a concept. Especially we need to be aware of this when we find ourselves concentrating on the cognitive aspects of the concept and ignoring the possibility that, for our students, it may be private, *affective* aspects that they need to clarify first. To teachers of mathematics and pure science, perhaps, this talk of private dimensions of a concept (especially of affective or emotional aspects) may seem quite beside the point. However, one does not have to stray far outside of pure science—into genetics, technology, and medicine, for instance—before we find ourselves dealing with value-laden concepts like 'the inheritance of intelligence', 'social utility', and 'health', that raise just the potential difficulties discussed.

Nine techniques have been mentioned above. Often you will not need all of them. It may be wise to start working through in the order listed above. And you will need to be very sure that your concepts are lacking in private dimensions before you can safely discard the last one. But, as for the others on the list, you may well find the boundaries of the concepts becoming clear enough for effective communication with students before you have applied them all. However, in certain situations you may decide that the most effective teaching strategy is to work through all the techniques—in company with your students.

CONCEPTS AND PRINCIPLES

We are rarely interested in a concept on its own. Usually we are more concerned with how it is *related* to other concepts. For instance, the concept of 'air' becomes of considerably greater interest when related to the concepts of 'heat' and 'rising', e.g., 'heated air rises' and 'cooled air descends'. These relationships between concepts are what I am here calling principles. They may, in various different subject areas, be known as rules, statements, generalizations, theorems, axioms, and so on. Here are some examples of such 'principles'.

1. The living standards of most of Britain's working population improved substantially during the first half of the 19th century.
2. The work done on a freely-moving body is equal to the increase in kinetic energy.
3. Wealth should be distributed more equitably.
4. It is not the author that writes his book, but the book that writes its author.
5. Crime is created by society attaching labels to certain forms of activity.
6. The square on the hypotenuse of a right-angled triangle is equal to the sum of the squares on the other two sides.
7. *Jude the Obscure* is the least characteristic and successful of Hardy's novels.
8. The principal anatomic changes of chronic hypoglycaemia are ·in the nerve cells of the brain.
9. A person's behaviour is fully determined by his genetic endowment and his history of reinforcement.

Clearly, such principles may well be untrue statements, or trivial, or unproveable. That last one, for instance—a principle from Skinnerian learning theory—is certainly unproveable. No matter how much detail we are given of a person's 'genetic endowment' and 'history of reinforcement', we cannot predict his future behaviour with any certainty. Nor is there any prospect that 'science' will ever make it possible to do so. Indeed, once the concepts involved were defined more precisely, it would probably become apparent that the principle is either untrue or else is tautologous and trivial: just an idiosyncratic way of defining 'behaviour'. We should always be suspicious of statements that claim, in effect, that 'all Xs are *really* Ys' (e.g., 'Everything we see in the world is a product of our imagination'). Such 'principles' are not usually giving us new information about one concept or the other. Rather, they are reducing one concept to the other. The implied relationship can have no practical consequences and limits the applicability of both concepts.

As part of our analysis of the concepts to be developed in a course, it is worth noticing in what kinds of principle (generalization, statement, etc.) they will be presented. In particular, how can the truth of the principle be ascertained? How is it justified? Let me mention just four kinds of statement:

- Empirical
- Evaluative
- Definitional
- Semantic

*Empirical*   These are statements whose truth can be checked by reference to facts. For example, 'Unemployment has increased in western countries, especially among young people' is an empirical statement. Whether or not we accept it depends partly, of course, on what we agree is meant by 'unemployment' and 'young people' and 'especially' and 'increasing'. But, given agreed definitions, the truth of the principle depends on facts and figures. Even if the facts and figures were not yet available (as in 'unemployment will continue to increase for at least ten years') such a statement would, nevertheless, be a question of fact.

*Evaluative*   These statements, however, are dependent on more than facts and definitions. Take the statement: 'A certain amount of unemployment is desirable'. What is being expressed here is a value-judgement. If asked to justify it, the speaker might say: 'It's a good thing because it provides a pool of available labour for new industries to draw on'. Such a reply might satisfy some people but not others. Some critics might say 'I don't believe that is worth the personal and social costs of unemployment'. In other words, we may disagree about evaluative statements, not because we differ as to the concepts involved or the facts behind the principle but because we disagree as to what is good, right, elegant, proper, worthwhile, and so on.

*Definitional* Our third category of statements is concerned purely with establishing the criteria for applying the concept. Such a statement on unemployment might be 'By unemployment I refer to the number of people offering themselves for employment who are unable to find jobs'. The concept is defined within the statement. As with many formal propositions in mathematics, for example, there is no way of disproving it by reference to facts. (Though if the statement had begun 'Unemployment means . . .' then it would have been a statement, presumably, about the factual issue of how the concept is usually applied; as such it would have been open to an empirical comment like: 'But doesn't it usually include . . .?') Nor is there any value judgement expressed in the statement (except the overall assumption, implicit in any such statement, that the definition embodies a worthwhile way of looking at things.) In short, the statement makes clear the 'rules of the game'. One cannot say 'You're wrong' or 'I don't agree'. And it would be silly to say 'But what does "unemployment" *really* mean?' One could however, challenge the adequacy of the statement, e.g., 'But your definition ignores people who have *stopped* offering themselves for employment—aren't they unemployed too?'

*Semantic* These are statements whose truth depends on what meanings we agree to attach to the contentious words in which they are couched. For example: 'Unemployment is inevitable in a free enterprise economy'. Now this is not an evaluative statement —no judgement is implied as to whether the alleged inevitability is a good thing or a bad thing. But it does look slightly like a definitional statement, i.e., 'unemployment is . . .' and it also sounds empirical, just a matter of checking to see whether unemployment is always associated with free enterprise economies. And that, of course, is where the semantic problem arises. For 'free enterprise economy' is not a concept like 'Britain' or 'the first half of the nineteenth century' about which one would expect fairly rapid agreement; nor is 'inevitable'. Thus there can be no easy verification of the statement. We have to say 'If you are using "free enterprise economy" and "inevitable" to mean this and that, then I agree' but 'If you are using the words to mean . . . then I disagree' and 'If you are using the words to mean . . . then I don't see how the truth of the statement can ever be established'.

I wonder if you agree with me on how to classify the principles I mentioned earlier (see page 77). Look again at each of the statements and decide whether it is chiefly empirical, or evaluative, or definitional, or semantic. (I would say the nine statements are, in order: 1. empirical, 2. empirical, 3. evaluative (semantic), 4. semantic, 5. definitional (semantic), 6. definitional, 7. evaluative, 8. empirical, 9. semantic).

*Mixtures and confusions*   As I have already admitted, the statement of a principle or generalization is often mixed. It may contain two or more kinds of statement within itself: definitional and evaluative, empirical and semantic, and so on. Consider the statement that 'Unemployed people should be punished if they do not accept whatever jobs are offered to them'. To come to terms with this statement we must (a) analyse the concept of punishment, (b) acquire factual knowledge about what kinds of people are unemployed and what kinds of job are offered to them, and (c) adopt some kind of moral, evaluative position as to whether, in any or all circumstances, some form of punishment would be justified.

Unfortunately, students may be unable, unless we give them explicit guidance, to distinguish between different types of statement. They may not appreciate what truth-criteria are appropriate. Thus they may accept as an empirical generalization a semantic statement that is actually crying out for conceptual analysis. This may happen particularly if it does not occur to them that some key concept in it can mean anything other than what they assume it to mean and the statement seems reasonable and attractive to them. Thus, a psychology student who reads that 'Psychology, like any science, must one day expect to provide a complete explanation of its subject—human behaviour' may be too captivated by the prospect of power to ask what is meant by the terms used, and how the statement can be verified. He will not ask the two basic questions with which our students should always face new principles: 'What do you mean?' and 'How do you know?'

We can help students by drawing attention to the nature of the statements we are making. It is very easy, for example, to start talking about a situation in an empirical way (describing what *is* the case) and gradually shift, almost unnoticeably, to an evaluative position (what *should be* the case). For example, we may begin by describing the level of unemployment or crime and then, perhaps by not challenging it, appear to be accepting it or condoning it as desirable or necessary. Then, without explicitly drawing the student's attention to it, we may let our definition change slightly, perhaps counting certain people as unemployed when they could not have been included by the original definition. All this can confuse the student and set him a bad example of academic argumentation for when he comes to write essays and so on.

Every discipline probably has its own distinctive mixture of these various types of principle and generalization, giving the discipline its characteristic flavour. Mathematics, for instance, is largely concerned with definitional statements which can be built up into a massive network of interlocking theorems. But mathematicians are sometimes concerned with real world (empirical) applications of their theorems. They may also apply evaluative criteria in choosing between alternative proofs on the grounds of elegance or economy. The social sciences, on the other hand, are much concerned with semantic problems and often have considerable trouble with the empirical aspects. Science and technology are chiefly concerned with empirical principles, though evaluative aspects are of growing importance in so far as practitioners of these disciplines feel it their business to consider what kind of society they should be helping to create. Disciplines like musicology, literary criticism and art history emphasize the evaluative, though not without a strong empirical basis. Western philosophy nowadays largely concentrates on semantic or conceptual issues, though with so much of the discussion centred on the works of eminent philosophers, the flavour is often distinctly evaluative.

CONCEPT MAPS IN ANALYSIS

Concept maps are a diagrammatical means of analysing the relationships among a set of concepts. Let us illustrate this using an example from Carroll (1964) who lists the criteria for using the legal concept of *tort*. This concept refers to a wrongful act, injury, or damage for which a civil action can be brought. Analysis of the many laws and courtroom decisions relating to tort reveals the following criteria for its use:

1. Battery
2. False imprisonment
3. Malicious prosecution
4. Trespass to land
5. Interference to chattels

6. Interference with advantageous relations
7. Misrepresentation
8. Defamation
9. Malicious intent
10. Negligence
11. Causal nexus (i.e., the wrongful act must be the cause of the plaintiff's injury)
12. Consent
13. Privilege
14. Reasonable risk by plaintiff
15. Breach of contract

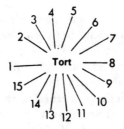

**Fig. 2.3** Simple concept map

Clearly, the analysis of the concept of tort involves at least fifteen further concepts! What bearing do they all have on the use of the word 'tort'? Must they all be present in a case for tort to apply? Is this how we must represent such relationships in a concept map? (See Fig. 2.3.) Fortunately, the relationship is rather more structured than that. The fifteen attributes need not all apply to any given tort. But they can be sorted into four groups and each group must be represented. That is, a tort can be defined by:

A  Type of act (any combination of one or more from 1–8 above)
B  Motivation and/or irresponsibility of defendant (one or both of 9 and 10)
C  Proven connection between defendant's wrongful act and injury claimed by plaintiff (11)
D  Agreements and responsibilities of defendant and plaintiff before and during the act (any combination of one or more from 12–15)

Hence, we can draw a concept map for 'tort' as shown in Fig. 2.4. Apart from helping us 'picture' the concept more clearly, this concept map might also help us in planning how to teach 'tort'

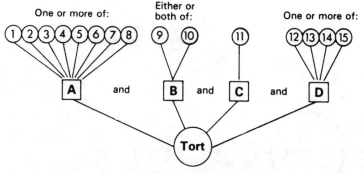

Fig. 2.4   Concept map for tort

in a course. Particularly, it might guide us on what to include and in what order, according to what kind of students we have, at what level, and what the overall objectives are. With some students, for example, we might have them recapitulate our analysis by examining laws and courts records themselves and arrive at their own structuring and understanding of the criteria for tort. With other students we might start with the four categories of criteria (A, B, C, and D) and exemplify these not with all fifteen of 1–15 but only the most common ones (e.g., battery may be a more frequent tort than misrepresentation; breach of contract may be more worth emphasis than absence of plaintiff's privilege, and so on). The content of our course might or might not include showing the student our concept map or having him draw up his own.

The concept map above can be seen as stating the relationships between a number of subconcepts that go to make up the concept of tort. Essentially it is a definitional statement—making clear the criteria to be used in applying the concept of tort. But it is also empirical in that the definition is not arbitrary; it is derived from the facts about how the concept is applied.

Now here is another kind of concept map, prepared by my colleague Bob Zimmer and it deals with the first law of thermodynamics:

The concept map shown in Fig. 2.5 is what we might call a 'noun–verb' diagram. With the words along the arrows it is clearly making a set of statements. It is certainly making an empirical statement: 'This is what happens when you put energy into a machine . . .'. But there are also definitional aspects: 'This is what we mean by "efficiency"'; and perhaps the whole diagram

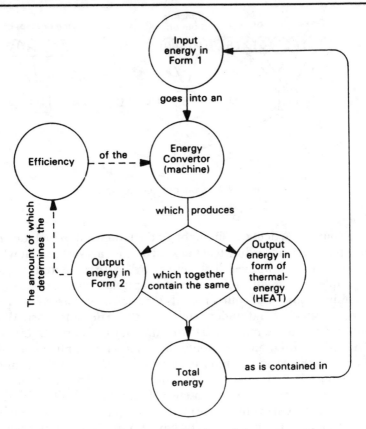

**Fig. 2.5** Concept map for first law of thermodynamics

can be said to be defining the first law of thermodynamics.

How might we use this concept map to decide upon the content of a course on thermodynamics? Here are some points we would have to explain to the student or things we might require him to do:

● Define energy, energy convertor, thermal energy, efficiency.
● Measure energy in its various forms.
● Give examples of different kinds of energy and energy convertors.
● Calculate the efficiency of particular energy convertors.
● Explain the basis of the calculation (e.g., by drawing a concept map).

Concept maps are a graphic reminder of the fact that concepts can rarely be grasped as separate entities. It is the *relationships* between them that should determine the content of our courses. In Chapter 3 we consider how to ensure the necessary relationships are indeed grasped by our students. That is, how we might best teach them?

# 3. Structuring your course

For me the word 'structure' has at least four important meanings in course development:

● *The pedagogical structure* What kind of system will enable the teachers' teaching to interact with the learners' learning? How will the course be organized?

● *The structure of events* What events or happenings can or must be scheduled in advance over the lifetime of the course—term by term, week by week, or even day by day? What events may arise *en route*?

● *The metaphorical structure* How do the participants think of the relationship between teaching and learning? What metaphors or analogies would best indicate how they see their respective roles?

● *The structure of ideas* What sequence of ideas might the student encounter during the course and how might those ideas be organized for optimum learning?

Each of these kinds of structure will be looked at in turn, although, as usual with categories in course development, none is entirely independent. Each interacts with the others. Most time will be spent on structure in the fourth sense above.

## Pedagogical structure

Within what kind of teaching–learning system will your course be operating? In the Open University, courses are intended for students studying at home. Many other institutions also offer such distance education courses, sometimes in addition to on-campus courses. Jordanhill College of Education in Glasgow offers a Diploma in Educational Technology for distance students. Several UK Colleges of further education offer 'flexistudy' courses (Green, 1979). Both Deakin University in Victoria, Australia and Waterloo University in Ontario, Canada, offer the courses studied by their on-campus students to their distance students also.

### Distance courses
The structure of the teaching–learning system for distance education courses is different from most on-campus systems. To begin with, it relies heavily on pre-prepared learning materials

such as textbooks, specially-written teaching texts, and tapes. Students will rarely, if ever, meet the teachers who developed the course, and may never meet any tutors at all. Furthermore, they may never meet other students.

Thus, the course is structured around the individual student working through material from which he is expected to learn on his own. This is often called self-teaching (or self-instructional) material. The student may be required to read, to write, to view television programmes or still photographs, to listen to radio programmes or audio-tapes, to perform practical work, etc., but there will be no-one to comment on what he is doing while he is doing it, or even immediately afterwards. Since neither tutors nor other students are around to give the learner help and encouragement, and guidance as to whether he is making sense of what he is trying to learn, the self-teaching materials must themselves provide this 'feedback'. Thus the student must use the materials not merely to teach himself, but also to tell himself whether he is learning. Therefore, self-teaching materials often incorporate questions, exercises and activities (together with answers and discussion of answers) to help the learner check his developing understanding as he goes. One variant of this approach I have called the 'tutorial in print' (Rowntree, 1979a). (See page 66 for an extract from such a text.)

So, the teaching–learning struture includes a means whereby students can gauge their own progress. In addition, it needs to find a means of retaining the student's interest in continuing with the course. Distance students can easily become discouraged, especially when they are aware of all the other things they could be doing with their time. Having no tutors around with whom to talk over difficulties, and no fellow students with whom they can compare themselves and get to realize they are not alone in having difficulties, they may start thinking they are really too stupid to continue taking the course. One of the first questions 'distance educators' are asked is 'What's your drop-out rate like?'

It has been said that many commercial correspondence colleges make their money like the mustard companies—who profit not so much by the mustard that people eat, as by that which they leave on the side of their plates. Most distance education institutions, however, like the Open University, will structure their courses with a view to maintaining the student's commitment. One way of attempting this is with regular public broadcasts (television or radio) for each of which the student needs to have prepared beforehand by getting up to date with his reading. These impose a timetable and a momentum that should pace the student through the course and encourage him when he may feel like slackening his efforts. However, there are usually reservations about using broadcasts alone to cover material that is so essential that the student would be unable to progress through the course without it. To do so would be to discriminate against students who, for one reason or another, may be unable to receive the broadcast regularly; one missed broadcast would be enough to reverse the intended effect, by causing them to give up their studies as a lost cause. Yet, if the broadcasts are nonessential they cease to be a very powerful pacing device.

Far more effective is the motivational device of requiring students to submit *assignments* regularly. Most distance education systems include in their structure the regular submission of essays, reports, calculations, etc., which will be marked, at the very least by a computer, and more usually by a human tutor who may also comment on the student's work. (Regularly timetabled assignments and broadcasts can also be seen as part of the 'structure of events' discussed in the next section.) This device works partly by giving the student valuable (and otherwise unobtainable) feedback on his work, and partly by relating him to another human being who cares whether or not he gets on with it.

There is also the possibility that these regular samples of 'work in progress' may count towards the student's overall grade for the course, though this is not a necessary feature of such a system. What is interesting is that the people who mark and comment may have had nothing to do with developing the course and the teaching materials. In fact, their role may be seen not primarily as teaching but as appraising how well the student has learned on his own—though they may be granted a secondary teaching role in remedying faulty learning or in enriching what the student has learned.

Indeed, a weakness in this kind of structure, as it operates in the Open University, anyway, is the divorce between the authors of the course materials and the tutor/assessors whose role may be somewhat unclear. Thus the institution may engage such tutors on the understanding that they are to act as assessors. Yet the authors of the self-teaching material may sometimes be heard resisting suggestions that they improve certain materials still in draft form by saying 'Well, if there are any difficulties the tutors will help the students sort them out'. At the same time, the tutors come under pressure from certain students who need help and who, in effect, are saying 'teach me what the course materials are about' but the tutor is perhaps not paid enough to spend the necessary time on this. In any case, he may be reluctant to do so on account of the fact that he disagrees with the line taken by the author of the course material.

Whether the tutors give 'remedial' or 'enrichment' teaching, or merely assessment comments, in a distance education system they will normally be given without tutors and students meeting— usually in writing but sometimes the telephone is used instead or as well. Some systems will build in occasional class meetings or tutorials spread throughout the course, or bring all students together just once during the course, say for a weekend or for a week's summer school on campus. Such an on-campus period may seem crucial for courses in subject areas that value practical 'hands on' experience (e.g., laboratory work in science). But the course will have to take account of the constraint imposed by its necessary structure, the practical work having to be concentrated into a week at a certain (possibly arbitrary) point in the course rather than running through its entirety (perhaps more organically) as might be possible in a normal on-campus course. A further constraint is that not all potential students may be able or willing to attend summer schools or even occasional class meetings. To include such events in the structure of a course is to shift from distance education towards on-campus education. So let us consider how the structure of on-campus courses might differ. (See Kaye and Rumble, 1981, for a worldwide review of distance teaching in post-secondary education).

### On-campus courses

The major difference with on-campus education is that students will be in regular contact with one another. Students are very much part of the pedagogical structure of an on-campus course— as *teachers* as well as learners. By whatever means the teaching on such a course is organized, and whatever its imperfections, students will learn a great deal from one another: not just about course-specific information and examples drawn from one another's experience and researches, but also about what is involved in being a student, both in general and on this course in particular. If students did not have this informal network of support, on-campus teachers would doubtless have to work very much harder to help students learn.

**89**

On-campus courses can also be structured around regular contact with teachers. I mention this factor only second because we cannot rely on teacher-contact being part of the structure to the extent we can student-contact. Discussing one's weekly essay individually with one's tutor over sherry and cakes is not part of the educational experience of most students. They may meet a particular teacher in small or large groups once or twice a week. They may be able to engage with him in discussion or in practical work; or they may be regarded simply as a lecture audience. Many on-campus students feel their contact with live human teachers is as slight as that of students learning at a distance.

This paucity of contact will often be due to worsening staff-student ratios. As such, it will be a constraint on the teaching–learning system to be bemoaned by staff and students alike. In some cases, however, on-campus courses will have been deliberately structured so as to maximize the extent to which students are enabled to learn on their own (not simply 'left to learn on their own'), with teacher-contact, while relatively slight, being highly significant. Such courses will have some of the features found in distance courses, especially the use of self-instructional materials.

To what extent do self-teaching materials form part of on-campus courses? To what extent might they usefully do so? Few courses in higher education, surely, assume that the student will do all his learning while in the company of other students and a teacher in the classroom. He will be expected to do at least as much work outside it, possibly two or three times as much. So what does he work on? Well, it is not for nothing that students are said to '*read* for a degree'. Even in the nineteenth century, at Oxford (home of the one-to-one tutorial), the university reformer, Mark Pattison, criticized university education for appearing to consist of 'writing essays about books about books'. In most subject areas, books (and other printed materials such as journals, periodicals) are the chief means of self-teaching.

Teachers vary greatly in the extent to which they aim to structure that self-teaching. It could be said that merely pointing the student in the direction of the library would be a kind of minimal structuring if we had *decided*, as a matter of pedagogical policy, to make the student decide for himself which books were most relevant to the course. More usually, however, the least he is given is a list of recommended reading. This may or may not be structured further by annotations suggesting, for example, rough priorities among the works listed, or some indications of strong and weak sections within each work.

We may structure the student's self-teaching yet further by stipulating a very small number of books, maybe only one or two, as 'set books' or 'required reading'. Even with a single set book, however, we may feel that students will need some help from us in coming to grips with it. We may write notes for them warning, say, about difficult passages that may need to be read several times; about weaknesses in the argument or evidence at certain points; about material that is now out of date; about ideas on which it would be well for them to turn to certain other authors for an alternative viewpoint. Such a commentary may be extended to include additional material we have written ourselves: summaries, new examples, case studies, exercises based on the text. (See also pages 173–174.)

In certain circumstances, we may find ourselves writing the bulk of the student's material ourselves. That is, we may decide to develop the main lines of argument ourselves, drawing on other authors for confirmation or contrast where appropriate, rather than accepting theirs as the central line of argument on which we merely comment. Clearly, this would be taking us towards producing the kind of self-teaching materials commonly (though not necessarily) found in distance education. The fact is that many on-campus courses in post-secondary education (and at 6th form level for that matter) are now structured around the systematic use of such self-teaching materials. This tendency was evident in the 1960s when university teachers began to recommend programmed learning texts as well as 'conventional' textbooks and then, perhaps recognizing the deficiencies of existing programmed texts, began to write and prescribe their own. (See, for example, Hogg, 1967; Reid, 1965; Stones, 1969; Stroud, 1969; Tribe, 1973).

Gradually, certain teachers began to assume more and more responsibility for guiding the student's self-teaching. They structured their courses in such a way that organized self-instruction carried the burden of the teaching, with teachers contributing mainly to encourage, appraise, and enrich the student's self-teaching. Perhaps the best-known proponents of such structures are two US professors, Samuel Postlethwaite (Biology) and Fred Keller (Psychology).

The Postlethwaite audio-tutorial approach, as it is called, was based originally around audio-tapes. Students spend most of their time working individually through specially prepared audio-tapes which guide them in performing experiments, reading from texts and journals, viewing short films or photographs, dissecting specimens or using the microscope on them, and so on. Students will have a different self-teaching task each week, perhaps introduced by a lecture and rounded off by a group discussion or quiz session. (See Postlethwaite *et al.*, 1971, for a full description.)

The Keller Plan, (see Keller, 1968; Keller and Sherman, 1974), or Personalised System of Instruction (PSI) as it is sometimes called, is based on the idea of *mastery learning*. That is, rather than going on to the next topic in the course, regardless, students are expected to demonstrate that they have reached a satisfactory level on the learning objectives appropriate to each topic. Students may learn from a variety of self-instructional materials, sometimes prepared entirely by the teacher but more often built around existing texts; and they are tested after each study-unit, usually by a more advanced student who is acting as a 'proctor'. Lectures and demonstrations by the teacher are used for motivational purposes rather than as sources of vital information. (See Bridge and Elton, 1977, for many contributions on the design, operation, and evaluation of such courses.)

The self-instructional courses one now sees operating in colleges and polytechnics and universities usually reveal many and mixed influences: programmed learning, Postlethwaite, Keller, and even the Open University, to name but a few. Literature on the subject is plentiful (e.g., Allen, 1978; Morton *et al.*, 1974; Pronay, 1979; Roach and Hammond, 1976) but see Hills (1976) for an analysis of the rationale of self-teaching and a review of many courses structured around it. In addition, Clarke and Leedham (1976) is devoted to papers about 'individualized learning' (self-teaching), mostly in post-secondary education.

What I have been trying to indicate above is that on-campus courses may, at one extreme, be structured around regular face-to-face teaching contact with tutors and with other students; while at the other extreme they may be structured around elaborate self-teaching materials. However, you may well feel like protesting that self-teaching materials are not the only means of enabling students to learn on their own. Indeed they are not; many people would feel that genuine self-teaching (as compared with self-administration of teaching pre-packaged by someone else) arises only when a course incorporates a *project* (see Cornwall, 1976).

The idea behind project work is that the student should be able to identify his own aims, subject-matter, and methodology which he will pursue with help and guidance from his tutor. Whereas, broadly speaking, one might say that self-teaching materials and packages—being prescriptive as to aims and content—are most obviously suitable in knowledge-oriented courses, projects lend themselves best to methodology-oriented courses. By pursuing his own researches, alone or as a member of a group, the student may acquire the necessary skills in obtaining information and developing his own responses to it. Nevertheless, the student doing project work may acquire considerable knowledge. My colleague Alistair Morgan (1976), in writing of projects in the study of architecture, suggests the aims as being to confirm and apply existing knowledge, to develop new knowledge, and to relate areas of knowledge.

Whatever the aims, the point here is that any course incorporating a substantial project component will have a rather distinctive structure. The decision to have students learn by project work will have many implications for other aspects of course development. There may be no predetermined subject-matter content; sequence of 'coverage' will be unpredictable; different students will need different learning materials and different kinds of teacher-guidance; no one method of assessment will suffice for all students; and most significant of all, the tutor will have a very varied role: he will be a counsellor on academic methodology, a guide to suitable learning resources, a subject-matter expert on some occasions, but on other occasions—where students are going deep into areas he is not too familiar with himself—a fellow-learner.

An extension of the project can be seen in courses requiring the student to leave the campus altogether for a period in order to apply and develop his learning in some appropriate 'real-world' situation. (For an extreme example, see Harrison and Hopkins, 1967.) Students of engineering or business administration may be attached to an industrial or commercial organization (e.g., as part of a 'sandwich course') and student teachers will spend part of their course as assistant teachers in schools. Normally, the students will be visited by their tutors and contact will be maintained. Nevertheless, tutors will recognize that such students are learning on their own and the determinants of that learning are largely beyond the tutor's control.

**93**

## The structure of events

Another kind of structure can be identified in a course by considering its key events or 'critical happenings': breaks, examinations, field trips, deadlines for student activity and so on. Such a structure of events, marking the closing and opening of different 'phases' within the course (see Broadbent, 1977), is paralleled in the structure of a musical composition or of a play in the theatre. Each will be broken into movements or acts, varying perhaps in tempo or tone, the movements structured around changes of key and the acts around dramatic confrontations and resolutions, but each taking the audience through a series of experiences in anticipation of some structural 'event' or in savouring the ramifications of one that has recently taken place.

### Critical events

So how do structural events operate within a course? What might they be? At what points within the course may they/must they occur? Even a project-based course will have such a structure based on such events. We may anticipate students having to decide on a topic, to settle on their approach, to collect their data, to analyse their data, and to produce a final report, possibly after having produced and obtained tutor comment on a draft report.

Each of the above steps will be a critical event within the course and some approximate timetabling will be necessary. Otherwise, students may spend too much time making up their minds about a suitable topic and collecting huge amounts of data, leaving themselves insufficient time for analysis and for writing up their conclusions.

Courses of all kinds have their critical events around which they can be or must be structured. To begin with, the duration of a course is normally predetermined by the conventions recognized within our institutions; it may have to occupy one or more complete terms or last for a multiple of a basic number of weeks, e.g., 8, 16, or 32. Again, the conventions of our institution may limit the number of possible starting dates and finishing dates for the course.

With the limits of the timetable agreed, its structure may be further defined by the timing of necessary events. These may be imposed by our institution, e.g., is there a fixed period for examinations? Alternatively, they may be decided by us on educational grounds, though still perhaps constrained in our choice by practical considerations, e.g., when will be the best time for the field trip? Thus we may begin to structure the course around the need to have covered all major topics and be ready to begin reviewing, say, two weeks before the examination. We can begin thinking what we need to do with students in the weeks prior to the field trip so as to use it to best advantage; we can allocate the time required for follow-up work afterwards. We can decide, in relation to other events, when it will be feasible to call for various kinds of assignment from students, and so on. Normally, we will end up with a rather broad timetable or structure of events, for the course as a whole; but, once embarked upon the course, we are likely to have a more specific timetable for the week ahead and a highly specific one for the particular day of the course that is about to begin, e.g., 9–11 a.m. lecture and group discussion; 1–3 p.m. practical work; 3.30–5.00 p.m. problem session.

### A case study

As an example, let us say we are developing a two-semester course on 'Health and Environment'. The course is based upon a relativistic definition of health as 'an index of success in adaptation to the environment'. It will begin by exploring this definition and comparing it with others; it will then consider various approaches to the improvement of health; and will then (the bulk of the course) examine a number of different environments, e.g., internal, social, natural, technical, economic, philosophical, political, etc., to probe the ways in which they interact with health as we define it.

The class (about 20 students) will meet for two hours once a week and will be expected to spend additional time on course reading. The 'pedagogical structure' of the course (the teaching–learning system) will comprise group discussion based on lectures and pre-recorded television tapes, supported by individual reading of primary source materials related to the themes of the course and a mini-project in the second semester.

The 'structure of events' is bounded by the two 13-week semesters with the Christmas break between them. What 'happenings' or deadlines shall we or must we insert within this framework? The television material presents no scheduling problem: it is on videotape and can be replayed whenever we wish. Similarly, the core reading materials can be presented to students at the beginning of the course; though individuals will supplement it from their own researches later.

The first seven weeks of the course will be devoted to concepts of health and their divers implications for approaches to the improvement of health. By the end of the seventh week we shall expect from students our essay on the concepts developed in the first six weeks. That seventh week, before we launch into environments, would be a good point at which to introduce the idea of projects. Although we shall not be expecting students to work on a project until well into the second semester, the prospect may already be causing them anxiety; so we shall need to discuss what will be expected of them, how they might set about it, what they can expect to get out of it, and so on. Also, the sooner they start thinking about possible topics the better.

So the essay and the discussion of projects will be key happenings halfway through the first semester. The next six weeks will be devoted to different environments and the demands they make on an individual's ability to adapt. At the end of this period we shall make use of the college's regular examination arrangements (though this is not obligatory) to schedule a test (probably multiple-choice) on the course reading so far. This can be the culminating event of the semester (apart from the Christmas party).

We considered delaying the test until the beginning of the second semester in order to encourage our students to keep thinking (worrying?) about the course during the rather long break. However, there is something else they can profitably be thinking about and that is the project. So, our next 'happening' will be a discussion with individual students about possible topics for their projects. This will be scheduled for the first week of the second semester and students will be asked to prepare for it over the Christmas break by writing notes on, say, up to three topics they would be interested in pursuing. Apart from anything else, this may encourage them to get ahead on the course reading.

So the second semester must begin with individual discussions about project topics. The first five weeks of the semester will be devoted to further environments and their implications for health. The subsequent five weeks will be spent on the project. So, one critical event that must be inserted at least two weeks before this, to allow for discussions as to practicalities, is the students' final choice of project topics. Also, to make sure that students do not neglect the course reading for this semester, which some may be inclined to do if the environments being looked at this semester do not relate too closely to their project-topics, we shall schedule a multiple-choice test in the week before they begin their projects.

For the next five weeks, students will be working on their projects. The tutor will be available during scheduled class hours for individual consultation as will the television tapes and other materials. Each student will be expected to develop *his own* structure of events during this period, but the tutor will keep sufficiently in touch to know when individuals need firmer guidance. The next critical event will occur at the end of the fifth project week when completed reports must be handed in.

The final three weeks of the semester will be devoted to discussions of the concepts and methodology developed during the course, how these have been exercised in the students projects, and how they might be applied in similar areas of concern. The culminating event will be an examination testing the students' ability to apply the concepts and methodology they have acquired to a totally new situation. The structure of events across the course as a whole can now be summed up as in Fig. 3.1 on page 98.

### *Implications*

Notice that such a 'structure of events' is not conceived in isolation from the other kinds of structure we are discussing in this chapter. For instance, the timing of critical events above clearly reflects the kind of course that is being devised (the pedagogical structure) and also the structure of ideas. The very fact that it has been produced at all may tell us something, in addition, about what I shall soon be going on to call the 'metaphorical structure' of a course.

Few courses are without some minimal structure of events. Frequently, however, it does not become apparent to students until after they have completed the course (if then). The composer Schumann once said of music: 'Only when the form is clear to you will the spirit become clear.' This may sometimes be true of students' perceptions of courses. Too often they are presented with a 'long, long road a-winding', featureless but for a final examination lowering distantly on the horizon. Students might often get more insight into the venture and more enthusiasm for it if we were able to begin the course by telling them (or negotiating with them, if that is our style) the chief events that lie ahead.

If you need convincing of the motivational value of discussing with students what lies in store for them, consider these plaintive comments made by one student a few weeks after the start of term (Beard and Senior, 1980, page 18):

**97**

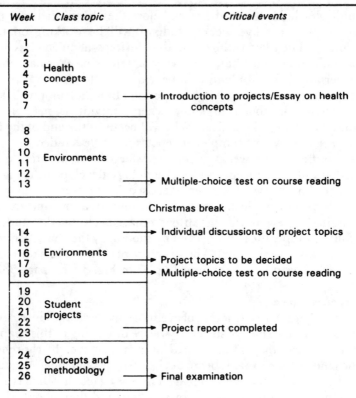

**Fig. 3.1** Health and environment (course structure)

'It's hard to see where all the separate sections fit together really. You keep sort of thinking you have a better idea and then you find out something else is going to happen which you didn't expect. . . . I only found out two days ago that the practical books are going to be handed in for assessment, which I hadn't heard anything about— it would have been nice to know before you started.'

Finally, we might observe that the structure of events will never have been completely determined in advance. Once a course is under way, it will create critical events of its own, and these will not always be the same for every student. The teacher, however, should be alert for them and ready to respond if necessary.

## The metaphorical structure

How do students and teachers perceive their relationships within the course? What metaphors or analogies would best indicate how they see their respective roles? To ask such questions is to recognize that a course is structured not simply by its teaching–learning methods, its critical events and its flow of ideas, but also by the way its participants *interpret* these and other features, in the light of their personal prejudices and expectations, and make decisions about their own and other people's intentions. A course is a social construction and two courses may differ profoundly in ethos because of the differences between their participants (teachers and students) in how they think about teaching and learning. The courses described by these two students, for example, would seem to embody quite different sets of metaphors:

> 'I'm taking Communications as an example because the way Dr . . . presents his lectures . . . is to give you an impression of the course and you go back and develop it for yourself. It's a kind of training in the way you approach a subject, and you develop it by yourself, and you trace things that you don't agree or rather things that you don't know. I don't know about university education— maybe sometimes it's a training of the mind. You read and you discriminate. . . .' (Brew and McCormick, 1979.)

> 'There's a fantastic amount of course work—lab. reports, writing up experiments, questions, drawing work you have to do—and it takes up two thirds of your time, and leaves you very little time for revision or trying to understand the lectures. . . . It doesn't train you to think, it's just mechanical, it's trotted out to you all the time, as though you were machines.' (Beard, 1979, page 23.)

### Students' metaphors

Some students have what is called an *expressive* attitude: they look to a course to provide opportunities for them to experience personal growth. They expect to express themselves through the medium of the course, enlarging their capabilities and gaining enjoyment in doing so. They will tend to spend most time on those elements within the course that are intrinsically rewarding or that, at least, might be expected to lead to capabilities that will be intrinsically rewarding at some time in the future. The personal growth metaphor is well-illustrated in the remarks of these two students (from Taylor *et al.*, 1980):

> 'I would like to think that [the course] might make me more interested and more interesting really—I want to feel that I've

had an exciting day; that I've learned something today, or read something today and so hopefully enrich me as a person.'

'I want a mind that can think about things on a broad scale more than just the latest football results. To stretch my mind I suppose— so I can think of things in a more analytic way and have a deeper understanding of what life's all about.'

Some students may be seeking such personal growth in understanding with a view to using it in a career. For example:

'In my work . . . I want to know the reason people react under various kinds of circumstances. So far, all I have is observations, you know, experiences. It's important because I hope it will help me to understand people more.' (Taylor *et al.*, 1980.)

However, a student who structures his course activities in accordance with the personal growth metaphor may come to recognise that the course itself is dominated by another:

'I tend to spend a lot of time on things I am really interested in, so I won't get a good degree. If I swotted away diligently, I would get a better degree but I wouldn't be so intellectually broadened.' (Miller and Parlett, 1973, page 56.)

The student above is observing the predominance of what might be called the games-playing metaphor. The system has its rules (whether legitimate or not) and, if we want to survive and prosper we must 'play the system' as if it were a game. The 'we' here refers chiefly to students, but younger members of staff may feel equally powerless to alter the rules. Another student is more explicit about this metaphor:

'What is the purpose of the examination game? . . . You know you want to get a certain class of degree within the system, but as far as assimilating knowledge properly is concerned, it just doesn't work, because if you're playing the game properly you're choosing all the time, and not getting an overview because you know there will be a certain question you have to answer.' (Miller and Parlett, 1973, page 53.)

Such a metaphor encourages students in an *instrumental* approach —valuing not the learning itself or the increase in capability it might bring about, but viewing it merely as the means towards some other end that *is* valued for itself—most probably the degree or diploma that, as a credential, might lead to improved income or status or to a more satisfying job. Here is a student who seems to have calculated just how little learning he needs to do in order to qualify for the job he wants:

> 'I'm in for a third at the moment. I think I'm better than a third, but I'm not all that bothered because I don't think our degree is recognised that much by industry. . . . As long as I'm getting a pass mark or reasonably above, then good—I'm not the sort of person to go all out to do the best I can.' (Beaty, 1978.)

An associated metaphor is that of the employer–employee relationship. As Howard Becker *et al.* (1968) pointed out, students may see grades as serving the same function as money in the wider community. They come to regard themselves as having a kind of implied contract with their tutors determining how hard they have to work in return for their 'wages'—acceptable grades. Unfortunately, as one of the students quoted by Becker *et al.* (page 59) seemed eloquently aware, the best-paid 'employees' are not necessarily those who produce worthwhile learning:

> 'There's an awful lot of work being done up here for the wrong reason. I don't know exactly how to put it, but people are going through here and not learning anything at all. . . . There's a terrific pressure on everybody here to get good grades. It's very important. . . . And yet there are a lot of courses where you can learn what's necessary to get the grade and when you come out of the class you don't know anything at all. You haven't learned a damned thing really.'

Students may well come to a course with the personal growth metaphor in mind, seeking enlightenment, yet settle, as a result of their experience, for a cynical, games-playing 'rate-for-the-job' metaphor. Needless to say, the latter type of metaphor leads a student to structure his own activities in accordance with the reward-structure (yet another structure!) of the course. Thus, he will be at pains to ascertain which parts of the course he can safely neglect; he will favour rote-learning whenever he finds it pays better dividends than striving after understanding; and he may find it prudent to side-step challenging topics or assignments, even though they might seem to offer him valuable insights or help in his weak areas, in favour of activities that make demands only on capacities that he knows he possesses already.

Some of my colleagues (see Taylor *et al.*, 1980) discuss four possible 'orientations' a student may develop to his courses— vocational, academic, personal, and social—all but the last of which may be pursued either for intrinsic or for extrinsic interest. Their interviews with students reveal how an individual may differ in the ways he responds to different courses, or even to different topics within a course. As one student said, talking of a Human Sciences course with three components, philosophy, psychology, and sociology:

> '. . . you've got to do a certain amount of course work and oh—I copy as many essays as I can and do the minimum amount of work in philosophy and psychology. [But] in sociology I just try to do as much reading as I can and then when I do write essays I always bring in much more—but I hardly ever answer the questions—I'm always much too concerned with other things of interest to *me*.'

Our contribution as teachers may undoubtedly help shape the students' metaphors. However, it is as well to recognize that there will always be students pursuing a 'social club' metaphor of higher education in which courses as such are allowed only a limited significance (perhaps equivalent to 'membership dues'). For example (from Taylor *et al.*, 1980):

> 'The outside activities that I do—radio and film unit and sport— are very important . . . and in some respects I tend to put off work because of them. I try to keep it balanced . . . this side of it is just as important as the academic side, and if not more important . . . because you can always study in a correspondence course or something like that but you can't get this kind of social thing and development anywhere else.'

### Teachers' metaphors

Teachers also favour a variety of metaphors and analogies in the way they think of teaching and learning. An individual teacher's metaphors can be expected to have some effect on those of his students. But the effect may be regrettably small. The teacher who really wants the students on his course to be expressive and take intellectual risks may find that his students are simply too attuned to the metaphors that predominate in *other* courses and in the institution as a whole to abandon their usual games-playing analogy.

Some teachers rely on a *medical* metaphor for their relationship, with students. That is to say, they see their job as being to diagnose some deficit or weakness in the student and then prescribe what they believe to be a suitable treatment. This treatment, ideally, should be based on the latest scientific research, and should lead to an improvement in the student's educational health. Unfortunately, the educational 'science' on which this doctoring metaphor is based remains infantile compared with medical science. And, even if it were as mature, the model would still be liable to the weakness that many medical doctors are accused of—treating the disease rather than the patient and under-estimating the psycho-social dimension. In educational terms, this would amount to failing to realize the significance to the student of his apparent educational weakness or of failing to take *his* diagnosis into account.

Another metaphor for teaching and learning is the process of *house-building*, described by my colleague Andrew Northedge (1976):

> The teacher is the builder and the student's mind is a plot of cleared ground on which he has to build. The house consists of bricks of knowledge and skill which are laid on top of each other. . . . As he works, the builder follows a plan, usually prepared by someone else, specifying in precise detail all relevant aspects of the intended edifice . . . he works towards a finished product—the house (in other words, perfect understanding of the selected course material on the part of the students).

The house-building metaphor incorporates a static view of knowledge: knowledge exists 'out there' and it needs to be reassembled in the mind of the student, by the master builder. And, until the edifice is complete, the new owner cannot be expected to get much use out of it. Andrew Northedge suggests as an alternative metaphor the idea of *cultivating a garden*. The teacher as gardener also starts off with the student's mind as an area of ground, . . .

> But this time I suggest we view the ground as already covered with vegetation (concept systems) some of which is clearly worth retaining and cultivating. Indeed the ground shows all the signs of having been tended by many previous gardeners. . . . In the garden, plants will tend to grow quite readily regardless of intervention from the gardener, and it is his aim to encourage certain plants at the expense of others. . . . The gardener does not work towards a precisely defined end. . . . He has broad plans as to how he wants the garden to develop (probably rather flexible ones, which change as possibilities within the garden reveal themselves), but he does not attempt to specify the exact dimensions that each plant (or concept

**103**

structure) is to achieve . . . there is never a stage when further constructive activity is not anticipated.

The gardening metaphor sees teaching and learning as a dynamic and organic process in which the 'ground' contributes as much as the efforts of the gardener to what is grown. In the house-building metaphor, on the other hand, the ground is inert and passive. The two metaphors give rise to different kinds of course and tie in best with (thereby reinforcing) different student metaphors. Thus, the house-builder, whose students may not see how any one brick relates to the overall structure until the edifice is complete, may well suit (or produce) the instrumental system-players who are prepared to give up the struggle to understand so long as they can hold the bricks in place long enough to pass the tests. The gardener, on the other hand, is likely to run a course that appeals to students interested in personal growth because it respects the individuality of his existing understandings and enlists his active cooperation in 'getting the best out of the ground'.

Of these two metaphors I prefer the second, though I would admit that some courses structured on the gardening model might have room within them—e.g., in the teaching of a body of routine techniques—for a little house-building. After all, many a garden has a shed in it. However, both of them (and especially the first) put too much emphasis, for my liking, on the teacher as builder/gardener. Students provide a plot of land, perhaps with workable vegetation, but they do not get signed on even as apprentice builders and gardeners. Hence, it is possible for courses structured on either metaphor, especially that of the house-builder, to be seen as doing things *to* the student rather than *with* him. Also, neither metaphor takes cognizance of the fact that the teacher will be working with many students (houses/gardens) rather than with one only. Consequently, neither considers the extent to which one house or garden might be influenced for good or ill by its neighbours.

My own favourite metaphor for a course is that of a *voyage*. Happily, 'course' is also part of the language of voyaging, e.g., 'setting a course for home'. I imagine a group of people joining together to make a journey that has something of the character of an expedition. All will embark with different hopes and expectations but each will have experience and skills of one sort or another that will be useful to himself and perhaps to others during the rigours that lie ahead. One of them (the teacher) will be the acknowledged leader. His seamanship and navigational skills have been well-tested and it is possible, though not essential, that he will have voyaged previously in the very waters to which the present expedition is bound.

The group may have a particular destination firmly in mind or they may be setting out simply to establish what lies beyond the setting sun (or the present boundaries of the discipline). Even if the destination is predetermined, the leader at least knows that the people who reach it will be different from those who started out. All will suffer a sea-change, being transformed as they respond to the largely unpredictable challenges they meet along the way. Once they reach their destination, each will see it differently. Even to the leader who has been there before it will no longer seem the same place—voyaging with his latest companions will have changed the way he looks at it. But all will agree that 'arriving' was the least important part of the adventure: what they have gained from the voyage came from the voyaging itself.

I like this metaphor because it sees a course as a social venture and stresses its open-ended and perhaps (intellectually) hazardous nature, while recognizing also the very important dimension of time. Obviously it would best suit those students who think in terms of 'personal growth' and is especially suitable when there is opportunity for students to work out their own purposes in relation to the course content and achieve their own perspectives on it.

That is all I am going to say about metaphors. No doubt, we can all think of many more metaphors and analogies for the teaching–learning process. But I am not going to describe them all, because I have no wish to be exhaustive (or exhausting). What I have given you are examples of a general observation: that we can often obtain illumination by considering the metaphors or analogies that appear to describe the way teachers and students think of what they are doing. So I have not given you ten or twenty teacher-metaphors to choose among when developing a course; but I hope I have said enough to make you think it worth your while asking what metaphors you (or other people) *are* using.

## The structure of ideas

A course can be seen to be structured around a sequence of ideas. This book, indeed, has structure in so far as its ideas are sequenced. In fact, there is more than one such sequence. For instance, there is the sequence in which I began writing the various chapters and the sections within them. And there is the (different) sequence in which I finished writing them. Then there is the sequence in which I have arranged them in the book. Most important of all, at least from your point of view, is the sequence in which you have chosen to consider the ideas in the book.

### Sequence in learning

What do we mean by 'sequence'? Why should sequencing in a course be any problem? Our interest in sequence arises because the student cannot learn everything at once. If he is to learn A and B, he must either learn A and then B, or B first and then A. (Unless he can learn a little bit of both A and B (but how much and in what order?) before going on to learn the rest of A and B (again, in what order?). But these may not be equally viable alternatives. For any given student, one of these sequences may be *better*—more 'learnable'—than others. For example, students who learn B first and then A may learn much more quickly and have a firmer grasp of the topic than those who learn A before learning B.

So, in enquiring about sequence, we are really asking whether one way of ordering the content of a course will be more helpful, educationally, than any other possible order. Should A come before B, or vice versa, and where does C fit in, and D, E, F, G, etc.? And we may have to recognize, even if we cannot do much about, the complication that what is best for one student may not be ideal for another. We are looking for a sequence that will suit the maximum number of people. Possibly this will mean we shall need to enable students to vary the sequence to suit their personal preferences, if this is feasible. (You will recall I suggested you should feel free to read the chapters of this book in any order you wished, having completed Chapter 1.)

In a classroom course, where one thing is presented at a time, we can be sure that this is the sequence in which students will tackle the course. Where students are learning on their own, however, e.g., from self-teaching materials, we cannot be so sure. For one thing, students may have access to material for several lessons all at once (or a variety of textbooks) and may choose not to read them in the order we have suggested. And even if they get only one lesson at a time they may well choose not to work stolidly through it from page 1 in the way we perhaps expected. In so far as we are guiding students through a course, we must be aware of the several possible sequences a student could take through it (or through any of its constituent parts). Then we shall be able to warn him of any paths that could be confusing or unproductive and to alert him when an opportunity arises for him to safely branch one way or another.

When planning a course as a whole we may identify many types of sequence. Here are the types I am going to discuss:

- Topic-by-topic (or parallel themes)
- Chronological
- Causal
- Structural logic
- Problem centred
- Spiral
- Backward chaining

Any of these can be developed within sections of a course as well as from section to section. So a course as a whole may contain many different kinds of sequence.

*Topic-by-topic*  This kind of sequence might almost be called 'no particular sequence at all'. That is, the course entails the study of a number of separate topics or themes, each of which is more or less independent of the others. None depends on any of the others having been tackled first; nor does any of them particularly equip the student for studying any of the others. The topics or themes are 'in parallel' rather than forming a necessary series. For example, a course on modern poetry might have the following sequence:

    Unit 1: Introduction—poetry today
    Unit 2: English poets
    Unit 3: American poets
    Unit 4: European poets

After studying the introductory unit the student would seem to be offered three parallel topics. Why should not 3, 2, 4 or 4, 2, 3 or 4, 3, 2 or 2, 4, 3 be as rewarding a sequence as 2, 3, 4? This is not to say that there might not be an 'obvious' sequence *within* a topic, e.g., from 'easier' poets to more difficult ones.

Here are the topics suggested recently for a course on *Contemporary Issues in Education*:

> Are standards falling?
> What are schools for?
> How can education be made more effective?
> Can parents help children to learn more?
> Teacher knows best? Rights and responsibilities.
> Equality in education: does it exist?

Can you see any obvious sequence? Is there any reason why any one of those topics should be tackled before or after any particular one of the others? Personally, I can see no necessary sequence among these topics. Different teachers (and students) might prefer different sequences, but it seems one could justify starting with any of these topics and moving on to any of the others. They would appear to suggest parallel rather than sequential treatment.

Please do not think I am decrying this kind of sequence. It is perfectly respectable in a course to, say, set up a framework of analysis or an investigative methodology in an initial unit (or lesson) and then introduce, as subsequent units, a series of parallel case studies to which it can be applied. There is no reason to insist that these 'case studies' or application units should be developmental in the sense that later units must build on the insights developed in earlier ones.

In actual practice, of course, what are originally conceived of as separate parallel units may turn out to assume knowledge of earlier ones—especially if the same teacher has been responsible for them all. This is all right when you are teaching face-to-face; and it *may* be all right also if you are teaching through self-instructional materials, provided you can rely on students working through the materials in a prescribed order. In this book, I have tried to avoid making any chapter dependent on previous chapters because I anticipated that readers might not follow my sequence and, indeed, I encouraged you to follow your own.

The topic-by-topic, parallel theme approach has one big advantage if you are producing the course with colleagues as a 'course team'. That is, each teacher can take a topic or a theme and get on with planning his or her section, more or less regardless of the others. There will be no need for a colleague to prevaricate with 'I can't plan my section until I see what Dr. Smith will be putting in hers'. However, assumptions about what other people will be saying can creep in, and the plans will still need to be discussed to see that they do not depend on teachers earlier in the course having introduced ideas or approaches which they have not in fact done.

So *casual* references to earlier units should be avoided if to do so means the student can be allowed flexibility of route. But if ideas really can be built up and developed from one topic to the next, the student may thus be enabled to operate more richly, more powerfully on later units than on earlier ones. This would probably be more motivating to him than merely having the freedom to choose his own sequence through topics that may still appear to him as 'just one damn thing after another'.

Even when a 'pure' topic-by-topic sequence is adopted for a course, with no development from topic-to-topic, there may well be a very strong and inescapable sequence *within* each topic. So let us go on to look at some of the other possible sequences.

*Chronological sequence* In such a sequence, happenings, events, or discoveries over a period of time are represented in the order in which they occurred. This order will obviously suggest itself with historical subject-matter, and this does not occur only in 'history' courses. It may be followed in dealing with the development of institutions, or of economic theories, or of scientific discoveries— whenever understanding of one event or of one stage depends on the understanding of a step or stage that occurred previously.

However, just because one's course has historical content, it does not follow that a chronological sequence is necessarily always the one to pursue. My colleague Clive Lawless has provided an example from an Open University history course, *The Revolutions of 1848*. The list that follows shows the titles of the four main parts and units within them. (In Open University parlance, a unit represents a study time of 12–15 hours.)

The Revolutions of 1848
Part I     Unit 1   Introduction to the study of revolutions and some interpretations of 1848
            Unit 2   Europe on the eve of 1848
            Unit 3   Document collection
            Unit 4   *Sentimental Education*: a Study Guide
Part II    France 1848–51
            Unit 5   France, February–December 1848
            Unit 6   France, January 1849–December 1851
            Unit 7   Interpretation of the French Revolution: Karl Marx and Alexis de Tocqueville
            Unit 8   Art in the French Revolution
Part III   Germany, Austria and Italy
            Unit 9   Revolutions in Germany

**109**

How far is this course sequence chronological? What else has entered into the sequence? Unit 2, Europe on the Eve of 1848, is certainly at the beginning while units 5 and 6 deal with later events. But the overall sequence is nation-by-nation (topic-by-topic) rather than chronological. Also, along with each block of three historical units, there is a unit on aesthetic subjects: literature, art, and music. These are meant to show how the revolutionary spirit was reflected in contemporary arts. This example would be sufficient to demonstrate that, even in historical studies, chronological order may provide little more than a bare outline which needs to be enriched by other patterns of sequencing.

*Causal sequence* This kind of sequence is closely related to the chronological. Learning based on a causal sequence follows a chain of causation for an event or a phenomenon, so that when the student reaches the end of the chain he can explain the final effect, the event or phenomenon itself. It applies where cause-and-effect relationships are being taught and where the objective is that the student should be able to establish and explain such a relationship. This kind of sequence might be relevant in meteorology or in geomorphology, where the student is establishing the cause-and-effect relationships that result in different weather patterns or different landscape formations.

This sounds straightforward enough: apparently just a matter of starting at the beginning and tracing through an obvious sequence of causes and effects. However, chains of causation are often not all that straightforward. For instance, let us just ask whether cause-and-effect relationships can be presented in linear sequence. The sequence below suggests how a narrow growth ring (tree ring) is formed in the trunk of a tree:

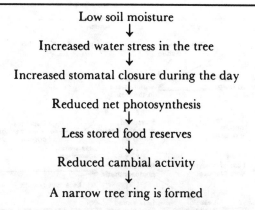

Low soil moisture
↓
Increased water stress in the tree
↓
Increased stomatal closure during the day
↓
Reduced net photosynthesis
↓
Less stored food reserves
↓
Reduced cambial activity
↓
A narrow tree ring is formed

The above sequence looks easy to master for any student who knows the concepts involved. But appearances are deceptive. The sequence represents the primary chain of causation involved. However, as the full diagram in Fig. 3.2 (page 112) reveals, the items in the chain have little sidechains of their own, showing the full complexity of the causal relationships.

Fig. 3.2 resembles the concept maps discussed in Chapter 2. Can the sketching out of such diagrams, mapping out the relationships (in this case, of cause and effect) between concepts, help us see ways of sequencing our courses? Here we might well want to begin by checking that students already have the concepts: 'solar radiation', 'xylem cells', 'water stress', etc. Or we might begin by establishing the primary chain of causation. Or we might start with one or other of the cause-and-effect clusters on either side of the primary chain. Another approach might be to work backwards from the final outcome, the narrow tree-ring, uncovering the causes in reverse sequence (e.g., if $z$ is caused by $y$, what causes $y$?). Fig. 3.2 makes clear that there are many alternative ways one could sequence such a topic to suit different students.

*Structural logic* Here we are talking about a sequence dictated by the logical structure of the subject. Sometimes it is clear that a certain topic cannot be learned without prior understanding of another topic. For instance, in basic number work, the idea of multiplication will not make sense unless you have already learned addition. And in order to carry out division you need first to be able to subtract.

Most subjects have a certain amount of 'structural logic' in them—either in the connection between one major topic and the

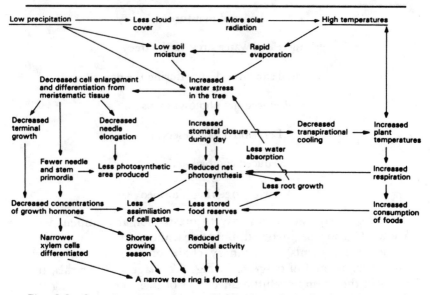

Fig. 3.2 Complex chain of causation in formation of narrow tree ring.
(After Fritts, 1969)

next or at least within such topics. Thus, in learning a new language it may be clear that the student must learn to discriminate between sounds in the language before he can imitate them in his own speech. In statistics, the idea of significance tests cannot be grasped without some prior concepts of probability. Before a student can comment usefully on the responses of literary critics to a particular dramatist's work, it is necessary for him to have read (seen?) some of his plays.

But the first question one must ask about the structural logic of a subject is 'Does it really have one?' Parker and Rubin (1966) suggest that the supposed 'structure' of a subject is not always easy to find and that different subject experts will disagree as to what the structure is. Many subject-matter experts and teachers act as though the way they learned the subject, or the way they see it now, is the best way or the only way. Yet students may find a different structural logic in the subject and still learn it thoroughly.

*Problem-centred sequence*   One can sometimes structure a course, or sequences within it, around the exploration of an issue or problem. A problem can be presented to students, or allowed to arise from their experience, and attempts to pursue solutions or interpretations of it provide a realistic context in which the teacher can help students learn the essential substance and intellectual skills of the subject.

For instance, an urban development course might focus on the problem of 'Why did Liverpool grow to be a more important port than Hull?' An interdisciplinary humanities course might develop a variety of approaches to the problem of 'Is man free?'. A technology course on the structure of materials might have a section based on the problem 'What is the most suitable material from which to mass-produce car bodies?' The *Contemporary Issues in Education* course, which I mentioned earlier, was to be based on six problems. The problem of 'Why are people the same but different?' posed within a biology course might lead to a genetics sequence like that described by Jim Eggleston (1971):

> The problems of measuring and systematizing continuous variations are defined and solutions are sought. Students may now be invited to speculate on possible causes of variation and conversely similarity. The students may at this point achieve some perspective of the nature and nurture problem to which Charles Darwin once addressed himself.
>
> Patterns of inheritance may be studied by systematically breeding such convenient organisms as fruit flies. Physical and mathematical models may be constructed to account for the results observed and their variation. Attention may also be drawn to the implications of these models and the possibility of a material, particulate theory of inheritance.
>
> The physical link between generations, sperms, and eggs are observed. With the aid of staining techniques and microscopes the behaviour and structure of chromosomes are studied and found to be consistent with the physical models which furnish the hypotheses which accounted for the observed patterns of inheritance.
>
> Anomalous results of certain breeding experiments then lead to a refining of the initial hypotheses, to the concepts of gene and locus. At a later point in this sequence of inquiry, the ways in which genes might work, the origin of variations and the conditions for the spread of genes in populations, are investigated.
>
> The facts and principles so discovered can be applied to evolutionary studies, to agricultural practice, to the proposals of the Eugenic Society; to the problems of racial differences and selection in education.

Clearly, causal and structural elements are also entering into the sequence outlined above. Likewise the technology course mentioned earlier, on the material for car bodies, contained a

**113**

causal sequence on joints and spot welding. It is to be expected, in any sizeable learning experience, that several kinds of sequence will mingle and interact.

*Spiral sequence* By this I mean the kind of sequence where the student meets a given concept again and again during his progress through a course, each time at a more complex or demanding level. Often this kind of sequence will recommend itself if your subject is of a kind where it appears the student cannot get deeply into any topic or concept before he is already acquainted at least with a great many more. Thus you may give him a brief tour of all the main conceptual landmarks before coming to examine them more closely and going on, later, to analyse each in still greater depth. At each new level, the student will treat the concepts in more sophisticated ways, relating them to a wider and wider network of more recently acquired understandings.

An example from elementary physics: the concept of 'force' might first be introduced as a 'push or pull'; then discussed in terms of acceleration, using graphs; and later on represented algebraically. This spiralling would tie in with Piaget's suggestion that we need experience with concrete realities before we can cope with pictorial representations of reality and with the pictorial images before we can handle more abstract representations. It also ensures that the student always has some kind of grasp, however superficial, of the whole field of enquiry.

I have not undertaken spiral sequencing in this text. To do so would have conflicted with my decision that you should be free to read the chapters in any order you choose.

*Backward chaining* Like spiral sequencing, the final form of sequencing I want to mention is also meant, among other things, to keep the student in touch with the whole subject or task throughout his learning. It is based on the work of Thomas Gilbert (1962).

Wherever objectives involve the learning of sequences (or 'chains') of activity or decision-making—whether simple chains (like tying a shoelace) or complex (like applying 'scientific method')—Gilbert urges the motivational value of teaching the *final* step in the chain first. Suppose your student is to learn a chain involving these main steps in scientific problem solving:

A. Recognize and state a problem
B. Form a hypothesis
C. Devise a test of the hypothesis
D. Carry out the test
E. Interpret the results of the test

Gilbert might recommend starting with step E. That is, you could present the student with data on steps A to D for a particular problem and teach him to do the interpretation. Then, taking another problem, you would present him with data on steps A to C and have him carry out the test before going on to interpret the results. Next, you could give him the results of steps A and B for a fresh problem and get him to devise a test, carry it out, and interpret. Next time, given a problem, he should be able to form a hypothesis, devise the test, carry it out, and interpret the results. After this experience the student should learn to recognize and state a problem for himself (step A) before running through the chain from start to finish.

Backward chaining is held to be more effective than forward chaining because, in the course of it, the student *completes* the sequence several times over instead of once only. Thus, he gets more frequent (and earlier) satisfaction and can always see the relevance of each new step in the learning.

In each 'run', Gilbert says that the teacher should teach a new step, remind the student of the last step he learned and then expect him to finish the chain unaided. Thus, a five-step chain like the one mentioned above, might need seven runs for complete mastery and we can represent them as in Fig. 3.3. Subsequent research has, of course, demonstrated that not all chains are best

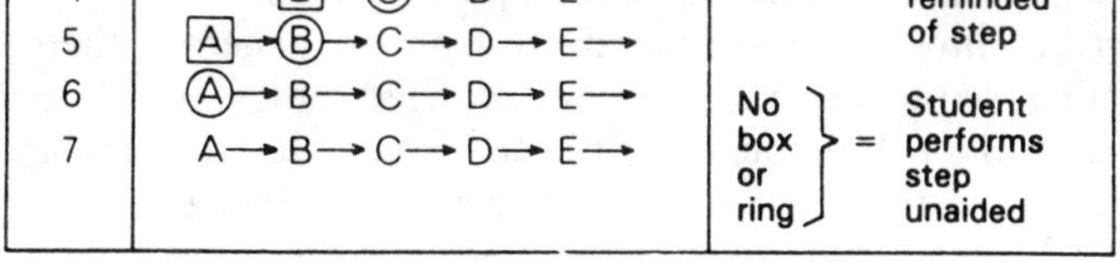

Fig. 3.3 Mastery of five-step chain

**115**

taught backwards. Nevertheless, the concept dramatically reminds us that the obvious way is not always the only way to sequence teaching. Backward chaining is now quite widely, and sometimes unexpectedly, encountered. It can be clearly recognized, for example, across the four-year structure of the industrial design course described by David Warren-Piper (1969) in which the student might

> . . . be told the design problem and how it was derived during the first year, would identify his own problems according to a specified procedure in the second year, would use a variety of procedures in the third year, and be able to justify a choice between procedures in the fourth year.

## Developing a sequence

So far, we have discussed a variety of sequences to be found in courses. But how do we decide on a suitable sequence for a course that we are planning? You may obtain ideas by analysing the concepts (as described in Chapter 2); or by sketching out a concept map; or by considering how your various learning objectives depend upon or lead up to one another. Very often, of course, you will find that a sequence 'just comes to you', without any conscious thinking on your part. (That is the way the sequence for *this* book is arriving.) In such a case, your task will be to evaluate it critically, and improve it. For example, beware of heaving a sigh of relief because you think you have discovered *the* logical order. And watch out for the possibility of conflict between logical and 'psychological' order.

### LOGIC VERSUS PSYCHOLOGIC

When considering the topics and ideas to be dealt with, it is natural to look for some kind of 'logical order'. But the logic we should look for is that which will ensure learning; and this may not be the same logic that would appear tidy to someone who knows the subject already. We need student's logic rather than teacher's logic. A much-quoted report by Robert Mager (1961) describes how he encouraged students to generate their own learning sequences in a course on electronics. Traditionally, electronics teaching begins with the simple (electron) theory and builds up to the complex (actual electronic devices). But every one of Mager's students, free to investigate the subject in his own way, wanted to begin with the fairly complex. They began by wanting information about vacuum tubes (radio valves), about how television pictures are formed and how a radio works, and about hifi and stereo sound reproduction; asking always about things before theory, concrete before abstract, function before structure, *how* rather than *why*.

In fact, there is often a conflict between logical and psychological order. The psychologically satisfying order is often from complex to simple, from the whole to the part, rather than the 'logical' reverse, even though this may be unavoidable in many passages of the course. The student who is learning to fly may well benefit from taking the controls of an aircraft before he learns the theory of flight in a simple-to-complex sequence. In other words, complex-to-simple and simple-to-complex sequences may co-exist within the same course, each serving different needs.

Psychological considerations may outweigh the chronological even in historical studies, where students may prefer to work backwards from where they are to examine, say, the current and recent state of affairs in Northern Ireland before they search for earlier and yet earlier influences. One is reminded of how Alexander Graham Bell was not motivated to learn about electricity until he had already conceived the idea of the telephone.

Michael Eraut *et al.* (1975a) report how an economics course was improved as a result of this realization: 'Previously it had been assumed that the most difficult aspects of learning economics were the concepts and techniques, and that their application would arise naturally. Now it seemed that the reverse might be true'. Indeed, despite the difficulty, students responded with enthusiasm to the discussion groups in which they were first given the opportunity to analyse economic problems with the help of a tutor and, *as a result*, found the learning of the relevant concepts and techniques to be easier and probably more satisfying.

HIERARCHIES IN LEARNING

One interesting approach to sequencing is based on the work of Robert Gagné (1965) who, like Gilbert, asks us to think (though not necessarily teach) backwards. Gagné suggests that we analyse each of the student's major learning objectives and seek out any hierarchy of 'enabling objectives' leading up to it. Each objective represents some operation that the student will be able to perform by the end of the course. Ask: 'What must the student be able to

**117**

do at each stage prior to attaining this ultimate performance?' (See Fig. 3.4 and the explanation below.)

If one of your student's objectives, say in literary studies, is 'to develop a tolerance for ambiguity', you may feel that he must first be able to recognize ambiguities, classify them, analyse their purposes or effects, compare them with related examples, and so on. But equally important would be affective traits that the student may or may not already possess, like open-mindedness, willingness to take risks, and a distrust of the superficial. The teacher and student, exploring together for possible hierarchical connections among such abilities and attitudes, might learn much both about what they mean by 'tolerance' and about one another's prejudices and predilections.

In analysing learning hierarchically, one can sometimes identify two or more separate *sequences* of enabling objectives that must converge at some point to result in the ability that is ultimately expected. For one example of such branching hierarchies, see Figs. 3.6 and 3.7 and note the accompanying explanation (pages 119–121).

One can sympathize with teachers who feel somewhat reluctant to start unravelling the hierarchy (or perhaps I should say *a* hierarchy, for many alternative structures might equally effectively 'enable' a given objective). But, whether they recognize it or not, the hierarchical principle does enter into their students' learning; and difficulties in learning may well be attributable to neglected steps in a hierarchy that has not been identified.

Notice, though, that this kind of analysis is unlikely to produce just one cut-and-dried, take-it-or-leave-it sequence. Apart from the fact that more than one hierarchy is usually possible, any given hierarchy, because of branches within it (and possible branches to topics *outside* it), may well show several possible routes. This will be discussed in a moment in connection with Figs. 3.6 and 3.7. In short, the analysis does not generate *the* sequence but rather reveals a variety of pathways. One of these will sometimes be identifiable as ideal, but often the variety is best used to accommodate the variety of learning styles among the students—'serialists', for instance, may choose one route, 'holists' a number of others.

*Concept Maps*  We can usefully bear in mind the possibility of hierarchies—of one idea entailing prior understanding of others—if we are trying to draw up concept maps of our subject area. Fig. 3.4 shows a simple example:

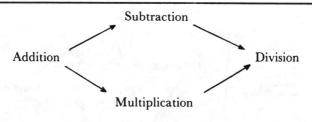

**Fig. 3.4** A simple hierarchy

An understanding of 'division' depends upon a prior under-standing of the concepts of 'subtraction' and 'multiplication' which in turn depend on the prior understanding of 'addition'. Thus, one's teaching sequence would begin with addition, go on to either subtraction then multiplication or vice versa, and finally to division. The above diagram is not dissimilar in principle from those produced in 'critical path analysis' or PERT ('pro-gramme evaluation and review technique').

Trying to draw a concept map can be a helpful way of high-lighting possible connections and dependencies between one's ideas. Just write each idea down on a large sheet of paper or a whiteboard from which they can easily be altered or erased, and look for possible or necessary links between them. Alternatively, they can be written on cards and moved around on a table top. The ideas may be linked by logical dependence, by time-sequence, by analogy, by opposition, and so on. Where you see a link, of whatever kind, draw a line between the two ideas; and, if the link is such that one idea must, or could usefully be treated prior to another, turn the line into an arrow to show the implied sequence. For example, look again at the tree ring growth diagram (Fig. 3.2) and at those shown at the end of Chapter 2.

Fig. 3.5 shows an initial sketch towards a concept map for a course on Diet and Nutrition. It contains ideas more or less as they first came to mind. Some of them will perhaps not be pursued in the eventual course; perhaps others will be brought in. The indicated links between ideas vary in their nature and strength, and several are still somewhat tentative. Further analysis suggests that the essential structure of ideas is as shown in Fig. 3.6, where arrows indicate that a hierarchy has emerged. Thus for example, knowledge of the 'components of food' seems to be the cornerstone

**119**

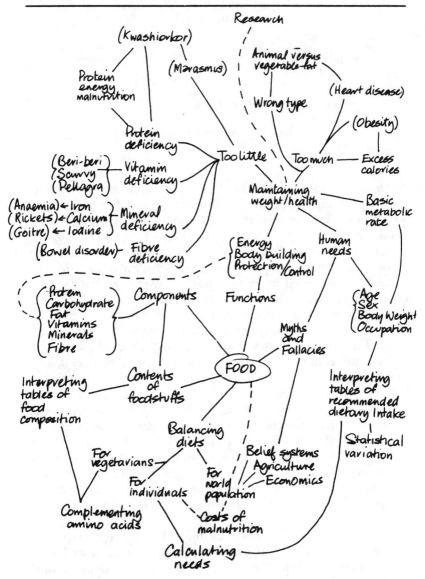

**Fig. 3.5** Initial concept map for a course on diet and nutrition

of understanding in this field. Finally, we may try to identify one or more linear routes through the topics. Fig. 3.7 is a flow diagram indicating two possible routes. After studying 'components of food' the student may be taken down 'the left-hand side of the

**120**

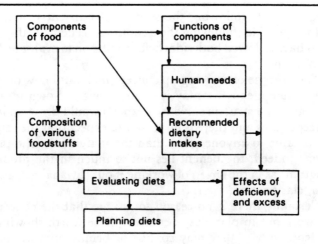

**Fig. 3.6** A hierarchy in the diet and nutrition course

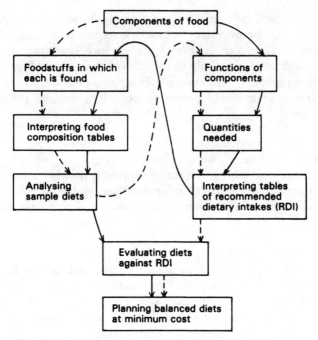

**Fig. 3.7** A flow diagram for the diet and nutrition course

diagram first (following the sources of nutrients) or down the right-hand side (following the quantities needed). Either way, he must have followed both sides before going on to evaluate diets and plan them.

The exercise of drawing up concept maps and flow diagrams is simply one means we may use to sort out our own ideas about sequence and structure. No two experts would draw up identical concept maps and there is no reason to expect that the results will be of value to anyone other than the individuals who produced them. Indeed, the benefit lies not so much in the product (the diagram) as in the *process* of working it out (by analysis, amplification, clarification, etc.).

Certainly there is no reason to assume that the concept maps we work out in planning a course will be worth showing to the student. In fact, they may confuse or bemuse him unless we are prepared to spend time explaining them. They are likely to contain far more detail than can be comprehended by someone who is not already as familiar as we are with the structure of the subject.

What may well be useful to the student, however, is a *flow diagram* showing the necessary or possible sequences through the main topics of the course. Thus, I suspect our flow diagram in Fig. 3.7 would be of more help to the student than would Figs. 3.5 or 3.6. For a more complex example, imagine a course that has 15 topics. Here are some of the possible sequences through them.

1. Topics 1–15 in that order.
2. Topics 1–15 in any order.
3. Topic 1–(2–14 in any order)–15.
4. A structure combining certain key topics (probably arranged in a set sequence) interspersed with enrichment/subsidiary/follow-up topics arranged in sets, allowing perhaps a choice from each (see Fig. 3.8).

STUDENTS' OWN SEQUENCE

Perhaps in the last few pages I have been putting too much emphasis on us (as teachers) thinking out sequences in advance of getting together with our students. Often this will be possible and desirable. But we must not forget that one way of developing a sequence, and structuring a course, is to help students do it for themselves. Ideally, it may be our aim that each student should be encouraged to construct and justify his own hierarchies, networks

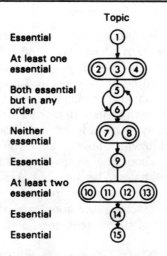

**Fig. 3.8** Possible and necessary paths through the 15 topics of a course

and sequences, just as he may learn to formulate his own objectives. For example, Harrison and Hopkins (1967), in their course for Peace Corps Volunteers, wanted to wean students from their dependence on expert, authoritative advice and enable them to take responsibility for solving problems on their own, often in the light of uncertainty, inadequate information, and the strong feelings generated by confrontations of value and attitude. Thus when students arrived expecting a traditional university classroom course they found that they had to design and sequence large parts of the course for themselves:

> From their arrival, the trainees would be encouraged to participate actively in the planning of their program. In fact, in a sense, there wouldn't be a program unless they planned it through determining what kind of a training program they needed in order to reach the objectives they had formulated.
>
> The program would be 'experience-based'. There would be ample opportunities furnished for 'doing things', such as organizing and operating co-ops, raising chickens and pigs, planting and tending gardens, approaching 'academic' subjects through research projects, etc. Trainees with needed skills would be urged to teach them to others, formally or informally. The emphasis, in short, was to be on trainee activity, not passivity.

**123**

## The microstructure of a course

Having dealt in this chapter with the broader issues of structure within a course, perhaps I had better end it by coming down to detail. This seems as good a place as any to make a few generalizations about the teaching of concepts and principles. As you will notice, I make remarks elsewhere about *how* to teach while discussing what to teach or in which order. In truth, the *how* and the *what* cannot really be considered in isolation. Thinking about what to teach, and in which order, makes you think about how to teach it. Thinking about how to teach it makes you think of yet *other* things that will have to be included. As stated before, course planning is a circular, iterative process. Early decisions, e.g., about content or teaching methods, are always liable to be altered in the light of subsequent ones, e.g., about sequence or assessment.

### *The teaching of concepts and principles**

In the next few paragraphs, eight aspects of the teaching of concepts and principles are mentioned. They should be equally valid whether you are teaching your students face-to-face on-campus or whether you are preparing self-teaching material for students learning at a distance. What they epitomize is the need for the 'microstructure' of a course to incorporate examples, student activity and practice, and feedback on activities.

ASPECT 1: ANALYSE THE CONCEPT OR PRINCIPLE
In the case of a principle you want to teach, what kind of statement is it? And what concepts does it incorporate? In the case of a concept, what attributes does it have? What are the criteria for applying it? Work through the steps of concept analysis, examining examples and nonexamples. You will need several of these for your teaching material. In fact, as I indicate with the concept of 'tort' in Chapter 2, one approach to teaching the concept would be to have students work through the analysis with you.

Let us say the principle we want to teach is the 'simple' one

---

* One note of apology: the examples in this final section may seem particularly trivial. This is the only way I can cater for readers from a wide variety of subject backgrounds. A high-level example that would be clear to a theoretical physicist would likely be neither comprehensible nor interesting to a political historian, and vice versa. It is hoped that these lowly examples will mean something to specialists of all kinds and that you will be able to think of parallel examples in your own subject area.

**124**

'area = length × width'. Or rather, 'the area of a rectangular figure = length × width', or rather '*one* way of finding the area of a rectangular figure is to multiply its length by its width'; or rather 'the area of a rectangular figure that is not a square, in which case you would multiply any two adjacent sides'—not quite so simple after all, perhaps! But, even sticking to the basic computational principle, we see that it involves the concepts of multiplication and of length and width, and of rectangularity.

ASPECT 2: TELL THE STUDENT WHAT HE WILL BE ABLE TO DO AS A RESULT OF UNDERSTANDING THE CONCEPT OR PRINCIPLE

In short, indicate the objectives or purpose of the learning. Tell him he will be able to recognize a Beethoven overture when he hears one; or distinguish between Art Nouveau and Art Deco in architecture and design; or suggest explanations for certain kinds of political structure; and so on. In the case of our principle tell him he will be able to calculate the size of rectangles. The purpose of this is to help the student direct his learning and monitor his own performance.

ASPECT 3: ENSURE THAT THE STUDENT HAS ALL NECESSARY PRE-REQUISITE LEARNING

Your analysis (Aspect 1) may have revealed concepts a student must already possess in order to grasp the new concept or principle. These will need teaching first if the student does not already have them. To acquire even a basic grasp of a simple concept like 'immigrant', the student must already have concepts like 'birthplace', 'place of domicile', 'travel', and (to distinguish immigrants from tourists, travelling businessmen, etc.), concepts like 'intention', 'duration of stay', and so on.

In the case of our 'area = length × width' principle, the student clearly needs a notion of rectangularity, in the absence of which the calculation will be irrelevant; he must be able to distinguish the long side from the wide one, or at least recognize that these are two adjacent sides; and he must know what multiplying involves, at least as an operation. Furthermore, if he is to understand the principle, as opposed to merely being able to apply it, i.e., perform a calculation, he must have formed some intuitive concept of areas, e.g., by grading rectangles in order of size or by comparing the number of, say, coins that can fit on surfaces he recognizes as being bigger or smaller than others.

You may need to carry out some kind of *diagnostic testing* early in

**125**

your course to establish which of the essential concepts your student already has. Any that he does not have he will have to learn. If he is working from self-teaching material, he may need to turn to some other source of instruction, or you will have to provide the necessary teaching within the course, perhaps as an optional sequence which many or most students will bypass. Anyway, lack of attention to necessary prerequisite learning— either not thinking about it at all, assuming the student has got all that is necessary, or hoping he can somehow struggle through without it—is one of the greatest barriers to effective learning, especially where the teacher and student are at a distance from one another.

ASPECT 4: PROVIDE EXAMPLES AND NONEXAMPLES OF THE CONCEPT OR PRINCIPLE

Here you will employ examples you developed during your earlier analysis (Aspect 1). There are several more detailed points we can make about Aspect 4:

*Provide several clear examples* Obvious as this may seem, it is rarely well done. To help him register all the criteria for a new concept, the student will usually need more than one example. But usually that is all he gets, e.g., one photograph of a river's meanders; one specimen of a metal fracture; one hearing of a major chord.

*Provide several clear nonexamples* Equally, to ensure his grasp of the criteria for using the concept or principle, the student needs several nonexamples, e.g., photographs of non-meandering rivers; specimens of metal that have been cut; hearing of minor chords. In the case of our 'area = length × width' principle, the student will need to recognize that it cannot be applied to shapes that do not have four sides.

*Provide borderline examples and nonexamples* Once the student can distinguish between clear-cut examples and nonexamples of the concept, he can be exposed to finer discriminations. Present him with borderline examples—examples that he might be tempted to regard as non-examples, e.g., he might not recognize an eel or a sea-horse as 'fish'. Examination of such borderline examples will help the student avoid *under*-generalizing the concept—being too restrictive in its use. With our 'area = length × width' principle, a

**126**

borderline example would be provided by showing how the principle applies to a square.

Conversely, the student needs to avoid *over*-generalizing the concept or principle. Thus, he will need to see borderline non-examples. These are cases to which he might think the concept or principle applies when in fact it does not. Thus, with the concept of 'fish', he might need to be shown that it does not apply to whales or tadpoles or sea-snakes, even though they all live in water. Likewise, our student of area may need to be persuaded that the length × width principle will not work even on shapes with four straight sides if the shapes do not contain four right angles—or two pairs of equal sides and two right angles, which amounts to the same thing. Showing how the principle can be extended by 'doctoring' parallelograms may be left until a later lesson!

*Go from simple to complex and from concrete to abstract in examples and nonexamples* (But notice the warning about psychological versus logical order on page 117.) In a way, I have already touched on the simple-to-complex idea in suggesting clear examples before borderline examples. But it is worth singling out for special mention. Make sure that your first examples of a concept or principle are not cluttered up with inessential elements. For example, in teaching the concept 'immigrant' it would be better to start with a person who has just arrived in your country intending to spend the rest of his life there than with someone who was born in your country but whose parents had immediately taken him abroad where he has remained for the last sixty years, returning now to spend the rest of his life in his homeland if he can adjust to it. In the case of 'area = length × width' an example of simple to complex would be to deal with rectangles having sides of, say, $3 \times 2$ before those with sides of, say, $3.42 \times 0.07$. Clearly, we would not want arithmetic to obscure the principle.

What about concrete-to-abstract? Generally speaking, a concrete example and nonexample should precede an abstract one. A real fish is more concrete than a picture of a fish; and a picture of a fish is more concrete than a verbal description; and a verbal description is more concrete than its name. If the student starts off on examples that are too abstract, he may well learn only a pallid, verbal ghost of the concept. Conceivably, he may for example, know that trout, herring, shark, etc., are fish but not recognize any of these creatures as fish if he saw actual specimens.

**127**

Again, he might even be able to give a verbal definition of 'fish' but be unable to relate the definition to actual biological specimens—because he had not seen any, or even pictures of them, while supposedly learning the concept. This results in a kind of verbal sophistication, accompanied by an impoverished ability to relate to the real world (even to 'real worlds' like literature or history), that is commoner than we would like in higher education.

How would concrete-to-abstract apply to 'area = length × width'? Perhaps we would have our students begin by cutting out cardboard rectangles and covering them with cut-out squares; then we might have them draw the squares; then they would do the calculation after merely measuring the sides; then they would apply the principle to rectangles they never see at all, merely being told the lengths of the two sides.

ASPECT 5: GET THE STUDENT TO APPLY THE CONCEPT OR PRINCIPLE
You may start by identifying examples and nonexamples of a concept for your student. But, as the course develops, you should encourage him to make such identifications (and increasingly subtle ones) for himself. Similar methods may be used in applying a principle. If the concept or principle has several dimensions and attributes (or criteria for use), which you are teaching one at a time, get the student to demonstrate that he can apply what you have taught so far before going on to teach more. For instance, going back to 'fish', suppose you are beginning with the fact of their living in water. You may give examples like salmon and sharks, and nonexamples like dogs and birds. Before going on to criteria like 'cold-blood' or 'scales' or 'no legs' (or whatever is essential), you might well give the student a set of creatures, only one of which (say a carp) lives in water, and ask him to pick out the fish. Your next exercise might involve him in selecting the fish, using new criteria, from a group of animals all of which live in water.

Furthermore, once a student's basic grasp of a concept or principle is established, you will want him to use it, along with others learned earlier, say in analysing a case study, solving a problem, or exploring a theory. Thus, the concept of 'fish' may be used in developing the idea of an evolutionary progression of life-forms from water to the land.

Getting the student active in using concepts and principles is an important part of this aspect. To accomplish this, we must leave

**128**

him something worthwhile to *do*. Here is Norris Sanders (1966) saying about textbooks what is often equally true of the way other teaching methods are used—television programmes, lectures, classroom lessons, and all:

> Although many are attractive, accurate, readable and understandable, they are also one of the biggest deterrents to thinking in the classroom, because the writers assume that students learn best by studying a polished product. The key function of the writer is to explain, and a good explanation is interesting, orderly, accurate and complete. The vocabulary suits the level of the student and complex ideas are clarified by dissection, integration, example and visual images. Thus, the textbook is weak in that it offers little opportunity for any mental activity except remembering. If there is an inference to be drawn, the author draws it, and if there is a significant relationship to be noted, the author points it out. There are no loose ends or incomplete analyses. The textbook is highly refined and as near perfection as a human mind is capable of making it—but the author does the thinking.

Immaculate exposition leaves nothing for the student to do except nod in agreement and commit *your* learning to memory. Such teaching, in whatever medium, resembles what my colleague, Brian Lewis, calls a 'mention list'—where we mention a number of things to the student in the hope that, later on, he will be able to mention them back to us. By implication, the Sanders paragraph tells us what our students should be doing—dissecting, integrating, exemplifying, and picturing ideas, drawing inferences and pointing out significant relationships, chasing up loose ends and bringing analyses to completion, rather than leaving all thinking to the teacher.

In this respect, it is worth remembering that you can often get the student to 'discover' the principle for himself rather than merely apply it once you have pointed it out to him. That is, you could provide him with a set of examples or case studies and get him to abstract the features or principles they have in common. I mention in Chapter 2 how the concept of 'tort' might be developed in this way. Again, our student of area could be given a series of exercises, involving covering rectangles with cut-out squares, that would culminate in him making the 'discovery' that the total number of squares on any given rectangle was the product of the two sides. Such 'discovery learning' often results in better motivation and retention, though it may be too time-consuming in some cases.

**129**

ASPECT 6: GIVE THE STUDENT FEEDBACK ON HIS ACTIVITY

This also sounds almost too obvious to mention. But is is often not done, even in texts that explicitly ask the student questions. Either the answers are not printed; or else only the bare answers are printed, with no indication as to the criteria by which they are justified; so the student who got the right answer may be ignorant as to whether he got it for the right reason, and the student who got it wrong has no knowledge of where his mistake occurred.

Effective feedback would ensure that the student knows why he is right if he is right and why he is wrong if he is wrong. If it is not a question of being right or wrong, then the feedback should give him the criteria for appraising his response himself and comparing it with other people's responses—yours for instance.

When teachers are meeting students in seminars, tutorials and laboratory work, etc., this feedback can be given face-to-face. (To a certain extent, students will give it to one another, but not necessarily reliably.) When students are learning from self-teaching material, feedback needs to be built into that material. Worthwhile feedback on students' written work (especially for distance students) may need to be given in writing. This is discussed in Chapter 5. The more quickly feedback can be given, the more valuable it may be to students. As one student put it (Ramsden, 1979):

> 'You give an essay in—I gave in two at the beginning of the second term and I didn't get those back till this term . . . you know it's a bit difficult when you're writing the next essay, because you want to know where you've gone wrong and the points that have been all right . . . by the time you've got it back after waiting a whole term you've forgotten what it's all about and it doesn't really mean much then.'

ASPECT 7: CONSIDER GETTING THE STUDENT TO VERBALIZE THE CONCEPT OR PRINCIPLE

We all 'get the feel' of a great many concepts and principles (e.g., 'family' or 'unsupported objects fall to the ground') long before we put them into words. Likewise, it is conceivable that our students may learn to apply a concept or principle very well, but subsequently be unable to describe the criteria for its use. This may not matter, indeed some concepts and principles, say in mathematics or science, may be impossible to describe in words. As Bertrand Russell once said, most of us can recognize a sparrow

**130**

when we see one but we would be hard put to describe its characteristics clearly enough for someone else to recognize one. Nevertheless, we should consider whether the ability to verbalize the concept or principle is important; and, if so, get the student to do it, perhaps at various stages of his learning. The point is simply that the ability to verbalize cannot be assumed from the ability to apply—or vice versa, of course.

It is worth remembering also that many students are able to *speak* ideas that they are yet unable to write clearly about. As one tutor (Zoellner, 1969) describes the situation:

> '. . . when I read the student's utterly opaque and impenetrable sentence or paragraph aloud to him. 'Mr Phillips,' I say, 'I simply can't make head nor tail out of this paragraph; what in the world were you trying to say?' When I pose this question . . . a large majority . . . open their mouths and *they say the thing they were unable to write.* 'Well, Dr Zoellner,' they usually begin, 'all I meant to say in that paragraph was that . . .', and out it comes, a sustained, articulated, rapid-fire segment of sound-stream, usually from five to fifteen seconds' duration, which communicates to me effectively and quickly what they 'had in mind' when they produced the impenetrable paragraph I hold in my hand.'

ASPECT 8: GIVE SUBSEQUENT PRACTICE WITH CONCEPT OR PRINCIPLE
This will happen 'naturally' in any sequential subject like mathematics or science. Later parts of a course will build upon earlier parts and whatever concepts and principles the student learned earlier, he will be constantly reusing them in learning new ones. With less sequential subjects we may need to make a special effort to keep earlier concepts alive in the student's mind. Even if they have no direct application in later parts of a course, they may, however, be referred back to by way of contrast, or as analogies with the concepts and principles that are then being explored.

In this chapter, we have looked at four different ways of conceiving of the structure of a course. In addition, I have introduced the idea of 'microstructure' which, strictly speaking, might seem more appropriate to understanding the shape of individual lessons (units/modules) within a course. I will end as I began, however, with a reminder that these structures do not develop independently of one another. For example, the kind of

**131**

pedagogical structure we settle for may well either stem from or help shape our metaphorical structure, while at the same time imposing a certain structure of events and limiting our freedom to experiment with the structure of ideas (and with the micro-structure). Furthermore, it should be clear that course structure both affects and is affected by the issues we discuss in all the other chapters of this book.

# 4. Your teaching methods and media

How are you going to teach your course? What methods and media will you be using? I do not want to labour the difference between 'medium' and 'method'. Writers tend to use the words interchangeably, sometimes confusing the issue still further by talking similarly of 'approach' or 'strategy' or 'mode'. What this chapter sets out to discuss can best be described as 'ways and means of facilitating teaching and learning'.

On hearing the word 'media' in an educational context, many people assume that the reference is to film and television. But a teaching medium is any means by which an educational stimulus is conveyed to a student. Thus the printed page you are looking at now can be considered a medium—so long as there is a chance someone might learn something from it. So we can talk of the textbook medium (or method, or approach, etc.) to teaching and learning. Films, audio-tapes, computer simulations, lectures, discussion groups, laboratory work, and projects are all means of learning. All can be regarded, then, as teaching methods or media.

### Influences on media choice

So how do you decide on methods or media? This will depend on four main factors. First of all, there is the type of teaching/learning system you will be in—what I call the 'pedagogical structure' in Chapter 3. For instance, if you plan to have students do a lot of their learning in face-to-face contact with one another and/or with you, you will tend to adopt different media than if you want to emphasize self-instruction or independent learning. On-campus courses are likely to use a different balance of media than courses where students are learning at a distance.

Secondly, your choice will depend on which methods and media you happen to be familiar with. Obviously, if you have never heard of simulation games, they will not be among the media you will be considering. Less strongly, you may have heard of them but not of any applications within your subject area; the result again may be that they simply do not come to mind when you are considering possible media. How often must it happen that we disregard a potentially valuable medium or method because

**133**

we are unaware it was available to us? All too often we choose only from among the media that we were taught by ourselves or that we have used successfully in the past. Ideally, we should be regularly examining reports of how media new to us have been used—even if in different subject areas and even at different levels of education—asking always whether they could be adapted to serve any worthwhile purposes of our own. Certainly the educational journals report abundant developments on which we might draw.

Thirdly, you will be influenced by what you believe to be the advantages and disadvantages of the media and methods known to you. Some methods will lend themselves to one purpose, some to others. If you want students, for example, to follow a closely reasoned argument you will possibly look for, or produce, an appropriate text. If you are aiming to change attitudes or develop social skills you will tend to choose methods involving the student in discussion with other people. The only limitation here is that our ignorance of certain media and methods may prevent us from making the most appropriate choice, or from using it as well as we might.

Finally, your choice of media will be constrained by what you regard as the practicalities of your situation. What media and methods will actually be available to you? Since some media are more expensive in money or time than others, which will you and your students be able to afford? And, to recognize the politics of teaching and learning, which media will be acceptable to your students and your colleagues?

Before we come to considering particular types of media and method, I would like to make a more fundamental distinction. This distinction is between the medium or method and the type of stimulus that a medium or method embodies.

## Types of stimulus

Different methods and media offer different forms of stimulus. That is, they appeal to different senses in our students. I would identify five different types of stimulus each of which, taken alone or in combination with others, can be conveyed by any of several media. And, between them, I believe they account for all possible media. They are:

● Human interaction (verbal and nonverbal).

- Realia (real things and events).
- Pictorial representation (still and moving images).
- Written symbols (words, figures, etc).
- Recorded sound (speech, music, 'natural' noises).

The medium you and I are using at present—a book—can present some of these kinds of stimuli but not others. Clearly it relies mainly on written symbols together with pictorial representation, e.g., maps, diagrams, photographs. Usually these images will be 'still', though a book can allow a sequence of moving images by printing them, say, in the right-hand bottom corner of every page and having the reader animate the sequence himself, achieving the illusion of movement by bending back the corners and then allowing them to flick through his fingers at speed.

Human interaction may be described in a book but it cannot be embodied therein. Nor, strictly speaking, can recorded sound(s). Though it would be possible to include a cassette for playing on a separate device or even, in some cases, to attach audio-tape to the pages in a way that would enable them to produce sound, again using a separate device. As for 'realia' (an ugly word, but difficult to improve on), a book usually conveys an educational message rather than itself being the message. If, however a history student were examining the handwritten diaries or account books from a family he was researching, then such books would be realia, i.e., real objects, produced without any educational intent. There is, of course, no reason why a book should not include realia (provided they are not too massive) between its pages. Dennis Wheatley demonstrated this rather neatly in one of his 1930s detective novels *Who Killed Robert Prentice?* (recently republished) by including 'clues' in the form of railway tickets, letters, newspaper clippings, and so on.

Let us now look at each of the five types of stimulus in turn and consider the media and methods in which each might be embodied.

### *Human interaction*

By human interaction I mean the stimulus that becomes available for communication whenever two or more people are aware of one another's presence, and begin responding, consciously or unconsciously, to one another's responses. The spoken word will often be the dominant element and the message communicated will often be cognitive—ideas, arguments, explanations are being expressed. But sometimes nonverbal elements are dominant—gestures, intonations, eye-contact, 'body-language'; here the message is largely affective and emotional—moods, feelings, attitudes, and values are being conveyed.

The intensity of the interaction—the degree to which each person modulates his thoughts and actions on account of responses from others—will vary from one teaching/learning method to another. Using the lecture medium, little interaction can take place (especially if the audience is large). With broadcast radio or television, none can take place at all. The responses of the listeners are usually either hidden from the lecturer or are ambiguous. So, he has no opportunity to adapt his manner or material to satisfy their individual needs. If the lecturer encourages questions from his audience then, of course, the level of interaction is raised.

For a high level of human interaction we might look to the tutorial medium, especially the one-to-one dialogue where both tutor and student respond directly to one another's verbal and nonverbal signals. Discussion groups, seminars, laboratory demonstrations and telephone conversations are other media embodying the stimulus of human interaction.

Perhaps one of the most promising of interaction media developed in recent years is that of role playing, and 'simulation' and 'academic games'. In such games, students act out a working model of some real-world human situation. They are provided with background data and with individual roles to play, together with constraints that may change due to 'outside' intervention or 'chance factors' as the game proceeds and they work in inter-acting groups with some kind of realistic problem to solve. They may find themselves coping, for example, with running the nation's economy, or competing as several industrial companies selling a similar product, or simulating a local election and so on. (For a useful overview of simulation and gaming, see McAleese, 1978 and Megarry, 1978 and 1979.)

Certainly, games appear to be an effective teaching medium, both cognitively and affectively. The essential concepts and structures of the real-life situation are built into the structure of the game and, like the decision-making processes involved, the student learns them by having to operate with them. In addition, he may well learn a considerable amount of factual information because he needs and uses it in a memorable context.

Games are particularly noted for the high·level of motivation they generate among students. There are many explanations for this: students are hooked by the relevance of the problem or issue; they are involved as producers rather than consumers of the subject-matter. They are freed from dependence on the teacher and are able to learn from one another; they are able to experiment safely with feelings as well as rational processes; they get a powerful and immediate response to their decisions and are aware of having an effect on the human environment. Human interaction can be intense.

Unfortunately, games are not always easy to arrange for students learning at a distance, unless you can bring them together from time to time. However, you may find it possible to design games in which such students can enlist the involvement of a colleague, friend, or spouse.

Clearly, media employing human interaction are not dependent on the presence of a professionally certified teacher. Students will learn from many other people in the community, especially from one another. (There will be more about this later.)

I have dealt with human interaction first because it is, in several senses, the primary stimulus. Obviously, it was about the first one we ever had. Again, it appears to satisfy a primary need—students need a human response to their efforts. The high drop-out rates on correspondence courses is often attributed to lack of human interaction; and if the Open University continues to maintain its relatively low drop-out rate, it may well be partly due to the attempts made to facilitate encounters between students, and between students and tutors. Self-instructional 'on-campus' courses have less of a problem in this respect.

Notice that media such as radio, television, and film can *demonstrate* human interaction to the student, but such demonstrations do not usually involve him, except vicariously. This vicarious involvement can be very valuable, especially for the student who has to work on his own; but seeing and hearing human interaction does not provide the same stimulus as being part of it.

However, with certain on-campus courses it may be appropriate, occasionally, to direct the cameras (and/or microphones) at the students themselves. Thus, tapes may be recorded of students teaching, interviewing, acting, engaging in a role-play exercise or a simulation game, and so on. Playback of these tapes may engender more than vicarious involvement ànd may lead to

**137**

renewed and intensive interaction. 'Microteaching' exercises are a well-researched development in this area.

### *Realia*

This is a word coined as a shorthand for real things, real events, real animals and, where the student merely observes rather than interacting with them, real people. The child learns from realia about as early as from human interaction. The smell and taste of his food, the brightness of overhead lights, the sound of slamming doors, the painfulness of fire, all these and others are building up what Gagné (1965) calls signal learning and stimulus-response learning from the moment of birth. Then, as the child becomes more mobile, he begins to respond to a wider range of realia: plants in the garden, complex toys, people at work or passing by in the street, cats and dogs and birds, events like the dropping of an egg or an altercation between adult visitors. From such realia the child learns much about the way the world works, about the nature of materials and how he can manipulate them, and about adult roles and relationships. Yet these realia have not been consciously organized with a view to teaching him anything.

When he gets to school, however, the child meets realia that are systematically organized and deployed with educational intent— sand and water, clay and paint, cuisenaire rods and counting frames and Montessori materials, visits to farms and seaside and factories and railway stations, flowers, shells, rocks and fossils, drums and recorders, insects, mammals, fish and birds—things he can see, feel, hear, smell, taste, and touch. As he gets older, the realia become more sophisticated—cadavers for dissection, antique documents, esoteric chemicals, complex laboratory equipment, visits to concerts and the professional theatre, field trips to archaeological sites and scenes of geographical or historical interest.

The significance of realia as a type of stimulus is epitomized in the rich learning from real things and events that can take place when working in the laboratory and especially 'in the field'. Keith Wheeler (1971), in the following quotation is talking of secondary education, but his remarks have considerable validity also for older students. He is saying that 'geographical imagination':

> . . . can only grow out of the first-hand experience of landscape and environment which can be had from fieldwork, because the child who has studied his own river, for instance, has a greater chance of

imagining accurately the development of a river like the Mississippi which he may never see. Or the 15-year-old who makes a land-use map of a farm during a field study is more able to appreciate the agricultural land utilisation in other parts of the world.

Such direct observation of and interaction with the real world lies behind much of the course content in post-secondary education. However, as he gains in experience the student is expected to work less with the realia and more with the symbolism (chiefly pictures and words) that can represent it. The ability to manipulate this symbolism is a vital part of the individual's cognitive growth and gives him a powerful tool for communication. Unfortunately, teachers often forget the need for preliminary experience with the realia of a *new* area of study. That is, adults new to the study of geography may have no less need than 15-year-olds to get their boots muddy along the river bank by going to see for themselves.

It is too easy to hurry the student on to a verbal facility with the subject before he can know what he is talking about. Harrison and Hopkins (1967) guarded against this in their training of Peace Corps Volunteers for Latin America by running the course at a primitive camp in Puerto Rico rather than in their classrooms at Yale University. Both medical education and teacher education in Britain have, in recent years, shown increasing interest in getting the students out of the lecture theatres and into the real worlds of hospitals and schools *early* in their training, before they become too immersed in theoretical studies.

The real worlds of hospital and school bring the student into contact not only with the realia but also, of course, involve him in highly relevant human interaction. Similarly, sandwich courses, involving lengthy attachments to commercial or industrial organizations, allow for total 'immersion' in a situation where realia and human interaction together can work powerfully towards the students' learning. As one student said about his sandwich course attachment (Beard and Senior, 1980, page 57):

> 'I was in a workshop operating a lathe. I couldn't see the relevance of it while I was there, but I have done since. I met people socially and was living in digs on my own. I think I matured a lot and got used to looking after myself.'

But even in more limited fieldwork, e.g., a geological visit to a quarry, or in laboratory practical work, human interaction is likely to be important as well as realia.

**139**

Realia can, indeed, be used along with any other form of stimulus in a variety of media from lectures and tutorials to a self-instructional 'package'. Where we cannot take or send the student to see the realia *in situ* (e.g., in a quarry) we may be able to bring some to him (e.g., a set of fossils). Practical work will be further discussed later.

### Pictorial representation

Here I am speaking of pictures and diagrams, which may be realistic or symbolic, still or moving. Photographs, 'artist's impressions', drawings, diagrams, graphs, charts, maps, are all pictorial representations of reality. Sometimes reality is too big for the classroom, e.g., the solar system; or too small, e.g., the heart-beats of a water-flea; or too slow, e.g., the sequence of cloud-types during the passage of an occluded depression; or too fast, e.g., the wing movement of a humming bird; or too inaccessible, e.g., peristalsis in the small intestine. At other times the reality is too dangerous, e.g., defusing a bomb; or too cluttered-up with confusing detail, e.g., classroom interaction between pupils and a teacher; or it may be invisible, e.g., the pattern of sound waves from an underwater echo-location device; or even extinct, e.g., dinosaurs. In all such cases, pictures may be able to overcome the disadvantages of the real thing.

With pictures we can control reality. We can make it smaller or bigger; we can speed it up—with time lapse photography; we can slow it down—by slow-motion techniques; we can take cameras and the artist's imagination where the human eye cannot go; we can picture what could not be safely observed in reality; we can emphasize using diagrams, editing, or selective photography—and eliminate confusing details; we can picture the invisible—using diagrams, animated or still; and, of course, we can picture scenes that never were, things and people and events that are not longer here to be looked at or have not yet come into being. Replicas and 'table-top' models—e.g., the development of a river delta, or the structure of a molecule, or the relative motions of planets in the solar system—can have many of the advantages mentioned above and are best regarded, perhaps, as three-dimensional 'pictures'.

This control of reality through pictures has its dangers, of course. Indeed we may be getting rid of extraneous detail (as we see it) if we present a student with a diagram or photograph or plastic model instead of real specimens, say, of a fruit or cell structure he is studying. We can thus ensure he concentrates on what we regard as the 'essential' features. But we need to be sure that we are not thereby impoverishing his learning unduly by denying him contact with a real specimen. If we can be sure he has had prior 'hands on' experience with the realia, we shall have less need to entertain such qualms.

A great many media are capable of presenting the stimulus of pictorial representation. Still photographs, paintings, cartoons, maps, diagrams, graphs, and the like can be made available as individual prints to be handled by students. They can be made large enough to display separately on a wall, incorporated into a poster or chart. They may be presented on film, as slides, or a film strip. They may be used along with other types of stimulus— in the pages of a book, on the visual display unit of a teaching computer, on a work card for use with an audio-cassette recording, on an overhead projection transparency for use during a lecture or tutorial.

If we want *moving* pictures or animated diagrams we may, if the sequence is sufficiently clear-cut (e.g., 'the dance of the molecules'), get away with presenting our pictures in a booklet so designed that its pages can be flicked through fast enough to give the illusion of continuous motion. Normally, however, we shall need to consider the medium of television or cine film, perhaps in association with other types of stimulus, say recorded sound or written symbols. (There will be more about this later.)

### Written symbols

The use of written symbols, and especially printed (or written) words, developed out of human interactions, realia, and pictorial representations. The written word is relatively accessible to teachers and students and is highly versatile as a generator, organizer, store, and disseminator of ideas. With print, the student can make an argument or explication stand still while he chews over a point; he can go back to the beginning and start again; see the whole shape of the argument 'in black and white'; and above all, re-read it whenever he likes, either considerably faster or more slowly than if it were spoken. Print affords us control over the 'reality' of the spoken words. Hence, although some subjects or disciplines do not rely so heavily on the written word in teaching, e.g., surgery or music or art education, for the majority it has become the most powerful stimulus of all. Whether students' reading ability is adequate to cope with the demands being made upon it is a matter we shall need to consider later on.

Written symbols—mathematical and technical symbols as well as words—are presented by a variety of media. The 'purest' medium of presentation is, of course, the book. Even here the stimulus of pictures may also be used. But students using computer-assisted learning are now used to seeing print (again allied with pictures) on their visual display unit. Slides and filmstrips may also present written symbols, perhaps along with pictures and diagrams. When written symbols are used in television programmes and cine films, they may be linked with recorded sound as well as pictures. As teachers, we generate our own written symbols, along with human interaction and other stimuli, when using the chalkboard, flip chart, or overhead projector. We may also prepare written material and present it to students through such media as lecture handouts, data sheets, work cards, posters, charts, self-instructional texts, and assignment exercises. Our handwritten comments on a student's assignment or test paper are a highly individualized use of the written word in teaching. (This is further dealt with in Chapter 5.) Students also use the stimulus extensively in making their own responses— test answers and geometrical 'proofs', letters and reports, notes and essays.

### Recorded sound

Here again, using this form of stimulus helps us control reality. Natural sound is ever-moving and we cannot persuade it to stand still for inspection. But we can capture it on tape, amplify it, slow it down, edit out confusing noise or extraneous detail and, above all, repeat it when, where, and as often as we like. The sounds we are interested in may be:

1. Physiological, e.g., heartbeats.
2. Mechanical, e.g., the knocking of a worn 'big end'.
3. Musical, e.g., a concert.
4. Conversational, e.g., foreign language dialogue.
5. Dramatic, e.g., a poetry reading.
6. Instructional, e.g., a lecture.
7. Environmental, e.g., birdsong.

Again, several presentation media are available. Recorded sound can be presented on audio-tapes and gramophone records. It can be presented on radio or as the 'sound track' of a television programme or cine film. On television and film, the stimulus of recorded sound can be combined with pictures and diagrams and with written symbols, but not with realia or human interaction. The 'missing' stimuli may, of course, be available in the teaching situation in which the sound recording is used. Thus, students working in pairs may discuss the taped instructions they receive while learning to handle a machine or conduct an experiment.

### Combining stimuli

As we have seen, any given type of stimulus can be conveyed by more than one medium. Similarly, a given medium can convey more than one type of stimulus. When two or more types of stimulus are put together in this way it is important to ensure that they do not conflict with each other, e.g., a film whose visual images are so powerful that the student is unable to pay attention to the spoken commentary. Considerable thought is needed to ensure that the types of stimulus complement and support one another.

It is also important to notice that several *media* can be used together within a particular learning situation; hence the so-called 'multi-media' learning packages that have figured so largely in the development of self-instructional courses. Samuel Postlethwaite (1964) and his colleagues at Purdue University describe one such multimedia, self-instructional (on-campus) course in first-year botany:

> Most of the factual information is acquired through independent study in a specially-designed learning center containing thirty booths. Each is equipped with a tape-player, and 8mm movie projector, a microscope, live plants, test tubes, diagrams and other materials pertinent to the week's study. Learning activities may include listening to short lectures, performing experiments, reading from texts and journals, studying demonstrations, viewing short films, discussions with the instructor and/or other students, microscope study, dissection of specimens, and any other study activity deemed helpful by the senior instructor or the student. Since the independent study is unscheduled, experiments do not have to be designed to fit into a three-hour time interval, and some experiments can take the form of miniature research projects.

## Choosing media and methods

We may well return now to the question mooted at the beginning of this chapter: 'In setting up a course, how do we decide when to use which media and methods?'

**143**

## *Media functions*

Before we can make a sensible choice of media we perhaps need to consider what functions they are to perform in the learning situation. Basically, they must present the student with a *stimulus* and evoke a *response*. But this basic stimulus-and-response requirement embraces a variety of subtle and intricately connected functions like the following:

- Engaging the student's motivation.
- Recalling earlier learning.
- Providing new learning stimuli.
- Activating the student's responses.
- Giving speedy feedback to the student.
- Encouraging appropriate practice.

These functions are discussed in greater detail in Rowntree (1974) and they underpin what I have to say about the 'microstructure' of a course at the end of Chapter 3 of this book. However, it should be apparent that presentation media using any of the learning stimuli mentioned earlier seem capable of tackling all six functions above, in some manner and to some degree.

But no single medium is superior on all functions, and for all students, in all situations. For example, human interaction·may be best at engaging the student's motivation, while print may excel in encouraging appropriate practice (in some situations). In some circumstances, appropriate new learning stimuli can perhaps be presented only by realia, while others will demand moving pictures, and so on. Ideally, we would choose a combination of media according to which is best for each function in a particular learning situation. If we are forced to settle for fewer media than we would ideally choose, we must use those that satisfy more of the functions than would any other combination. (This is not to deny, of course, that the problem we are often faced with in actuality is how to make the best of whatever happens to be available.)

What other factors shall we take into account when weighing benefits and disadvantages of various media? The main ones are: relationship to objectives, students' learning preferences; the need for variety; availability/accessibility, and cost.

## *Matching with objectives*

Sometimes, our choice of media is strictly limited by the nature of our objectives. In other words, it may be necessary to ensure the

**144**

kind of stimulus presented by the media is appropriate to the kind of ability the student is aiming to acquire. Thus, if the student is learning to 'distinguish between valid and invalid inferences that might be made from a particular historical source', the printed word may well be a suitable stimulus. But if he must 'state whether a musical passage played on the piano ends on the tonic or dominant', no amount of printed words or musical notation, or even human interaction, will help him unless he also has access to the stimulus of sound, either from recordings or a real piano. Again, the student who must 'identify which of a set of soil samples are sand, which clay and which loam' may get some help from words, printed or spoken, but he will be unable to make the discrimination until he gets his fingers on the realia—some soil specimens. Similarly, if the student is to be able to 'describe the motion of an amoeba' he must see one moving, or else he will be merely describing someone else's description; if microscopes and amoebae are not available, pictures will have to suffice—moving pictures of course. But if we are helping our student towards affective objectives, changes of attitude, for instance, we will probably feel that none of the above media will be very helpful, and, instead, look for one involving intensive human interaction, e.g., simulation games or group discussion.

But usually a given objective can be achieved with the help of any one of a number of media. In fact, if it is not as obvious as in the paragraph above that one medium is essential, it probably does not matter which is used.

### Students' preferences

So, most objectives will not help us too much in choosing media. What about the possibility of choosing media to suit the different learning preferences of individual students? If more than one type of stimulus is appropriate to a given objective, we might aim to provide the student with the one that suits him best. Unfortunately, research allows few generalizations to help us here—apart from the rather obvious reminder that poor readers may learn better from spoken or recorded words than from printed material. Followers of Marshall McLuhan (1964) are inclined to suggest that our students nowadays, soaked in television, may have a more pictorial thought process than earlier generations did. But would this imply we should try to teach pictorially, or rather to avoid pictures in the hope of developing other kinds of thought process in the student?

**145**

Different students may well have different styles and preferences. Some will thrive best on human interaction, while some prefer print; yet others will not be happy unless they see the real thing, and so on. It may be difficult to predict the distribution of preferences in advance, let alone to cater for them all.

If we are in doubt about our students' preferences we may be able to go in for 'media overkill'—tackling each objective with several media in the reasonable expectation that between them they will satisfy all students. Since we have no exact science of who can best learn what from which, a certain amount of redundancy is unavoidable. I know one Open University professor who says what he wants to say in his printed course book, then says it in sound on radio, and then says it again, with pictures, on television. He argues that no one student will need it all three ways, but that all three are needed to make sure everyone gets it his own best way!

VARIETY

All the same, one can have too much even of one's preferred medium. Any medium or method, however appropriate to your educational purposes, will fatigue and bore the student if it is the only one you ever use. Variety is one good reason for combining media, even where one medium could (in theory) perform all the necessary functions. Hence the lecturer may enliven or alternate his 'talk and chalk' by handing out worksheets, by using the overhead projector, and by occasionally incorporating tape-slide presentations. As one student says, in appreciation (Beard and Senior, 1980, page 19):

> 'He's a good lecturer, he knows what he's going to say next, but he puts life and feeling into it and jokes about it; and he shows us slides which I think break it up—people need a break from writing all the time.'

Similarly, students learning on their own may rely chiefly on reading, but may usefully be provided also with audio-tapes, practical work, and opportunities for group discussion.

### Practical considerations

Now let us look at two practical constraints on your choice of media. What is available and/or accessible? And can you and the students afford the costs involved?

**146**

## AVAILABILITY/ACCESSIBILITY

Is the medium on which you are planning actually available for you to use? And, assuming it is, will it be accessible to students?

For example, you cannot make film or television programmes unless you have production facilities available. Even if you can make the programmes, can the students manage to see them? For on-campus students you would need film projectors or video cassette players or a closed-circuit transmission system, not to mention an administrative system for scheduling group or individual viewing. If your students were studying 'at a distance', there might need to be a television broadcasting system that could make time available to show your programmes, and you would certainly need to be sure students had access to television receivers.

.Even the Open University was able to choose its media—print and broadcasting chiefly—only because the delivery system existed *already*. That is, Britain has a good postal service, through which printed materials (and 'home experiment kits') can be sent to students, and the BBC's broadcasts reach all parts of the British Isles. Furthermore, students can confidently be expected to have access to radio and television receivers, and to record players or audio-cassette players. In time, we may be able to assume they also have access to video-tape players and even home computers.

On the other hand, even the Open University is now facing severe restrictions on its use of television as a medium. As courses multiply, the BBC is no longer able to provide adequate transmission time. Alternatives are being investigated—e.g., video-tape replay machines for group viewing in local study centres—but such alternatives do raise a whole new set of problems, especially those relating to cost. In any case, I think it quite likely that a shift in emphasis from television to other media—especially the medium we call 'audio-vision' (individual student activity guided by an audio-cassette recording accompanied by some combination of print, still pictures and realia)—will lead to a net increase in learning.

## COSTS

Cost is an inevitable constraint on your choice of media. How much will it cost you to teach with a particular method or medium? How much will it cost your students to make use of it? For example, designing a series of laboratory exercises may cost you a great deal in time and materials; but students will incur no costs (other than learning time) in working through those exercises. On the other hand, you may recommend students to buy a set of textbooks, thus incurring no expense yourself but requiring students to pay for their use of that medium.

Film and television material can be expensive both to make and to use. Making a programme will be costly in time, even if your institution has already acquired the expensive equipment and facilities required. Whether you are making your own material or are using material produced by others, you will need to ensure that viewing facilities are available. Either you or your students will have to pay for those facilities.

Perhaps the most reasonable approach to costs is always to ask yourself the question: 'Can another medium do an acceptably good job, more cheaply?' Thus, do not spend months writing a completely new text on your subject when you could achieve similar teaching effects by spending just a few days writing a commentary and supplement for students to use with a book that exists already, and is cheap enough for them to buy. Similarly, if you feel an urge to make a television programme, ask yourself whether moving pictures are really necessary—could you achieve comparable results by providing students with *still* pictures and a commentary on audio-tape (audio-vision or tape-slide presentation)?

### Summary

Perhaps I can best sum up with a set of questions to ask when choosing media and methods:

1. Which media and methods are available to me and to the student?
2. Do any of our learning objectives imply particular types of stimulus and particular media?
3. How would I wish to use each of the available media? (More of this follows in the next section.)
4. What would it cost me (and the student) to use these ideal media?
5. Would less expensive media and methods be acceptably effective?
6. Do the chosen media and methods offer the student sufficient variety of stimulus and activity?

## Using media and methods

The one question I rather neglected in the previous section was 'How would I wish to use each of the available media?' The answer depends to a very large extent on two factors:

1. The kind of situation one is teaching in, e.g., on-campus or at a distance.
2. The type of teaching/learning system one wants to encourage, e.g., the extent to which you wish to control what students learn and how they learn it.

These two factors working together are responsible for what, in Chapter 3, I call the 'pedagogical structure' of the course.

So, different structures may demand different media and methods. Or, at least, the balance between media will differ. More significantly, however, any given medium or method will be used in different ways.

Let us think, first of all, how this applies to the two most common media. Undoubtedly the most noticeable teaching method with on-campus courses is the *lecture*. Similarly, the most obvious medium for distance courses is the *book*. Though even with on-campus courses students may spend much more time reading than attending lectures. Interestingly, the emphasis with a lecture is on teaching whereas with reading it is on learning.

### *The lecture method*

In many institutions, lectures are seen as the natural and proper way to 'impart a body of knowledge'. Students' timetables may demand that they be lectured at for several hours a day, leaving little time for other forms of learning. This may suit certain kinds of student—those who will be content to feel that all the knowledge they will need is being neatly assembled for them and handed out in convenient hour-length packages. Similarly, many teachers will be basically content with this arrangement. After all, it does put them firmly in control of the situation, and it also enables them to feel that at least they've 'covered the syllabus'. If the students appear not to have taken much of it in, well 'that's up to them, they're not schoolchildren now'.

But I do not wish to decry the lecture method as such. Lectures have their place, so long as they are used sparingly (the variety criterion) and appropriately (the criterion of relevance to objectives). Certainly lectures are economical in that they let one

**149**

teacher speak to a large number of students all at once. And a good lecturer on a good day can do a lot for his audience. He may be able to review students' past learning in such a way as to give them new insights as well as some glow of satisfaction at having conquered the terrain being described. Similarly, from his own pinnacle of mastery, he may be able to survey the terrain ahead of them, identifying major landmarks and pitfalls, thus saving his audience considerable time and trouble when they come to explore it for themselves. In doing so, he may be modelling for them a 'master performance', letting them see (and perhaps identify with) the thought processes of the specialist pursuing the call of his discipline. For many students this may be highly motivational, even inspiring—filling them with respect for their teacher and for the subject, and with confidence in themselves as favoured disciples. As one student describes it (Ramsden, 1979):

> 'If they [lecturers] have enthusiasm, then they really fire their own students with the subject, and the students really pick it up. . . . I'm really good at and enjoy [one course], but that's only because a particular tutor I've had has been so enthusiastic that he's given me an enthusiasm for it.'

However, such teaching may be comparatively rare. Too often a lecture will be given by a teacher who is nervous about the students or does not really know the area of the subject he has been asked to lecture on, or who does not know what students are supposed to do with his information anyway, or who lacks presence and even audibility. Consequently, for these and other reasons, students often have very patchy and peculiar perceptions of what has been said in a lecture. Thomas (1972) found that the level of students' learning declines steadily after the first few minutes of a lecture until interest picks up again when the lecturer begins to indicate that the end is in sight. And what students do remember of a lecture is likely to fade from memory fairly rapidly. McLeish (1968) suggests 40 per cent recall of main ideas immediately after, falling to 20 per cent one week later.

IMPROVING ON LECTURES

For the teacher who needs to give lectures come what may, there are many things he can do to increase their effectiveness. Such books as Beard (1979), Bligh *et al.* (1975) and UTMU (1976) make many sensible and practicable suggestions. However, many of them amount to abandoning the lecture method in its pure and undiluted form as, in essence, a means of *presenting* information to the student.

Indeed, as I mentioned earlier in this chapter, the main weakness of the lecture method is that it allows only one-way communication (or 'munication' as I called it in Rowntree, 1975). The lecturer has little or no opportunity to ascertain how his discourse is being received by students and so modify it accordingly. Conversely, students have no means of influencing it by asking for it to relate to their own individual concerns, perceptions, and puzzlements. In short, there is no feedback—neither to the lecturer telling him how well he is getting his message across, nor to the student telling him whether he is making sense of what is being said.

Consequently, many lecturers make their first step away from 'munication' towards communication by allowing for questions at the end of the lecture. Some may go further and allow questions *within* the lecture. By such means students are enabled to check out their reception of the lecturer's message and, to a limited extent, get that message to touch on their own concerns. (Such a method is common enough in secondary school teaching, where teachers cultivate the skill of being able to maintain a logical development to their lesson while at the same time asking and receiving questions.) However, even with a class as small as 30 students, and even if the lecturer is prepared to spend as much as 30 minutes dealing with questions, either very few students will be able to enjoy this facility personally, or, if all do, the enjoyment thereof will be exceedingly brief.

So, still remaining within what is basically a lecture situation, some lecturers will move towards even fuller communication. That is, they will enable the students to communicate with (and learn from) not just the lecturer but also one another. One way of doing this might be to ask each student to write down a question he has about the lecture, or an answer to a question posed by the lecturer. This he may then be asked to discuss with his neighbour. Then each pair may be asked to discuss their responses with another pair and agree on a single question or comment to be put to the lecturer by one of the four students in a general 'plenary' discussion.

This basic approach—individual thought followed by discussion with at least one other student—can be adapted for use with almost any size of lecture group and even the terraced seating of a lecture theatre does not rule it out. It can be used as an

**151**

exercise following on from the initial presentation made by the lecturer or it can be used, once or even several times during the presentation, as a means of structuring it.

Such an approach has many advantages, apart from leavening the lump of an hour of solid teacher-talk and, at the same time, relieving the lecturer of the strain of being the constant centre of attention. More significantly, such an approach begins to address different objectives, different styles of learning, and different beliefs about the nature of knowledge. It assumes that students can learn from comparing their own perceptions of a situation with those of others; that their differing backgrounds and values will be of positive value to one another in coming to grips with new subject-matter; and that they will be improving both their ability to express themselves cogently and to cooperate with others. Above all, it ensures that every student has to do more than merely internalize the lecturer's presentation. He is forced to *think*, both about its subject and about the thoughts of his peers.

### Group learning
Such are the benefits of discussion (as opposed to presentation) of ideas that some teaching sessions will abandon the lecture element altogether. Or it may be attenuated to a five minute introduction or be replaced by students having done preparatory reading and/or writing. Such sessions are commonly timetabled as tutorials or seminars; but Bligh *et al.* (1975) list and describe many variants: buzz groups, square root groups, brainstorming, horseshoe groups, case discussion, syndicates, group tutorials, individual tutorials, seminars, free discussion groups, sensitivity groups, and so on.

These different methods all have their different advantages and make a variety of demands on the organizational and social skills of teacher and students. All I want to draw attention to in the present context is the degree to which they call for the teacher to move away from the role of presenter towards that of facilitator. Instead of acting as the fountain of all wisdom on whom all eyes and ears are turned, he can become more a provoker of self-discovery and peer-teaching, in which attitudes are liable to change as well as cognitive understanding. He will be helping students with the struggle to articulate their own grasp of the subject-matter and to learn also from the way their colleagues challenge or elaborate one another's initial suggestions. As one student described such situations (Beard and Senior, 1980, page 60):

> 'You get put on the spot and it's amazing how much you pick up when you're under pressure. When you're actively participating you learn a lot from whatever people have to say; the tutor's just guiding the argument.'

Even the tutor may learn from such exchanges. Graham Holderness (1973), rebuking the kind of teachers who regard students' personal viewpoints and anecdotes as irrelevant interruptions to their teaching, puts it like this:

> Discussing *The Rainbow* with a group of Open University students and hearing the personal responses, the individual contributions of a wide variety of ages and occupations—the 'irrelevant anecdotes' of a farmer, an ex-miner, an engineer, a schoolteacher, a single woman, a married woman, a woman with children—to my mind enriched the reading of that book infinitely. It came to life as I had never seen it before—and I had taught it many times.

## SELF-HELP GROUPS

Some group work may be pursued without a teacher present. Or, at least, if a class is split into several groups, the teacher may move round spending just a few minutes with each group in turn; not with a view to intervening in the discussion but mainly so as to be familiar with the kind of issue likely to arise in the later plenary session. Such 'tutorless' groups are a further step in the direction of requiring students to think for themselves. With students learning at a distance, where tuition may not be easy to provide, such groups—'self-help groups' as the Open University calls them—may be the only way for students to learn with (and from) other human beings. Even so, their viability will depend on a large enough number of students living close enough to one another to get together frequently. And they may need help from the course organizers in the shape of suggested topics or materials, around which to structure their sessions, e.g., simulation exercises or games. In Rowntree (1976) I encouraged the formation of 'syndicates' of three or four students who meet together two or three times a week to compare notes and review syllabus topics together. Such self-help groups and syndicates are sometimes described as engaging in 'peer-teaching'.

There is abundant literature on teaching in small groups. Among books worth consulting for advice are Abercrombie (1969 and 1974), Bligh *et al.* (1975), Cantor (1972), Hill (1969) and UTMU (1976). For a useful review of peer-teaching, see Goldschmid and Goldschmid (1976).

### Practical work

Such activity is often justified by reference to the old Chinese proverb: 'I hear, and I forget; I see and I remember, I do and I understand.' Practical work includes demonstrations, laboratory work, clinical experience, fieldwork and, in many cases, projects. Again there is plenty of advice available on how to use such teaching methods (see Beard, 1979, and UTMU, 1976). My interest here is in pointing out that the list of methods above (from demonstrations to projects) illustrates once more the progression from teacher-controlled presentation methods to increasingly individualized, student-controlled learning methods. Interesting problems arise also in deciding how to incorporate practical work into courses for students learning at a distance.

Demonstrations are clearly a means of *presentation*—showing students how something or other is done. The knowledge students acquire of the technique will be cognitive—perhaps they will be able to describe how it is done—but they may not be able to do it themselves (or at least not very adeptly) until they have tried it out.

This leads us into laboratory work in which students are usually involved in setting up and carrying out 'experiments' or tests following the guidance given on worksheets, and then writing up the results for checking by the teacher. This method is something of a holy cow in the teaching of science and engineering. It is one that eats vast quantities of money, equipment, space and student time. Yet many people are beginning to question how essential it really is. For instance, science students in the Open University are sent Home Experiment Kits, replete with materials and equipment to carry out experiments carefully integrated into the course. Yet as many as 25 per cent of students appear never to open the package—without suffering any visible academic loss. And students in other universities complain at the often perfunctory and pedestrian nature of the tasks they are expected to perform ('cookbook science'), especially if they suspect other, less-qualified, people will be performing any such work for them in their subsequent careers.

PURPOSES

So what do teachers believe to be the purposes of laboratory work? Below is one set of desired outcomes I have seen suggested. It is worth asking just which of them actually do appear to need physical contact with the realia. Laboratory work should improve students':

1. Theoretical knowledge.
2. Knowledge of apparatus and instruments.
3. Ability to handle apparatus.
4. Knowledge of procedures.
5. Ability to suggest a hypothesis in order to solve a problem.
6. Ability to select procedures to solve a problem.
7. Ability to carry out procedures.
8. Observational skills.
9. Concern for accuracy.
10. Capacity for independent thinking.
11. Ability to interpret and evaluate experimental data.
12. Ability to write coherent reports.
13. Capacity for self-directed learning.
14. Ability to work effectively with others.

It seems to me that only purposes 3 and 7 definitely do demand some kind of 'hands on' experience (though 13 and 14 seem to suggest *projects*, which will be discussed later); but some of them (2, 4, 5, and 6, for instance) might be equally well attainable through the examination of a series of photographs under guidance from print or an audio-tape. Similarly, even the observational skills and accuracy mentioned in 8 and 9 might be exercised through study of events recorded on film or video-tape rather than of the events themselves. Likewise, 11 and 12 sound like activities that could be performed just as well in the library as in the laboratory.

No doubt there would be losses as well as gains in thus moving away from the realia towards relying on representations of it. However, no-one is suggesting an end to laboratory work but merely that its use be directed towards the purposes only it can satisfy and that more cost-effective means might be found of satisfying those other peripheral purposes that have accreted around it.

PRACTICAL WORK AT A DISTANCE

Where practical work with realia is thought necessary it can be

**155**

arranged, even for students learning at a distance. Sometimes such students can be brought together occasionally in a laboratory or workshop, in 'summer schools', or 'weekend practicals'. But usually it will be necessary to send the laboratory to them. I have already mentioned the Home Experiment Kits used by (most) Open University science and technology students. These may contain rock specimens, chemicals, microscopes, photospectrometers, or whatever is appropriate to the subject.

To acknowledge that the Open University is not alone in this activity, I will illustrate it with an example brought to my attention by my colleague Clive Lawless. Below are listed the contents of a kit sent to botany students of Macquarie University which has external undergraduates throughout the state of New South Wales in Australia. The kit, consisting of relatively cheap and simple materials, enables students to carry out a surprisingly wide range of experiments on seed germination and plant growth which are listed directly after the kit's contents.

*Items in kit for seed germination and plant growth*
Plastic tray with holes in base to allow drainage, to be used for growing large number of seeds.
Blotting paper to line tray and provide moist surface for seeds.
Plastic bag to cover tray loosely. (This retains moisture in the early stages of germination.)
Packets of seeds.
Disposable Petri dishes in which to grow seeds or isolated plant organs and tissues.
Filter paper circles on which to support plants and tissues.
Glass rods to support filter paper at surface of solution in Petri dishes.
Plant growth substance (2,4-D giberellic acid).
Disposable pipettes for diluting growth substance solution.
Glass marking pencil.
Waterproof graph paper as scale for measuring growth.
Masking tape to use in making light-tight box on which to grow plants.
Supplementary items supplied for experiment on: breakdown of starch by germinating seeds.
Roll of 'Testape' (Eli Lilley) to determine glucose concentration in solution.
Spall specimen tubes (1 to 2 dozen).
(Students need to supply a small quantity of sodium hypochlorite,

which is readily available from pharmacies, to sterilize seeds and some methylated spirits to sterilize instruments.)

*List of experiments and topics utilizing kit*
*Plant structure*
Some differences between spores and seeds.
Structure of angiosperm seeds.
Seed dormancy and requirements for germination.
Anatomy of monocotyledon and dicotyledon seedlings.
Structure of meristematic and vaculate cells.
*Water relations of cells and tissues*
Inhibition by seeds.
Osmosis.
*Metabolism of germinating seeds*
Respiration, starch breakdown and sugar production.
Production of amylase by germinating seeds.
Effect of temperature on amylase synthesis.
Action of gibberellin on breakdown of starch via induction of amylase synthesis.
*Growth of the seedlings*
Mitosis in root squashes; action of metabolic inhibitors.
Role of cell division and cell expansion in growth: gamma irradiated and normal seedlings.
Cell differentiation.
The locus of plant growth root and shoot growth.
Tropism geotropism and phototropism.
Growth analysis of young plants relative growth rate and net assimilation rate.
Effects of inorganic nutrients on plant growth.
Seedling development in light and dark.
*Plant growth substances*
Production of auxin by apices apical dominance.
Effect of auxins on shoot elongation using coleoptile sections: time course of expansion: auxin concentration use of inhibitors.
Effect of auxins on root growth using cucumber and cotton.
Auxin bioassay.
Morphogenetic effects of auxins.
Sequential response of pea stems to auxin and gibberellin.
Effect of gibberellin and CCC on the growth of dwarf beans.
Control of flowering.
Control of cell division by an interaction between auxin and kinetin.

**157**

As a matter of fact, this Macquarie kit proved so successful with external students that it was subsequently adapted for use by on-campus students. Normal 'laboratory' sessions were superseded by an 'open' laboratory in which students worked independently with the kit under guidance from an audio-tape (Adamson and Mercer, 1970). Such on-campus use of a self-instructional kit is clearly very similar to the audio-tutorial described by Samuel Postlethwaite in the paragraph I quoted on page 143. Keller Plan courses (see page 92) can also incorporate such activity.

Incidentally, the Macquarie students were able to carry out the experiments successfully and obtain good experimental data, but were often unable to effectively evaluate the data without the help of a tutor. This is just a reminder that such individual learning does not do away with the teacher; it simply changes his role from that of presenting a stream of information and, perhaps, continuous feedback, to that of designer of a system in which students can generate their own information and their own feedback, with the teacher re-entering the system at the point where his wider experience is needed to help the student make sense of what he has learned on his own (or with his peers).

THE USE OF MODELS

It is worth pointing out here that relevant practical work may sometimes be made possible far more cheaply than would be implied by Open University and Macquarie home experiment kits. In some cases, practical work may be based not on realia but on *models*. This was clearly essential with one Open University course (*Renaissance and Reformation* A201) in which students needed to understand how the Greek astronomer, Ptolemy, managed to explain the irregular motion of the planets without having to abandon the idea of uniform circular movement around the earth. (Since this idea was, of course, incorrect, his explanation had to involve a rather complex set of concepts—'excentric', 'epicycle,' and 'equant'.) Although the Ptolemaic system was explained in the text and demonstrated on television, the course team felt that students would still need 'hands on' experience if they were to grasp the abstractions. So the course materials included a 'do-it-yourself Ptolemaic universe kit'—two sheets of A4 card on which were printed various shapes which, when cut and pushed out, could be placed on the turntable of a record player. With the turntable providing uniform circular motion, a student could physically manipulate the orbital speeds and shapes of orbits until the role of Ptolemy's concepts became clear.

Another course (on geology) provides similar sheets of printed card from which the student can make three-dimensional models of faulted blocks (of rock). By moving these around he can see how the surface distribution of rock-types, as shown on a geological map, compares with what might be under the surface. Such a 'concrete operational' experience is presumably necessary before the student can cope with symbolic representations (e.g., maps) or verbal descriptions. Clearly, written symbols cannot convey the experience. Watching other people do the manipulations, e.g., on film or video-tape, would not be very helpful either. Even the 'realia'—faults and outcrops that a student might inspect if he visited a quarry—would not give the same kind of understanding. Indeed the realia might make more sense to the student *after* he had learned from manipulating the models.

### Projects and independent learning

In this section, we started by thinking about lectures. We then went into group learning and practical work, and now I want to say something about projects. Underlying this sequence was the idea of a teacher progressively loosening his control over what and how the students learn. Projects can represent the decontrolled extremity of this process. A project (discussed also in Chapter 3) is a substantial programme of study organized around some problem or topic. Ideally, if it is to be distinguishable from a 'mere' exercise, it should be giving the student considerable latitude in his choice of topic and/or study activities. The student may work alone or with others on a topic of common interest. The work will normally result in some end-product, e.g., a report, a portfolio of designs, a computer programme, a working model, an annotated anthology of poems, or whatever is appropriate. But the emphasis is likely to be not so much on the product as on the *processes* of research and learning.

THE TEACHER'S ROLE

The teacher will not be acting as a presenter or communicator of knowledge. Indeed the student may well be working in an area that is slightly outside of his teacher's detailed knowledge. Rather, his role will be that of adviser. He will begin by helping the student identify and formulate a relevant topic or problem that is manageable in the time available. Then he will help him to find appropriate sources of information, to organize his data, to interpret it, to plan a report, and so on. Some students will need more help than others at different stages, but the teacher's role is that of 'expert-student' rather than 'subject-expert'. That is, he is concerned to help his students develop a methodology to determine their own content. This he should be able to do even if students are tackling content that is fairly new to him; his insights as an experienced and expert student enables him to contribute to the students' learning by questions along the lines of: 'What do you mean? How do you know? What other evidence might exist? How else could you analyse this? What sources of bias are there? How would you relate this to . . .?' and so on.

In effect, by getting students to teach him their content, he is teaching them the methodologies of enquiry in his discipline. In doing so, he needs to exercise very nice judgement in avoiding imposing too much direction on a student's own efforts after knowledge while at the same time avoiding the opposite error of giving so little help that the student becomes overwhelmed by the demands of his self-appointed task and loses his sense of direction.

WHAT IS INDEPENDENT LEARNING?

When interpreted as I have indicated above, a project becomes a medium of *independent learning*. Like 'integrated', 'inter-disciplinary', and a variety of other recently introduced educational jargon, the term 'independent learning' tends to be used as if to seek or confer approval, but it gets applied in seemingly diverse circumstances.

Few would quarrel with the idea that students in post-secondary education should be acquiring the skills needed to learn independently. After all, if they are to continue learning at all in the rest of their lives, they will be doing so, as a rule, without formal help from teachers and without the carrots and sticks of syllabuses and assessment by others. Hence, so the argument goes, students should be practising independent learning as part of their education.

But *of what* is the student's learning meant to be independent? Of the work of other students? Of the aims imposed by a teacher? Of learning methods imposed by a teacher? Or what? Some teachers would call a student's learning independent if it were pursued at the student's own pace, without his being either hurried along or slowed down by having to keep roughly in step with other

**160**

students. But this is to confuse independent learning with 'solitary learning' or 'private study'.

On the one hand, the solitary learner may be highly dependent on the teacher in that he may be working to attain a very specific objective that was prescribed for him. He may even be expected to learn from highly prescriptive material (e.g., a programmed text) that even decides for him *how* he is to reach those objectives.

On the other hand, the independent learner—let us say that means one who has some control of his ends and means in learning—does not necessarily have to be a solitary learner. He may benefit from, and indeed may feel he needs the stimulus of group discussion to air his developing ideas and obtain comments and criticisms that will help him improve them further. He may also attend lectures and may even seek specific information from a teacher on a point that is troubling him. (The teacher will thus be used as a learning resource himself.) So a student may well be pursuing independent learning in company with others—the criteria are whether he is free to choose between that and other learning situations and/or whether he is free to take from it just whatever he deems personally relevant and no more.

Incidentally, similar confusions (with solitary learning, and with learning at one's own pace from materials) attach to the use of the terms 'individualized learning' and 'personalized learning'. Learning can surely deserve neither of these epithets unless the objectives a student pursues, and the means and materials he uses, have somehow been chosen to relate to his personal needs and interests (and of any like-minded colleagues) rather than to the convenience of the teacher or the class as a whole. Such individualized or personalized learning might differ from independent learning in that these ends and means, though related to the individual student's needs, may have been defined by his teacher.

But we cannot really expect fully independent learning—with students deciding both how and what they are to learn—within our system of formal post-secondary education. This is because, at some point in the process, teachers are always required to assess what has been accomplished and issue some kind of certificate of approval. Project work, for instance, raises quite knotty assessment problems which are discussed in Chapter 5. Students can hardly avoid speculating as to whether what they are doing, however acceptable to them, will also be acceptable to their assessors. As one student put it (Miller and Parlett, 1973, page 53):

**161**

'What is the purpose of the examination game? . . . You know you want to get a certain class of degree within the system, but as far as assimilating knowledge properly is concerned, it just doesn't work, because if you play the game properly you're choosing all the time, and not getting an overview because you know there will be a certain question you have to answer.'

Perhaps the only 'certificates' that reward truly independent learning are honorary degrees (in those cases where they do reward learning rather than public service) and higher doctorates such as some universities award on the basis of published work to those of their graduates who *subsequently* make significant contributions to knowledge in their field.

So how would one classify the Keller Plan, discussed in Chapter 3? It is a system based on self-instructional materials, not unlike the Postlethwaite audio-tutorial system mentioned earlier in this chapter. It requires the student to work (usually alone) through a series of packages or modules, with his competency on each being tested before he is able to move on to the next. Such work could perhaps be individualized/personalized to some extent if different students were tackling different modules according to their differing needs or were able to choose from a variety of ways of tackling them. But there would be little independence about such learning since students would still be choosing rather than creating their own purposes and strategies.

There is a definite limit to the extent to which learning that is based on self-teaching (on-campus or at a distance) can be independent. The most we can expect is that such materials will not be so tightly structured and packaged that they can be used in one way only and towards but one goal. Rather they may be structured to allow students to choose and discard from among them and combine them with other resources and experiences in personally meaningful ways. Such would probably be true of the Open University course, *Art and Environment*, mentioned in Chapter 2, page 40.

There is no reason, it seems, why students should not pursue independent learning 'at a distance'. Many Open University courses now incorporate projects (see Henry, 1978). One, in technology, consists entirely of a project, whose ends and means are decided by the student in consultation with his tutor. Such courses provide more individual tutorial time than usual, but relatively little in the way of prescribed learning materials. Students will be helped to track down their own reading material, and other learning resources. This brings me to the second of the two most common media mentioned at the beginning of this section—reading.

### Reading: books and other printed material

It is no anachronism to speak of students 'reading' a subject or 'reading for' a degree. Despite the key role of lectures as a teaching medium, and the proliferation of a new technology of education, students are still expected to spend a large part of their time reading books, journal articles, and other printed materials. The proportion of their total study time so spent will vary from one kind of institution to another and even from one subject to another. Arts students, for example, are likely to spend a much greater proportion of their time on reading than on classwork; while the reverse is likely to be true for science students. In fact, Peter Mann (1973 and 1976) distinguishes between 'doing' subjects (maths and science, engineering, etc.) and 'reading' subjects (law, philosophy, sociology, etc.). But his researches indicated that students can get a degree, even in arts and social sciences, on lecture notes alone.

Bligh *et al.* (1975) after reviewing a number of investigations into how different kinds of student spend their time, reckon that a typical student in Britain spends 20 or more hours a week on individual study. Some of this time will be spent in writing notes, essays, or reports and some may be spent with other media such as audio and video-tapes, but we may well suppose that reading will occupy a large part of it. For students learning 'at a distance', print is likely to occupy nearly all their time; for instance, few Open University students will spend more than one hour a week with television and radio programmes, audio-tapes, or other media; most of their 12–15 hours is devoted to reading.

Despite the fact that books and journals are a prime learning resource, both off and on campus, they are given little attention in books about teaching. The comprehensive and authoritative *Second Handbook of Research on Teaching* (Travers, 1973) devotes less than one of its 1400 pages to textbooks. The equally voluminous *Encyclopedia of Educational Research* (Ebel, 1973) manages eight pages of data about text books, though virtually none of it is concerned with how students use them and learn from them. This may reflect a relative lack of research on the use of books. And since books tend to be used privately, and in ways very much at the whim of individual readers, it may be that their use does not lend itself to investigation by traditional experimental research methods. Yet

**163**

even at the level of anecdote drawn from the practical experience and qualitative research, books about teaching and learning contain little discussion about the use of textbooks and other print material. Revelations can be expected, however, from the kind of research into student learning that I discussed in Chapter 1, e.g., Marton and Säljö, 1976 and Pask, 1976. In what remains of this section, let us remind ourselves of the advantages and disadvantages of print as a medium and consider how reading materials may be selected and used.

### ADVANTAGES AND DISADVANTAGES

We have touched upon the benefits or advantages of print already in this chapter. Printed materials are profuse and highly accessible. That is, the student should have no trouble getting hold of a diversity of books and articles on any given subject. This enables the student to embark upon truly independent learning. He does not have to be bound to the viewpoints presented him by his teacher, or by any single author. Furthermore, print is relatively cheap to use: for the most part, print involves no complex viewing equipment. It is also convenient to use: the student can turn to it when and where he wishes, e.g., at a library table or on a bus journey.

Printed material is flexible in that any given item can be used in different ways by different students, or by the same student on different occasions. He may read an entire book carefully with a view to mastering all its main lines of argument; he may read certain parts carefully and ignore others; he may skim rapidly through it all to remind himself of what he has already learned elsewhere; he may use its index to pick out a few important details he needs knowledge of; he may or may not make notes on it; he may or may not follow up some of the references given in its bibliography; he may or may not discuss its ideas with other students or a tutor; and so on. And, as I said earlier, print enables the student to make the argument or explanation stay still while he pauses for thought or skips backwards or forwards through its pages to review a point or see what lies ahead.

Against these advantages must be set several disadvantages. The first is that students may not know what they ought to be reading or why. That is, they may not have adequate criteria (whether given them by a teacher or developed on their own) for deciding which books or articles might be most relevant to a particular topic of study. Without such criteria they may be overwhelmed by the diversity of material and the conflicts of viewpoint contained in it. Secondly, students may not be able to read. Put so bluntly, this may sound ridiculous. I do not wish to imply that they would be unable to look at a paragraph of text and tell you what it says. But reading in college and university is liable to demand a higher order of skill than is involved in what the primary schools sometimes call 'barking at print'.

My concern would not be with whether students could tell you what the paragraph says but with whether they could tell you what it means. Can they identify the main idea? Can they distinguish between main ideas and supporting detail? Can they see how the main idea of that paragraph relates to those of section/chapter/book as a whole? Can students recognize the significance of that particular paragraph in relation to others? Can they relate it to any ideas or associations of their own?

In addition, assuming the paragraph in question is actually worth the students' attention, would they have been able to track it down for themselves? For many students, the way to read a book is to 'begin at the beginning, go on to the end, and then stop'. The idea that a book will normally contain an index that will help one to decide which parts of the book (if any) are worth reading seems to have passed them by. So they read laboriously from word to word, getting so bogged down in detail (and anxiety about whether they will be able to remember it and which bits they ought to remember anyway) that they cannot see the wood for the trees. Certainly they are not reading critically, neither challenging the internal coherence of what they are reading nor testing it against their own experience. Such slow, undiscriminating reading is probably more common than we imagine. It is often linked with, and to some extent caused by, the students not really knowing why they are reading that particular piece of print and what they might hope to get from it.

All this is not to suggest, of course, that students are likely to be any more deficient in reading skills than they are, say, in listening skills or in observational skills. So other (nonprint) media that rely on other skills may also be putting some students at a disadvantage. One can compensate for this to some extent by using *variety* of media—ensuring that each student will get at least some opportunity to exercise his best learning skills, and to some extent by media *redundancy*—ensuring that any important 'message' is available through several different media.

The third disadvantage of print stems from the relatively *sparse* nature of written communication when compared with speech. Written language is tighter and more compact. A writer strives for his one best way of saying things, whereas in speech he might express the same thought several different ways. Similarly, his examples are likely to be fewer and, where he wishes to build upon a concept mentioned earlier in the text, he is likely to refer the reader back to it rather than 'waste space' repeating the relevant aspects of the concept. Also, the grammar and syntax of written language are less flexible than those of speech, making it more difficult for him to convey certain nuances. Again, the writer has to do without gesture, intonation, pauses, and changes of speed or volume, all of which can be used to help a listener grasp subtle shades of meaning.

Another aspect of the compactness of writing is the conceptual density it often displays. Even if a text begins gradually, defining and exemplifying each new concept as it is introduced, there may soon come a time when the writer needs several of these 'in play' at once; and, if he is to advance his argument, he cannot keep repeating definitions or giving yet more examples. So he must rely on readers keeping up with him as the plot thickens. Here are two examples from standard texts, one in economics and one in science, and therefore using the compression of symbolic notation as well as technical terms:

> Let us now consider what will be the shape of the supply curve of the industry where entrepreneurs are heterogeneous, but all other factors are homogeneous. So far as the short-run supply curve is concerned, the fact that entrepreneurs are heterogeneous will make little difference. It will still represent a lateral summation of the short-run marginal cost curves of the individual firms. . . .

> If we work in free space so that $\mu r = 1$, and use the same current $I$ for the two wires, we can obtain $I$ in terms of the fundamental units of mass, length and time used for measuring $F$, $l$, and $a$, and the value we assign to $\mu c$.

It seems inappropriate to name the authors here—not because I am suggesting the writing is poor (I am not) but because practically any other two textbooks I have within reach would yield similar passages. In fact, both passages play fair with the reader in using only concepts that have been introduced already. But the reader is being worked hard to relate them all together.

In the economics passage, the reader is being invited to visualize a hypothetical 'curve', distinguishing between 'long

**166**

term' and 'short term' (not to mention 'supply and demand'), and between 'heterogeneity' and 'homogeneity', and recalling what 'entrepreneurs' and 'lateral summation' and 'marginal cost curves' are. In the science passage, to follow the analysis of McClelland and Ogborn (1977) in whose article I found the passage quoted, the reader must identify five physical symbols, have some idea how the two wires are arranged, understand why three quantities are measured and one is assigned, and realize that special meanings are being attached to the terms 'free', 'fundamental' and 'value.'

A fourth disadvantage of print (with one exception which I will mention later) is the fact that the student cannot interact with it. He cannot interrogate it as he might a human tutor, asking for further examples or for a reminder of hazy concepts. He cannot ask it to comment on *his* response to one of its ideas. He cannot get it to respond to his individual needs. Again, print is not the only medium to suffer from this disadvantage.

Notice that the disadvantages or difficulties I have outlined above (and perhaps you can think of more) are to do with print as such and *not* with how well or poorly the medium is used. An inept or inconsiderate writer can use the medium to such baleful effect that the unfortunate student's difficulties become insuperable. As teachers developing courses, it is our duty to consider how we might best enable our students to overcome or avoid the disadvantages and difficulties, while benefiting as fully as possible from the very real advantages of print. I suggest we approach this aim through careful selection of texts, through helping students to develop their reading skills, and through supplementing existing texts, where necessary, with material of our own.

THE SELECTION OF TEXTS

Who chooses the books and articles our students read? Unless they are wished upon us, along with an imposed syllabus, either we choose them, our students choose them, or some are chosen by each of us. How can we ensure that they are chosen wisely— whether by us, by our students, or by both? A wise choice demands that we have some rational criteria that will make sense to colleagues in the same field. (Even if they would use the same criteria to make a different choice of material.)

Most courses will present students with a book list or reading list of some kind. Too often this can be a document of formidable length with no indication as to whether any of its many books and

**167**

articles are more relevant than others, let alone to which parts of the course each might relate. Seeing at once, or very soon, that he will not have time to read everything, the inexperienced student may give up the idea of reading anything at all. The lecturer may well protest that it is his intention to spend his first session going through the list with students and commenting on each title in turn. This would be commendable indeed, but his task might have been simpler had he given students a list with some of these comments and annotations already built into it. A reading list should answer the following questions that students might reasonably ask:

1. What basic books and articles do we all have to read? At what point(s) in the course do we need this material?
2. Which additional material would you recommend if I wish to study any of the topics in greater depth?

As an example, the extract below shows how 'further reading' is suggested to students by Roach and Hammond (1976) for each section of an undergraduate zoology course:

> Most books on freshwater ecology have introductory chapters dealing with the general, physical and chemical features of inland waters. The following will give you further information on these aspects:
> Macan, T. T., & Worthington, E. B. (1951) *Life in Lakes and Rivers* Collins: London, pp. xvi + 272. This is a well-illustrated, authoritative, but relatively non-technical account of freshwater life; Chapters 2, 4 and 9 are appropriate to this Section.
> Reid, G. K. (1961) *Ecology of Inland Waters and Estuaries* Van Nostrand Reinhold: New York, pp. ix + 375. Parts II and III relate to this Section.
> Ruttern, F. (1963) *Fundamentals of Limnology* University of Toronto Press: Toronto, pp. xvi + 295. Section A deals with the Physical and Chemical background.
> Russell-Hunter, W. D. (1970) *Aquatic productivity* Macmillan: London, pp. xiii + 306. Chapter 6 deals with eutrophic and oligotrophic lakes.

In fact, we might look to a reading list to contain the following:

1. A basic text to cover all the topics of the course (if any such exists) and/or a number of basic texts, each covering a different topic.
2. Alternatives to any or all of the above (where they exist; and where it is feasible that some students may prefer one author's

style of presentation to another's; and where it will not matter that different students are working from different texts).

3. A topic-by-topic list of further reading—books, articles, and primary source materials.

4. A list of any important reference works.

5. A commentary on the texts listed (perhaps to be discussed further in a class session) indicating their strengths, weaknesses, and unusual features, together perhaps with some guidance as to how the texts might be used. (The purpose of this is not only to help the student in his approach to the material listed but also to help him be critical and comparative in hunting out additional material on his own account.)

6. If there is to be no separate 'study guide' to the course, you might add a section indicating where to look out for current publications, newspaper reports, radio and television programmes, films, etc., on the subject.

The list should give full details of authors, titles, publishers, date and place of publication, and in the case of articles in journals and periodicals, the relevant page numbers. The student should be told whether he is expected to buy his own copies and, if not, any special arrangements that exist for consulting the material in the library. Needless to say, local bookshops and libraries should be given a copy of the list, so that they know what to expect. It can be very painful for a lecturer to have to explain to his first class that *the* set book for his course will not be available in the bookshop for another three weeks! (For the viewpoints of lecturers, librarians, students, publishers, and bookshops, see Mann, 1976).

But how do we choose the titles for the list? With inexperienced students and/or a very basic course, we may be highly prescriptive and require the reading of just one very comprehensive volume. With more experienced students and/or a higher level course, we may offer a great deal of choice or even set students free to establish their own reading lists.

Much will depend on our objectives and the kinds of learning activity we wish students to engage in. If our course is knowledge-oriented and stresses the mastery of a body of highly organized information, we are likely to settle for a single, definitive (and probably rather fat) text. If our course is methodology-oriented, we may wish our students to be considering a variety of viewpoints and to be examining primary source materials also; in which case we will no doubt list a variety of text materials, giving students

**169**

considerable guidance on how to choose among it and add to the list with materials they root out for themselves with help perhaps from abstracting journals. We should also be clear about how the listed readings are meant to relate to the other media we are using. Which are preparatory? Which are alternatives to our lectures? Ideally we should choose texts that offer different ideas or different emphases from those that are provided in our lectures or other media.

Given such considerations, we may still have several possible candidates for a limited number of places on our list. In Chapter 6, I consider the evaluation of possible texts (and other learning materials) for a course. On page 246 I offer a checklist for judging the academic acceptability of a text and, on page 254, another for judging its likely educational effectiveness. Neither of these may be appropriate to your subject, but you may think them worth looking at now with a view to developing your own version.

Finally, it is as well to be realistic about the quantity of material we put on our reading list, especially if we are getting students to buy books. Even paperbacks are becoming very expensive and students are increasingly reluctant to purchase unless they are convinced the books are absolutely essential. So, we must make sure that our reading list will cost students no more than they will be willing to pay for a single course, remembering that they may be taking other courses that are making similar demands on them. And it is as well to check that the books we recommend are still in print!

IMPROVING READING SKILLS

In his survey of students' use of books, Peter Mann (1973) came to the conclusion that 'undergraduates are on the whole, un-instructed about the use of books' and that 'lecturers could do a lot more than they do . . . to improve the situation'.

In fact, if we discuss reading lists with students in the kind of way described above, we will have begun to improve the situation. Such discussion leads into consideration of how to find one's way around the literature of one's discipline and, in particular, how to use the facilities and resources of an academic library. With the help of library staff, we can guide students, (and to the extent that some of them may be proficient already) help them guide one another, in carrying out a literature search, using catalogues and classification systems, retrieving and storing off-prints and papers, generating their own card index bibliographies, and so on.

**170**

Students are likely to need occasional guidance on tracking down and obtaining print material, and on dealing systematically with it, throughout their programme of studies. The needs of a first-year student are likely to be different from those of one in his second or third year. Yet it would clearly be a waste of effort to attempt, at the beginning of a student's first course, to pump him full of all the information-processing know-how he will need in the rest of his educational career. Something needs to be done at the start, but teachers on subsequent courses and in subsequent years will need to make their contribution also. This calls for a certain amount of collaboration between those teachers in agreeing an acceptable joint strategy. Otherwise, as often happens at present, it is too easy for any one of us, responsible for just one course, to protest that we have got a syllabus to cover, our time-allocation is short enough as it is, and we cannot spare any of it for teaching skills that should have been taught earlier or that are just as much the responsibility of teachers on other courses our students are currently taking.

Absence of agreement with colleagues, however, should not prevent us doing what we can for students' reading skills on our own courses. At the very least we can seek out and recommend appropriate books on study techniques (e.g., Buzan, 1973; Maddox, 1963; OU, 1979; Richards, 1943; Rowntree, 1976; Webster, 1967). Such general advice is better than nothing, but we may be able to help our students relate it to their own studies by basing occasional class sessions on such books or on exercises of our own.

Students, faced with what seems to them enormous quantities of print, may seek advice on how to read faster. Undoubtedly most students could learn to read considerably faster than they do, and many speed-reading courses exist to teach them. However, the comedian Woody Allen reminded us of the dangers with his remark: 'I've just taken a speed-reading course. Very useful. I read *War and Peace* last night, took me 20 minutes. It's about Russia, isn't it?'. Gains in speed are possible, however, without loss of comprehension; but it is doubtful whether any huge increases in speed are maintained much beyond the training period (see Carver, 1973).

Generally speaking, what may do students more good than increasing their top speed is to develop a strategy that will enable them to *vary* their speed according to what and why they are reading—skimming, scanning, and skipping, or carefully

**171**

savouring each nuance of a literary image or ruminating on each new step in a philosophical or mathematical argument. One widely recommended approach to tackling a text is the so-called SQ3R system. SQ3R stands for Survey-Question-Read-Recall-Review. The basic idea is that the student should begin with a new text by surveying it—looking at the table of contents, chapter headings, and summaries, skimming the book to see whether it might suit his purpose. If it seems relevant he should then make note of questions that this preliminary skim will have raised and which he will hope to answer in examining the text more carefully. He should then read it, section by relevant section, pausing at the end of each to recall what he has read, making any necessary notes, and then checking the accuracy of his recall by looking back through the text to review.

Different disciplines will call for students to use texts in different ways, and different students will also find their own preferred ways of handling print. It can be time well spent to schedule some class reading sessions in which students can learn from one another's approaches. My colleague, Graham Gibbs (1976), has given much useful advice on running such sessions. Here is the kind of exercise he suggests:

1. Give each student a copy of a short paper (e.g., 5 or 6 pages of A4) covering some topic of general interest.
2. Ask students to read it, imagining they will have to write a paragraph on it in a week's time. Tell them they will have time to read it all.
3. Stop the students unexpectedly after two minutes. Ask them to write down whatever they can about the paper, without looking at it.
4. After two minutes ask the students to form pairs and compare what they have written with their neighbour. Ask them to discuss how they came to write the things they did and why they started reading in the way they did.
5. After five minutes ask them to read right through the paper without further interruption.
6. Ten to fifteen minutes later, ask students to form pairs again to compare their reading. Ask them to go through the paper explaining how they read it and why they read it that way.
7. After ten minutes, ask the pairs to form fours to generate a list of DOs and DONTs about reading, based on their experience of this session.

8. After fifteen minutes, bring students together for a plenary session in which each group is asked to offer one piece of advice (perhaps illustrated from the paper). Everyone else in the class will be invited to comment on the usefulness of each piece of advice.

Another such exercise is based around giving students copies of a book and telling them that they are about to attend a tutorial on it and have just one minute to find out what it is about. This exercise should bring out the idea that a book may contain only one or two central notions and that there are ways of getting a fair inkling of them quite fast, e.g., by looking at the preface or at the blurb on the dust jacket or by reading only the first and last paragraphs of each chapter.

Learning from print is not, for all students, as straightforward as it may be to us. If it is part of our course, we should ensure that our students know all of the experienced readers' 'tools of trade', however commonplace some of them may seem. As William Taylor (1980) reminds us: 'We should not be ashamed to state and share the apparently obvious with our students and our colleagues. For the simplest tip, as for the oldest joke, there is for everyone a first time of hearing'.

SUPPLEMENTING THE TEXTS

Apart from our concern about choice of reading material, and about helping students improve the appropriate skills, there is one more thing we can do to help them avoid the disadvantages and difficulties of print and get the maximum benefit from their texts. That is, we can *supplement* those texts.

To some extent we have begun this process the moment we offer students a selective bibliography, especially if we have distinguished between essential, basic reading, and material that may be used to deepen understanding in a particular area. Yet we may go further, as I have suggested, and annotate our bibliography, writing a mini-review of the strengths, weaknesses, and special features of each text listed.

From here we can move towards producing a *study guide* for the course or for each section within it. Such a guide might contain, for example:

● The lecturer's overview of the course or section.
● A concept map showing how the main ideas and topics are related.

**173**

● Suggested learning objectives.

● An annotated bibliography.

● Guidance on which chapters/sections to read and which to ignore.

● Alternative explanatory material prepared by the lecturer— to be read instead of sections in the text that are thought inaccurate, biased, out-of-date, etc.

● Local or topical examples or case-studies that will be more immediate than those (if any) in the texts.

● Questions and exercises based on each text, to be tackled by individuals or by discussion groups.

● Suggestions for practical work or laboratory activities.

● A glossary of technical terms.

● A self-checking end-of-section test.

Clearly, so ambitious a study guide could become highly prescriptive and would be edging towards the kind of learning envisaged by the Keller Plan or Postlethwaite's audio-tutorial approach. How far one wishes to travel along that road, from minimal structure to week-by-week programming, must depend on the kind of course one is operating and the level of sophistication of one's students. I would hope that it would be one of our objectives that students should learn to survive with less and less structuring from us as they progress through their educational careers. Eventually, all the independent learner may need (even in a knowledge-oriented science course) is a reading list and a set of typical examination questions. But most of our students will not at present have achieved those ultimate powers of self-direction.

COMPUTER ASSISTED LEARNING

Earlier in this section, I suggested that one of the disadvantages of print is that students normally cannot interact with it. They cannot interrogate it, getting answers to their questions or getting the text to comment on their responses. There was some attempt to cater for the latter at least in 'branching' programmed texts in the 1960s; but the procedure was somewhat artificial and cumbersome. However, it seems that students may now be getting the opportunity to interrogate print, or interact with it in a much more satisfying (because more life-like) way, when that text can be presented on the 'visual display unit' (screen) of a computer.

For two decades the sceptics among us have been saying 'Computer assisted learning is the thing of the future—and always

**174**

will be'. But the ubiquitous silicon chip seems to have transformed the situation almost overnight. The most obvious factors militating against widespread use of computers—size, complexity, and, above all, cost—seem to have vanished. Remarkably versatile and compact computers are now available so cheaply (and likely to become cheaper still) that we are more or less honour bound, at last, to check out their purported educational capabilities—can they teach? There is no lack of literature, but perhaps the most useful surveys are provided by Richard Hooper (1977) in his report of the five-year national development programme in computer-assisted learning in the UK and by Kemmis *et al.* (1977) who, besides profiling a number of UK computer-assisted learning projects, explore the nature of the learning and understanding involved.

A useful general introduction to the educational issues is provided by Nicholas Rushby (1979). Following Kemmis *et al.* (1977) and Mcdonald *et al.* (1977) he discusses four forms of computer assisted learning.

1.  The *instructional* form in which the computer is used as a patient, personal tutor. The student is led systematically through a body of subject matter which he is expected to master. This form is related to programmed learning but, being able to consider fairly lengthy type-written responses from the student rather than merely one-word answers (or alternative answers in the case of a multiple-choice question), and being able to consider a sequence of responses from a student rather than merely his latest, it can deal much more flexibly and individually with the student than can a programmed text in deciding what to say to him or what material to show him next.

2.  The *revelatory* form in which the emphasis is on the student's perceptions rather than on a subject to be learned. The computer simulates a particular situation or system (e.g., a nuclear reactor, the processes of mountain building, or an ailing patient) and the student is able to call up information that will enable him to experiment with the situation and reveal the underlying theory.

3.  The *conjectural* form in which the student is able to formulate and test hypotheses, e.g., about a body of historical data from parish registers, census returns, etc. This may involve him in developing his own programmes, e.g., to write a programme modelling the behaviour of a semiconductor junction whose results he can compare with those obtained from experiments.

**175**

4. The *emancipatory* form in which the computer frees the student from what Mcdonald *et al.* (1977) call 'inauthentic labour'; that is, labour that makes a student's learning possible but is not valued for its own sake. Thus, the computer may be used to search vast amounts of data or perform complex calculations at speed.

It is impossible to do justice to the emerging claims of computer assisted learning in the space available to me here. However, it does seem to offer learning opportunities—and ways of learning from print, in particular—that cannot easily be provided in any other way. Whether those forms of learning are likely to be relevant in your subject-area and whether they are worth the cost, particularly the cost of teacher's time in devising teaching capable of adapting to a multiplicity of students, is left for you to investigate for yourself.

## Learning to use media

Who needs to learn how to use the media and methods of teaching and learning? Both the teachers and the students. I began this chapter by mentioning that one of the limitations of our choice of media was the extent of our familiarity with them in all their variety. As professionals, we should be at pains to increase our awareness of new media and be alert to new applications of old ones. For myself, as you may have sensed in the previous section, I am beginning to feel uncomfortably ignorant about computer-assisted learning. Perhaps it has no application for the kind of teaching and learning I want to be involved with. But I shall need to know considerably more about it than I do at present before I can be sure, one way or the other. No doubt you too can identify media or methods (e.g., simulation games, Keller Plan, audio-vision) that could be worth learning more about.

But, of course, one really learns how to use media not by reading about them and hearing about the experience of others, but by using them oneself. Ideally, our use of media and methods should be one of continuous *experiment* in which we are not only intro-ducing innovations in response to new circumstances but are also open to the realization that our older or even discarded methods may be due for rehabilitation. In this process, the responses of our students will have much to teach us about our use of media. In turn we have much to teach our students about how to get the best out of the learning system. We certainly cannot assume that all we have to do is teach and they will learn. They simply may

**176**

not have the skills to learn from the methods we use. Thus, we must do all we can to make sure they understand, and can cope with, our methods. This responsibility is even greater if our students are learning at a distance. For they will be denied the on-campus benefit of being able to learn from one another and pick up advice from older students who have been through it all before.

I have already spoken of the need to discuss approaches to books and reading with our students. Similarly, we may help them look at the various ways of making notes from lectures or books, of writing essays or laboratory reports, and of organizing their study time. If our course involves much use of radio or television, students will need to learn how to learn from broadcasts; for many, television programmes, and radio even more so, are something they are used to letting wash over them, expecting to be entertained. To get them to listen alertly, expecting to learn something, demands a major shift of psychological set, and may need to be worked up to through specially prepared 'listening exercises'. Again, if discussion groups are to play a large part in your course, you cannot necessarily rely on students already knowing how to get the best out of them, or alternatively, being able to pick it up as they go along. You may find it worth discussing the processes involved with your students, or even starting with some self-conscious learning-to-learn activities suggested by writers like Abercrombie (1974) and Hill (1969).

With any major *innovation* in teaching method, there is little doubt of our forgetting to discuss its implications with students. If we are introducing, say, simulation games, computer-assisted learning, Keller Plan, or even projects, students will express so many anxieties, confusions, and maybe even hostilities, that the first running of such a scheme will probably raise as many questions about the method as about the subject matter it is teaching. The danger is that once the method is established to our satisfaction, we may forget that each new course brings students for whom projects, or whatever, are just as new and full of terror as they were for the students with whom we first tried the method. Therefore, to extend the much-quoted dictum of the sergeant-major ('First I tells 'em what I'm going to tell 'em; then I tells 'em; then I tells 'em what I've told 'em'), we also need to tell 'em HOW we're going to tell 'em (or to help 'em find out for themselves), and give them whatever help they need in learning how to learn from our media and methods.

**177**

# 5. Assessing your students

What is the difference between assessment and evaluation? In the Open University, and quite widely in the UK, we use the words to refer to two different activities. Elsewhere (in North America, for instance) the word 'evaluation' is often used for both. The difference is this: you assess your students but you evaluate your course. Your assessment of students will be part of that evaluation, but only part. So assessment tells you what and how well your students have learned.

Usually it is the teacher who is trying to find out what students have learned. Sometimes, however, the student is assessed by someone who has not taught him, e.g., by an 'external examiner' or by other students. Sometimes, indeed, it may be the student himself who is trying to find out about *his own* learning—self-assessment.

Here is how I define assessment:

> Assessment is an attempt to get to know about the student and find out the nature and quality of his learning—his strengths and weaknesses, or his interests and aversions, or his style of learning.

So, in Chapter 5, I want you to think about planning an assessment strategy for your course as a whole. Such a strategy will provide the context in which you will later be able to decide detailed assessment plans for individual sections of your course. These are the questions to be discussed:

- Why assess?
- What shall we assess?
- How shall we assess?
- What shall we do with the results of assessment?

## Why assess?

Why do we try to find out about the nature and quality of a student's learning? In what he says is 'undoubtedly an incomplete list', Brian Klug (1974) has identified no fewer than thirty-two reasons for formal assessment. In my book on assessment (Rowntree, 1977), I concentrate on what I believe to be the six main reasons commonly advanced:

- To aid in selection.
- To maintain standards.

**178**

- To motivate students.
- To give feedback to students.
- To give feedback to teachers.
- To prepare students for 'real life'.

I do not have space here to discuss these six purposes in detail. They are not entirely without overlap, however, and no doubt we could do with a seventh 'miscellaneous' category to catch a few purposes that are less commonly voiced.

I believe most teachers in post-secondary education will already be well aware of assessment being used for all the purposes mentioned above. Not all will be relevant in each and every assessment situation, however. Indeed, some teachers may dispute the relevance of certain of the purposes (e.g., selection, or preparation for life) to any of their assessments.

What all teachers should be conscious of is the abundant potential for confusion and conflict among the purposes. For example, an examination that is made tough enough to maintain the highest standards may be so demoralizing that student motivation declines. Again, if teachers are not clear which purposes are meant to be served by a particular assessment exercise, or if students and teachers differ in their understanding of what is expected, the assessment may turn out to be less than revealing.

The scope for conflict is brought into sharper relief if we take that list of six purposes and boil it down to the *two* that I believe underlie them. These we can identify by asking how assessment— or the knowledge about a student that results from it—is *used*. It is used :

1. to *teach* the student and/or
2. to *report* on him.

That is, the assessor may use what he knows of the student to help him learn and/or he may report what he knows, e.g., as a grade, profile, reference, etc., to other people, e.g., other teachers, potential employers, etc.

I shall be pursuing both of those uses of assessment in more detail in the final section of this chapter. Let us simply recognize here the scope for conflict in roles when a teacher is also doing his own assessing. In (1) he can clearly be seen by students as tutor, guide, and friend. In (2) he may be seen as inquisitor, judge, and informer. Thus, students who could use his guidance may be reluctant to reveal the knowledge of their difficulties that would enable him to help them; they may fear being marked down as 'dense' or as 'weaker brethren'. I do not wish to make overmuch of this potential conflict of roles; with sensitivity and goodwill it can be minimized. But it never goes away entirely and is responsible for much of the mixed feelings both staff and students have about assessment.

## What shall we assess?

If it is to be educationally valid, assessment should be clearly related to the purposes and objectives of the course. Your assessment strategy should enable the student to demonstrate the knowledge, skills, and attitudes he has acquired or improved upon during the course. Some of these will be assessable week by week; some only after several weeks of learning. Some objectives will be so dependent upon the impact of the course as a whole that a valid assessment will be impossible until the student has completed it. For example, medical students might be assessed immediately after the relevant teaching session on whether they can, for example, list the signs and symptoms of rheumatic fever, or the characteristics of presystolic murmer, or whether they can elicit a patient's history in a systematic and sympathetic fashion. But whether they can identify a patient suffering from rheumatic heart disease may be an objective that is only assessable after they have had many weeks of experience. Much higher education requires of the student that he *integrates* a number of separate objectives; not merely that he has attained them and can exercise them separately.

Assessment exercises that relate to a set of topics or to the course as a whole, may require the student to operate on a higher, more integrated level, than does the assessment relating to any one particular section of the course. For example, compare the following three questions which might appear in the examination for a course on 'health and environment'. Which would appear to demand most, and which least, of the student?

1. Describe the principles of natural selection.
2. Compare and evaluate the medical model and the adaptational model of health.
3. Outline some of the problems in health and environment to which this course might need to address itself if it were rerun

50 years from now; and indicate how such problems might be explored using approaches developed in this course.

It should be obvious, even if you know little or nothing about the subject-matter, that these questions demand answers differing in depth, breadth, and quality. Question 1 demands nothing but recall. The student is being asked to remember and reproduce a verbal description. It will not necessarily even be in his own words. Furthermore, the question concerns just one topic from within the course.

The second question seems to require rather more analysis on the part of the student. It is possible, of course, that he may have been thoroughly taught the similarities and differences between the two models; in which case he will be, to some extent, exercising recall. Even so, the question requires him also to evaluate the two models; thus it seems to be testing his critical ability as well as recall. Question 2, then, is operating on a higher level than question 1. It may also be wider in the sense that the student may need to draw, for examples, on more than one topic from within the course.

But, of all these questions, it is the third that makes the highest intellectual demands; and also requires the student to integrate what he has learned from the entire course. Presumably the student will not have encountered this problem before. He is being asked to build on what he has learned of current problems of health and environment to conceive a future scenario, and then show how the methodology he has learned might be related to it. Clearly, this calls for considerable insight and imagination as well as knowledge. To have got inside his subject to this considerable degree, he will need to have studied the complete course and be able to draw its threads together in what may be a very personal reworking of its themes and methods.

### Knowledge versus skills

The point I am trying to make is that different exercises on the same general area of knowledge can involve very different cognitive levels in constructing an answer. Several authors have developed different classifications of the levels involved. The simplest offers just two categories:

1. Knowledge
2. Intellectual abilities and skills

The kinds of mental activity covered by that second category are well-displayed in the widely known classification produced by Benjamin Bloom and his colleagues (1956). Starting from knowledge, he distinguishes a further five cognitive levels:

1. *Knowledge*: ability to remember facts, terms, definitions, methods, rules, principles, etc.
2. *Comprehension*: ability to translate ideas from one form into another, to interpret, and to extrapolate trends, consequences, etc.
3. *Application*: ability to use general rules and principles in particular situations.
4. *Analysis*: ability to break down an artefact and make clear the nature of its component parts and the relationship between them.
5. *Synthesis*: ability to arrange and assemble various elements so as to make a new statement or plan or conclusion—a 'unique communication'.
6. *Evaluation*: ability to judge the value of materials or methods in terms of internal accuracy and consistency or by comparison with external criteria.

Bloom would say that these categories are arranged in order of difficulty—level 3 being more demanding than level 2; level 4 more than level 3, and so on. Furthermore, he would expect that the ability to operate at one level would pre-suppose that the student could also operate (on the same subject-matter) at all the preceding levels. The fine distinctions among the higher processes and how they are related will remain a matter for debate (e.g., see Gribble, 1970; Ormell, 1974; Pring, 1971; and Rowntree, 1977, pages 102–7). The important point to note, however, is that these higher level processes or abilities somehow *transform* the remembered or given data and *go beyond it*.

How are you to ensure that your assessment exercises make the appropriate demands on students? The appropriate levels of activity may be indicated in your course aims and objectives. It is then up to you to devise ways of ascertaining that students can fulfil those intentions by displaying the implied abilities. This is not always easy to achieve. It is generally easier to set tests at the lower rather than at the higher cognitive levels. If you are not careful you may find, for instance, that your assessment is operating chiefly at Bloom's levels 1, 2, and maybe 3.

Another way of getting at those higher levels is to ask how we can test cognitive *skills* rather than merely knowledge. Some people would define a skill, of course, as the knowledge of *how to do* something. But this would be to miss the point and leads to the fallacy that we can test a student's skill by asking him how he would do a certain thing. The essence of a skill is that it can be used to create something (perhaps even new knowledge) or change the state of something. So, in order to assess a skill, we must ask our student to create or change something. It would not be enough for him merely to tell how he might set about doing so.

PHYSICAL, SOCIAL AND COGNITIVE SKILLS

Some skills, like those in vocational education (e.g., carpentry) or musical education (e.g., clarinet playing) or medical education (e.g., suturing an incision), may have a strong *physical* component. Some skills will have a strong *social* or affective component (e.g., the medical examination of a patient, the negotiation of a pay agreement). But most of the valued skills in higher education (including many of those with a physical or social component) are essentially *cognitive* skills. They involve the higher-level intellectual processes like analysis, interpretation, synthesis, and evaluation. Scientific experimentation, essay writing, philosophical argumentation, literary criticism, engineering design, are all examples of such skills—or 'clusters' of skills. So, we do not judge the novitiate literary critic by his knowledge of what other critics have already said about certain poems or by his ability to describe (as another piece of knowledge) how a literary critic might set about responding to a poem. We judge him by his skill in actually producing some worthwhile responses himself to a poem he has not thought about before.

Pure knowledge, without the higher order skills involved in being able to see which of it is relevant and apply it accordingly, is not much use to anyone. As Oliver Wendell Holmes said in his *Medical Essays* (1882), rebuking the medical educators of his day:

> What is this stuff with which you are cramming the brains of the young men who are to hold the lives of the community in their hands? Here is a man fallen into a fit; you can tell me all about the eight surfaces of the two processes of the palatebone, but you have not had the sense to loosen the man's neck-cloth, and the old women are still calling you a fool.

Assessing skills, as I've already suggested, is far more difficult than assessing knowledge, whether we are talking about cognitive,

**183**

physical, or social skills. For one thing, the students will need to be given more time in which to achieve anything assessable. Secondly, it is often difficult to get other assessors to agree on criteria of judgement. Thirdly, some teachers convince themselves that they do not need to assess skills. They may take certain skills for granted in their students; e.g., they may assume that the student who can draw a certain kind of graph could also interpret it, or vice versa. Or they may assume that a student who is knowledgeable in his field can be relied on to acquire all the higher skills by practice, later on. Or they may commit the fallacy of assuming, for instance, that the student who can describe standard procedures for carrying out a public opinion poll would also be able to carry out such a poll successfully himself.

Often there is considerable justification for making some assumptions like those above. But they are not necessarily valid; they may lead to serious mistakes and injustices in assessment. On the one hand, students who can recall an impressive amount of detailed information, but who lack the practical, social, and cognitive skills to apply it effectively, may be undeservedly 'licenced' as practitioners. On the other hand, students with a real practical and creative flair, but an inability to recall volumes of information, may be penalized because their considerable skills have not been assessed.

In practice, the distinction between knowledge and skill is not always clear-cut. One possible way of distinguishing between them is to ask how many times a student will need to practice whatever is involved before he can be reasonably assured of competence. If he achieves mastery after reading or listening to one or two explanations and attempting one or two exercises, then probably it is knowledge which is involved. But if he can practise doing the same thing over and over, gaining in mastery each time, then at least some element of skill is involved. (In Chapter 2, this is discussed in terms of infinitely improveable objectives.)

In deciding the assessment strategy for your course, you will need to think about the methodological and procedural skills used by experts in your subject or discipline. Which of them should you be looking for in your students? You will also need to consider which skills must be assessed directly (e.g., by presenting students with the kinds of problem that experts tackle), which can be inferred from other abilities, and which can be taken for granted. And what kind of knowledge must you expect students to display?

If you are teaching on campus, and are in regular, close contact with your students, you may feel that there is little need for formal assessment of skills. Perhaps you will feel that you can assess students' progress day-by-day and give help where necessary. Thus you may ensure that no-one can get through your course without at least some practice in the basic skills of your discipline. However, it is important to test the higher skills directly and not simply to infer them from lesser skills or from knowledge. Unless students are directly assessed on the higher abilities, they may see little incentive to practice them, and so fail to develop their potential.

These strictures carry even more force if your students are working with self-teaching materials, especially if they are learning 'at a distance'. With such a student, the development of higher level abilities certainly cannot be taken for granted. He may be strongly tempted to view the learning task in terms of memorizing the course materials. After all, he may not be in regular contact with a tutor or even with other students, and so will have no-one to emulate. Hence, if he is to develop skills he must see them modelled very explicitly in the teaching materials and must be given practice in applying them. His own skills will need to be assessed, if only to help him improve at them.

ASSESSING KNOWLEDGE AND SKILLS

In the following sequence (based on some ideas of my colleague Roger Harrison), let us consider some assessment objectives and decide the kind of skill or knowledge involved in each. For each objective, we shall ask: how would we attempt to test it, and is the cognitive level high or low?

1. Prepare a rainfall map of a given region from the data supplied.
2. Assess the adequacy and balance of a person's diet.
3. Explain the significance of tears and weeping in *King Lear*.
4. Plan an experiment to confirm or repudiate a given hypothesis.
5. Criticize a previously unseen short story.
6. Design a device that can be used to advantage by a person with a particular kind of physical handicap.
7. Visualize the physical features of an unknown region from a map.
8. Diagnose the illness from which a given patient is suffering.

1. Preparing a rainfall map could be largely a matter of knowledge. Provided the student knows how rainfall data is translated into symbolic form, he may be able to produce a

**185**

reasonable map, even at his first attempt. Little in the way of decision-making skill, or even physical skill, would be required. The knowledge might almost be tested by a multiple-choice question—asking the student to say which of a number of given rainfall maps best matches the data—rather than by asking him to draw one.

2. Assessing a person's diet will certainly involve considerable amounts of knowledge, e.g., of the nutritional composition of various foodstuffs and the quantities needed by people of various age, sex, occupations. In fact, the student would not be expected to carry the detailed information in his head but to look it up in standard tables. The essence of the assessment lies in his ability to analyse the person's diet into its components, evaluate those components, and come to a decision. A certain amount of skill is involved here (at the 'application' level) but higher-level interpretative skills are unlikely to be called upon, and little improvement (except perhaps in speed at using the tables) could be expected to result from practice.

3. Explaining the significance of a particular motif in a Shakespearean play could be a matter of almost pure recall. Only if the student has not previously read, or been involved in, discussions of the significance of 'tears and weeping' will he be called upon to exercise his higher level skills of interpretation and synthesis. An essay would seem the obvious assessment method. But in a drama course students might be asked to act or direct some scenes from the play according to their interpretation.

4. Planning an experiment would appear to demand considerable skill in problem-solving as well as extensive knowledge of scientific method and experimental procedure on which the student can draw for analogies. The student has to analyse an hypothesis that is presumably new to him, and develop procedures that may even be unique to him. We could test this by means of an essay or in conversation. Though if we were interested also in the student's practical or organizing skills, we would not be able to infer them from his answer; we'd have to get him to carry out his experiment.

5. Criticizing a previously unseen literary work certainly involves a high level skill (or set of skills). It cannot be done by the application of formulae and routines. The student can be expected to get better and better at it, as his perceptions and judgement mature over the years. An essay would be the obvious form of

assessment, though the student's critical acumen might also be appraised in group discussions.

6. Designing a device for use by a handicapped person calls upon high level problem-solving skills, as well as an extensive knowledge, both of technological principles and of the problems faced by the person he is designing for. Ideally, the student would be required to build a prototype of his device and then develop it further with the help of people with the relevant handicap. Thus, his social skills would also be called upon in working closely with these 'client-colleagues'.

7. Interpreting a map is a skill that demands more than the knowledge of conventions needed in objective (1). Visualizing a terrain calls for more than the ability to recognize relevant symbols on a map and give the names of the features they represent. It calls for systematic observation, deciding what to look for next, inferring relationships between separate items, and for imaginative hypothesizing. It can be expected to improve with practice, especially if the student gets feedback from photographs or from visits to the terrains. The skills could be assessed by asking the student to describe the terrain orally or in writing. Of course, this would not give us direct access to the picture in his mind. If we suspected that the student's language ability was inadequate to do justice to his mental picture, we might consider asking him to sketch pictures of the terrain. And if we had doubts about his sketching ability, we might fall back on asking him to say which of a set of photographs looks most like what he has in mind. In the end, only the student himself can fully assess his ability here, by comparing his mental picture with the real terrain or a set of photographs.

8. The diagnosis of an illness is based on a considerable amount of knowledge. In addition, it requires a high level of social skill in interacting with the patient, and cognitive skills in the interpretation of signs and symptoms presented by the patient (not all of which may be relevant) and decision-making on the basis of clinical tests. Various aspects of this process can be tested separately; e.g., the student may be given a patient's case history and symptoms and may then ask for the results of any additional tests he might need before making a diagnosis. Computers are being used to good effect for this purpose. However, the only true assessment method is to see how well the medical student performs when faced with a number of real patients, where he has to integrate both the technical and the human aspects of his work.

**187**

Between them, computer-testing and clinical work may allow for both breadth and depth of assessment in this area.

### *Attitudes*

Yet there is more to education, even in colleges and universities, than cultivating knowledge and improving the higher cognitive processes. There is also an affective domain, concerned with feelings, values, and commitments. For example, Hirst and Peters (1970) ask, in the case of science: 'How do [students] come to care about getting their facts right, being clear and precise? How do they come to abhor what is irrelevant, inconsistent, and false?'

Most teachers are concerned to develop their students' values and hence their attitudes, if not to life in general then at least to particular aspects of their academic work. Medical education is often shown to be particularly concerned with socializing medical students into adopting the range of attitudes expected of doctors by other doctors (e.g., Horowitz, 1964; Silman, 1972). For example, doctors are expected to subscribe to the ethics expressed in the Hippocratic Oath. But most professions and disciplines have some such implicit notions about the attitudes a practitioner might reasonably be expected to display towards the discipline, towards fellow-practitioners, towards 'clients', and towards people from other disciplines. (See part 4 of Pateman, 1972.) There is more to being a lawyer (engineer, pharmacist, geographer, etc.) than knowing the law (engineering, pharmacy, geography, etc.).

Consider the following questions, agreed by one group of teachers as being important in assessing the work of their students (EDC, 1969):

- Are they capable of intense involvement?
- Do they initiate activities which are new to the classroom?
- Do they talk to each other about their work?
- Can they listen to each other?
- Do they challenge ideas and interpretations with the purpose of reaching deeper understanding?
- Are they charitable and open in dealing with ideas with which they do not agree?
- Can they afford to make mistakes freely and profit from them?
- Are they intellectually responsible?
- Are they self-propelling?

In fact, these questions (and many similar ones) were suggested by a group of science teachers (and elementary school teachers, at that); but the attitudes implied would surely be desired by most disciplines, and at all levels.

Before we consider the assessment of such attitudes, it is worth recognizing that we teachers have some responsibility for fostering them. Thus, for example, students will not get a chance to become self-propelling if we programme their every move or if we leave them, from the start, entirely to their own devices. Similarly, we cannot expect them to become intellectually adventurous—so they feel they can 'afford to make mistakes freely and profit from them'—if our assessment system penalizes imperfections in everything a student ever says or does.

### ASSESSING ATTITUDES

Attitudes usually express themselves in how a student exercises his knowledge and cognitive and social skills. I have already suggested, for instance, how the cluster of skills involved in the medical examination of a patient will contain social or affective elements—revealing the trainee doctor's attitudes to patients and perhaps his beliefs about the role of medicine. Similarly, the teacher of English may see in a student's essay on Wordsworth something of his attitude not only towards Wordsworth but also to literature, to the discipline of literary criticism, to the relationship of art and truth and revolutionary responsibility, and all manner of things.

There are dangers, however. Teachers are even less likely to agree about the nature and quality of the attitudes expressed than they are about the level of cognitive skill a student is displaying. What one teacher sees, another may not, even in the same utterance. And even if both see the same thing, they may value it differently. Husbands (1976) suggests, in only mild parody, how the ideological bias of an examiner may affect his marking:

> It could be that the free-enterprise economist, for example, having read a rather mundane effort that was nonetheless written from his own standpoint, says, 'What a pedestrian attempt! Forty-five, I suppose. But at least he doesn't drop a lot of leftist slogans. Okay, fifty-two.' Or the Marxist sociologist may read a strongly pro-functionalist effort and conclude 'Quite well argued. Sixty-two, maybe. But he refuses to get to grips with the real issues. Fifty-seven'.

Even when one makes a point of trying to be objective, it can be

**189**

hard to judge the quality of an argument without being affected by the point of view expressed.

Furthermore, can the teacher be sure that the student has not faked his attitudes? This may be a particular problem in distance education, where the tutor may never meet his student face to face. At the very least, a student who suspects that certain opinions would count against him, e.g., the medical student who strongly supports abortion or euthanasia, might take care not to reveal them or else might tone them down. At worst, he might cynically wear what he perceives to be the ideology of his teacher, with the firm intention of casting it off as soon as he is no longer subject to that teacher's assessments.

Despite the dangers, we cannot teach without assessing attitudes. In some courses, e.g., in the training of social workers or counsellors, they may be our main concern. (Consider also the assessment implications of Carl Rogers' course objectives on page 48.) But even if they are not our main concern, they will still manifest themselves and can affect, for good or ill, the way we teach a particular student. Perhaps the dangers become more potent, however, when we use assessment not for teaching but for *reporting*. Given the problematical nature of our assessments of attitude, we should think twice before passing them on to anyone else, e.g., in a profile or reference. And we should only ever pass them on in the clear understanding that our perceptions covered a limited period of contact between us and the student, and might anyway be an artefact of the relationship between us.

### Summing up

Assessment is not all of one kind or all at one level. It may concern knowledge, skills (cognitive, social, and physical), and attitudes. In the area of knowledge and cognitive skills, we can assess abilities ranging from simply remembering factual data and routines, up through skills like analysis and evaluation (using remembered or given data), towards the creative formulation and solution of problems (perhaps generating new knowledge in the process). In the affective area, the most basic attitude we might look for is simply the student's interest and his reaching out towards a new experience; at a rather higher level, he may be seen actually to value and care for what he is interested in; and at the highest level we may observe that the student seems to have developed coherent attitudes and a strong commitment towards, say, the topic (e.g., optics), the subject (e.g., physics), the field

**190**

(e.g., science), the type of endeavour (e.g., academic enquiry), and so on. In all kinds of assessment, however, there lurks the risk that we are assessing not what we think we are assessing but something else, and usually something lesser, instead. So how are we to assess?

## How shall we assess?

Let us say we are fairly sure about what would be *worth* assessing. We may even have a list of aims and objectives for the course. Perhaps some of them will be rather broad and the list is always likely to be amended once the course is under way. But we shall want to know the extent to which our students have attained whatever objectives loom large during the course. But when shall we find out? At the end of the course, during it, or both? And by what means shall we find out? First, let us give a few moments' thought to who does the assessing.

### Who are the assessors?

It would be easy for me to write as if you were completely in control of how your course will be assessed. But this may not be the case at all. To begin with, you may be producing the course with one or more colleagues so your assessment strategy will have to be negotiated with them. But even if you are working alone, or with a group who are agreed on an ideal assessment strategy, you may not be able to put it into effect without modification. It may have to be adapted to fit in with the general assessment policy of your department, or even your college or university, or of some external validating body. The external body may allow you considerable autonomy in designing your own syllabus and assessment strategy. But it may require your assessment procedures to be 'moderated' in some way, e.g., by having samples of your students' work assessed by teachers in other institutions to ensure that standards are comparable throughout the country. In the most extreme case, assessment may be out of your hands entirely, and totally under the control of an external examinations body.

Universities generally conduct their own assessment of students. Most, however, insist on *several* internal examiners contributing to a student's overall assessment. This, it is hoped, will minimize the possibility of results being influenced by mistakes or personal prejudices. Effectively, the student may be judged by the whole department or even several departments rather than by one or two individuals. British universities use the additional safeguard of having one or more *external* examiners from other universities to help set and mark each examination paper.

Once we ask 'Who are the assessors?', we discern that several people may be involved. More precisely, we may ask:

● Who decides the syllabus to which the assessment must relate?
● Who decides precisely what students are to be asked to do for assessment purposes?
● Who carries out the assessment on a particular student?
● Who acts upon the results of that assessment?

Thus, the syllabus may be decided by an outside body, by the teacher, by the students (e.g., in a project-based course), or by some combination of these and others. Any one of them, alone or with others, may decide what the student will be asked to do for assessment purposes, e.g., the examination questions he is to answer. Again, the person(s) carrying out the assessment, e.g., marking a student's essay, may or may not have designed the question. For example, in distance education the marking may be done by tutors who played no part in planning the course or deciding the assessment questions.

Indeed, as I make clear in Chapter 4, *self*-assessment by students is especially vital in distance education. Similarly, in on-campus Keller Plan courses, assessment may even be carried out by a 'proctor'—a student who is more advanced in the subject. The person who acts upon the assessment results, e.g., by teaching the student or reporting on him, may be someone different again. Thus, the proctor just mentioned may report his students' marks to the tutor in charge of the course. Obviously, if any two of the above roles are performed by different people, then it becomes important to communicate intentions and perceptions clearly from one to another. For instance, the designer of an assignment may need to produce written guidelines to let markers know what he would like to see rewarded in students' responses to it.

So who plays which role in assessment? You will know the position in your own institution. Perhaps you are quite free to decide the syllabus, set the assessment exercises, fix the standards, do the marking, and report the results in whatever way you please. But perhaps you are free to do none of these or some of them only. Whatever is the case, you cannot afford to ignore the issues discussed in the rest of this chapter.

### When shall we assess?

For many teaching institutions, there can be only one obvious answer to that question—at the end of the course. ('When else could we assess; we can't find out how well students have done the work until they've done the work!') But, of course, it is not really that simple, since students will have done some of the work before they have done all of it. So, in certain circumstances, it will be possible, and may be desirable, to assess students on some aspects of their work *before* they get to the end of the course. Then the end-of-course assessment can concentrate on those aspects not already tested.

Just as some institutions use end-of-course assessment only, e.g., 'final exams', some base all their assessment on the student's work *during* the course. This may be called *continuous* assessment, intermittent assessment, cumulative assessment, or some such name. Yet other institutions combine continuous assessment and end-of-course assessment. The Open University is one example.

So your assessment strategy will have to include a decision on whether you will assess work done during your course, at the end of it, or both. Any one of these three alternative decisions could be the right one, educationally, according to the nature of your course and the type of work your students will be doing. Let us look at the advantages and disadvantages.

END-OF-COURSE ASSESSMENT

For most people, this will automatically suggest an examination. Probably the 'traditional' three-hour examination in which the student has to answer, within the time-limit, a number of previously unseen questions, chosen from a larger number, without access to books and reference materials, and without consulting any of his colleagues. Examinations do not have to be like that but, for the moment, let us use that as our example of end-of-course assessment.

End-of-course assessment has a number of advantages. It means that neither students nor teachers need be much concerned with assessment for the greater part of the year. It thus reduces the tensions on students during their everyday work and makes less acute the conflict between the teaching and examining role of the teachers. It is a test of what the student has succeeded in getting out of the course as an entity, rather than of what he could do at some time during the course but perhaps can do no longer. Ideally

**193**

it will test his grasp of the subject as a whole rather than of individual, discrete sections of knowledge.

On the other hand, end-of-course assessment has much against it. It encourages some students to postpone any real effort until very late in the course. It puts far too high a premium on reaching the summit of achievement on one particular occasion and renders the student far too much at risk from the effects of ill health, stress, or bad luck. Finally, in the time available, it is possible to test only a relatively small proportion of the student's total knowledge and abilities. Here is how one student (quoted by Siann and French, 1975) describes the situation:

> 'I work hard and consistently all year, I am frequently commended for my tutorial contributions—I also know that my hard-earned ideas are noted and stored away by less vociferous students, yet, because of the truly fearful stress which I feel each time, I know my exam results cannot reflect the best.'

On the other hand, another of their students says:

> 'The idea of Edinburgh University becoming a three-year holiday camp, all expenses paid, galls me, and I am reactionary enough to believe that the 'threat' of exams (i.e., the inherent threat of failure and becoming an outcast) is the only reason that the library doormats are cleaned.'

CONTINUOUS ASSESSMENT

However, as these students' remarks (from Beard and Senior, 1980) make clear, continuous assessment may also be stressful and no less efficacious in motivating students to work:

> 'I like the idea of assessment by tests and essays, but you've got to accept the fact that it is hard work. It is continual pressure. . . .'

> 'It's a lot easier to work gently all through the year than to make a mad rush just before exams.'

> 'I don't mind continuous assessment for practicals but I'd prefer a major exam on theory. I think [continuous assessment] is more strain.'

And according to another student (Cowell, 1972):

> 'Comparing continuous assessment with examinations is like comparing months of nagging toothache with the short sharp pain of having a tooth removed.'

Theoretically, the advantages and disadvantages of continuous assessment are almost the exact opposite of those of end-of-course assessment. Continuous assessment is clearly able to take into account a wider range of examples from the student's work, but it may unduly emphasize separate parts at the expense of the whole. If all a student's work is to be counted, some students may find this an intolerable strain. They may regard their teachers with chronic suspicion if they fear that almost anything they do may be 'noted down and used in evidence'! Continuous assessment, however, may take many forms. It could, for instance, take the form of weekly exams. Only in its most extreme form is every piece of work submitted by the student graded and taken into account. Perhaps it is agreed in advance as to which pieces of work are to count for assessment and grading purposes, and which are not. Perhaps it is agreed that all pieces of work will be assessed (in the sense of being judged and commented on) but that only certain ones will be graded. Or perhaps all are to be graded, but the poorest grades (say the poorest two out of eight) will not count.

There is no clear-cut balance of advantages between end-of-course assessment and some form of continuous assessment. A lot will depend on the nature of the subject matter, the length of the course, and the nature of the institution in which the students are working. When students are 'learning at a distance' (away from regular contact with tutors or other students), some form of continuous assessment seems to be almost essential. Unless they are required regularly to submit work which counts towards their assessment, such students may find it all too easy to postpone effort or to omit doing exercises which are essential to the learning process. This need is nothing like so acute when the student is learning 'on campus' and can be appropriately exhorted by his teachers or set an example by his fellow students.

However, end-of-course assessment will be essential if we wish to test the student's grasp of the whole, rather than simply of the parts. And the prospect of having to somehow 'account' for the whole course at the end of it may well encourage students to take a more holistic approach to their learning in the first place, rather than regarding the course as a series of hurdles each of which has to be leapt in turn and then forgotten. Perhaps a hybrid system, in which the final result depends on both continuous assessment and an end-of-course examination, has much to recommend it.

There is another compromise that is worth considering: end-of-course assessment does *not* necessarily have to be restricted to work done at the end of the course. That is, students can be asked to collect together examples of the work they have done during the course—presumably having had it commented on by tutors at the time—and hand it in for final assessment and grading at the end. This would be particularly suitable, for instance, if the student had been working on some kind of project during the course and was expected to produce a dissertation by the end of it. However, the student might equally turn in a 'portfolio' of essays, photographs, designs or whatever was appropriate to his subject.

We can thus divide up continuous and end-of-course assessment like this, with an overlap:

| 1. Continuous assessment of | 2. End-of-course assessment of | 3. End-of-course assessment of |
|---|---|---|
| work done *during* course | work done *during* course | work done *at end of* course |

In (1) the student can know, as he goes through the course, how much each piece of work is contributing to his final overall assessment. In (2) he may get some idea from the comments of his tutors, especially if they will be doing the eventual grading. In (3) he will get no idea of his ultimate, overall assessment, unless his tutors help him predict it on the basis of his course work—even though that work itself is not going to contribute to his grade.

## What assessment methods shall we use?

OPEN–CONTROLLED ASSESSMENT

What means of assessment do we have at our disposal? To begin with, we can consider how far we want to *control* the students while they are carrying out their assessment exercises. At one extreme the student must answer previously unseen questions without access to reference sources but within a rigid time limit. At the other extreme he is free to choose his own assessment task (or at least is given a task long before it is due to be completed) and he tackles it at his own pace, consulting whatever sources and people he wishes, the only constraint being that he must complete it by a certain date. We can call the first kind of assessment *controlled* and the second kind *open*.

The rigidly controlled exam is generally held to be fairest for all students, since all are treated alike. However, it may not be so fair as it appears, since students are not all alike, and some may find the examination constraints far more stultifying than others. A student's performance in the highly artificial exam conditions may not necessarily bear any very close relationship to his performance in more relaxed real-life situations. As one British university teacher (Jones, 1969) said: 'although much of our work, whatever profession we follow after graduating, has to be done against the clock, our *best work* generally isn't'.

An uncontrolled (open) test, however, is not necessarily a fair or valid indicator of the student's knowledge and skills either. After all, some students may, unknown to the assessor, get considerable help from others—perhaps even getting others to write their assignments. In a distance learning institution like the Open University or the external degree wing of London University, a controlled examination may offer the only opportunity to check that the person who writes the assessment exercise is actually the student who is registered for the course! And even then, passport photographs may need to be demanded to deter imposters.

In recent years, assessment has tended to become much more open, reflecting changes in teaching methods. Typical of this trend is the increasing use of more-or-less student-initiated project work. Such work is easy to justify educationally, but it does raise assessment problems. For instance, how does the assessor allow for the possibility that some students' work may be less impressive than that of others because they have chosen to tackle more difficult problems? How does he allow for the fact that he had to give some students more help than others in developing their projects? And how can he tell how much help from others the students may have had? How does he grade an individual student's contribution if the project has been developed by students working as a *group*? These problems are tricky, but not insuperable. In that last case, for example, the teacher may give a total mark to the group and, since they know best what contribution was made by each individual, leave them to decide whether to share it out equally or give some a larger proportion of the mark than others.

There are several factors over which control may or may not be exercised in planning assessment exercises:

● Is the student to be assessed at a set time and place, or does he complete the work at his own speed and simply have to hand it in by an appointed time?

**197**

● Is the student to be given no prior notice of the task to be performed (unseen examination)? Or is he to be given the question beforehand and have time in which to prepare himself to answer them? Or is he to be given a general indication of the field in which he will be tested, but the precise wording of the question left unstated?

● Is he to work from memory? Or is he allowed access to notes, reference books, or text books? If he is allowed access, is there to be any restriction on what materials he may have access to?

● Finally, what is the nature of the task set the student? Is he to confine himself to precisely worded questions set by an assessor? Or is he to define his own problems and explore his own insights in a field indicated only very generally by the assessor?

There is, of course, a continuum between controlled and open assessment exercises. We cannot expect any given exercise to fall neatly into one category or the other. It all depends what it is being compared with. Thus, an examination is generally a rather controlled exercise. But an examination that allows students to bring in reference materials will be more open than most. Yet even this type will be less open (i.e., more controlled) than an examination that allows not only the use of reference materials, but also publishes the questions in advance. Nevertheless, we can use this 'open-closed' continuum along with the 'continuous versus end-of-course' distinction already made, as a way of classifying possible assessment activities.

Consider how each of the following assessment activities might be classified using each of those two distinctions.

(a) An essay to be written in the student's own time.
(b) A dissertation on a mini research project to be completed by the end of the course.
(c) An examination in which students are given advance notice of the questions and are allowed to bring in reference books.
(d) An oral examination relating to the project a student has carried out during the course.
(e) Class tests each week during the course.
(f) A set of multiple-choice questions to be answered by the student at home.
(g) An assessment by observation of practical, 'on-the-job' activity at the end of a theoretical course.

(h) A final exhibition of student course work at which assessors give grades.

(i) A traditional 3-hour unseen examination.

The method shown below is how I would classify them:

| | 1. Continuous Assessment of work done *during* course | 2. End-of-course Assessment of work done *during* course | 3. End-of-course Assessment of work done *at end of* course |
|---|---|---|---|
| Controlled ↑<br><br><br><br><br>↓<br>Open | (e) Class tests<br><br><br><br><br>(a) Essay—own time<br>(f) Multiple-choice questions at home | <br><br><br>(h) Final exhibition<br><br>(b) Dissertation on project | (i) Traditional 3-hour exam<br>(d) Oral exam re project<br>(c) Exam with questions in advance plus reference books<br><br>(g) Observation of practical |

It is fairly easy to decide which column each activity belongs in. The only one I had the slightest hesitation about was (d), the oral examination relating to the student's project. Clearly, it is end-of-course assessment. But is it of work done during or at the end? I decided that what was being assessed was *not* what the student had done during the course though this would be crucial to the result. Rather it was his work in the actual oral situation—at the end of the course: what he was able to say *then* based on what he had done earlier.

There is more room for disagreement as to the relative positions of certain activities within a column—on the 'controlled-open' continuum. In column 1 both (a) and (f) are much more open than (e); I regarded the essay (a) as being rather more controlled than the objective test because a tutor would be more likely to realize if any essay was not a student's own work than he would if the student submitted someone else's answers to multiple-choice questions. In column 2, (h) and (b) are about equally open; I have guessed that the 'final exhibition' might be slightly more controlled than the dissertation in that several deadlines will have

**199**

been met by the pieces of work it contains. In column 3, I have made observation of practical experience (g) the most open, because control is often difficult to apply in real-life situations. As for (d), I have no doubt that an oral test is considerably more controlled than an examination in which the student can use his books and knows what questions will be asked. It gives the student much less opportunity to hide his ignorance or confusion by means of clever question-choice and ambiguous writing. Equally clearly, the three-hour traditional examination is the most controlled form of assessment.

TYPES OF ASSESSMENT EXERCISE
Apart from the degree of control required, we must decide among the various possible types of test or assessment exercise. There are many ways of getting to know about a student's knowledge, skills, and attitudes. Here are some that occur to me:

| | |
|---|---|
| essays | teacher-observation |
| short-answer questions | projects |
| multiple-choice questions | practical tests |
| oral quizzes | self-reports |
| classroom discussion | student presentations |
| telephone conversations | examinations |
| exchange of letters | simulation games |
| problem-solving | |

In your situation, not all the above methods will seem equally useful or practicable. If your students are learning 'at a distance', and you are not in immediate contact with them while they are working through your materials, you will have no opportunity for teacher observations, classroom discussion, or simulation games. Alternatively, if you are meeting your students regularly on campus, you are unlikely to see the relevance of letters and telephone conversations.

I find that most assessment exercises belong to one or other of two broad-types:

1. *Paper-and-pencil exercises*—like essays, multiple-choice questions, and project reports—where there is a physical *product* to assess.
2. *Situational exercises*—like discussions, conversations, performances, or displays of students' practical skills—where we assess a *process* or activity that may or may not result in a product.

Tradition has usually favoured the paper-and-pencil exercise, producing a written or graphic record which can be examined at leisure by the assessor(s). Such a form of assessment will be particularly convenient in distance education. However, not all forms of understanding can be expressed in written or graphic form. Nor are all students capable of so expressing their nevertheless real talents. We must beware of the danger of using what is traditional (or easier) when it may not be the more appropriate. If we are interested in assessing processes, e.g., the manner in which a student performs a particular kind of dissection, we must think of a way of assessing the student while he performs that process. It would *not* be appropriate to ask him merely to show us the completed dissection (a product) nor to write us an essay (another product) about how he would do it.

### PAPER-AND-PENCIL EXERCISES

Even when a paper-and-pencil exercise is considered to be appropriate or essential, it does not necessarily have to take the form of the traditional essay. Objective tests—using multiple-choice questions of one kind or another—have many useful features for assessing certain kinds of learning. They can test the student's knowledge of many aspects of the syllabus in a relatively short time. They are quick, easy and cheap to mark, and there would be no doubt about different markers agreeing on the grade a student had earned. In fact, they can be marked by someone ignorant of the subject-matter, or even by a computer. Additionally, they can sometimes offer students who cannot write very fluently to demonstrate the extent of their knowledge.

On the other hand, they are difficult to devise and, therefore, are usually expensive. Often they cannot be justified unless, over the life of the course, hundreds of candidates will take the test. They seem more suitable for testing knowledge of facts and routine procedures than for testing higher cognitive skills. Therefore, they are likely to seem relatively trivial. They are clearly incapable of testing the candidate's ability to present an *argument*—an analysis, interpretation, or evaluation, reviewing what he sees as the relevant facts and coming to some kind of conclusion about them. They cannot test the student's ability to make judgements, only his ability to recognize good judgements among the alternative answers offered him. They do not, therefore, constitute a true test of some of the abilities we are likely to be most interested in.

The succession of questions below, which I analyse in greater

**201**

detail in Rowntree (1977), illustrates what may be lost in moving through increasingly specific 'own answer' questions towards the ultimate strictures of a multiple-choice question.

Qu. 1 What aspects of the political system of modern Sweden seem to you most worthy of comment?

Qu. 2 Comment on the political stability of modern Sweden.

Qu. 3 Explain the political stability of modern Sweden.

Qu. 4 Identify and discuss three factors that might help the political stability of modern Sweden.

Qu. 5 Identify and discuss three factors that might help explain the emergence of a stable political system in Sweden despite the massive social and economic changes engendered by processes of modernization.

Qu. 6 Which *three* of the factors listed below might best help explain the emergence of a stable political system in Sweden despite the massive social and economic changes engendered by processes of modernization?

(a) Affluence

(b) Gradual economic development

(c) Traditional legitimacy

(d) Civic culture

(e) A homogeneous political culture

(f) Equality

(g) Congruent authority patterns

(h) Elite consensus

(i) The habituation of mechanisms of conflict resolution

(j) Political institutionalization

One by one, the questions become more specific, leaving the student less and less responsibility for deciding what is significant about the situation referred to and in what terms to respond to it. The final multiple-choice question, of course, tests only whether students can identify the three crucial factors. Further multiple-choice questions would be needed to take each of the ten suggested factors in turn and ask 'If this was one of the three factors you chose, which of the statements below best explains the contribution made by that factor.'

Many students feel frustrated by objective tests as a form of assessment, because they are unable to argue with the answers offered or express the fine distinctions that they may think are necessary. There is also the danger that we may not realize that students may have arrived at the right answer for the wrong reasons if they are not required to justify their answers. A possible half-way house, then, is the 'semi-objective' question in which the student is required to *select* an answer from a set of alternatives, but is also invited to *explain* his answer in a sentence or so. This type of question merges into the short 'own answer' question, in which the student, instead of being asked to write an 'essay', which will take him anything from 30 minutes to 1 hour, is required to answer a set of short questions, each taking 5 to 10 minutes and being answered in only a few lines.

There are many other ways for students to produce responses of their own, besides writing short answers and essays. Students could, for example, if the subject seemed appropriate, be asked to write a letter as if to the editor of a journal, to review a book in their field, to build a working model, to produce a research proposal, to script a television programme. In some subject areas, expression of *feeling* may be as relevant as reasoned argument. In such cases, the student's own answer may be expressed in the form of poems, photographs, drawings, songs, plays, dance, and so on. However, some of these last forms of expression are taking us beyond paper-and-pencil testing, and into 'situational' testing which we will look at in a few moments' time.

My colleague Nicola Durbridge recently compared all the tutor-marked assessment exercises set by the Open University during one year. She found an immense variety among them, and you may find it helpful to consider the types she described. First of all she split the assignments into 'single-task' and 'multi-task', the latter type having several shorter exercises rather than one long one. Then she went on to establish the existence of many varieties within those two categories:

| *Single-task* | *Multi-task* |
|---|---|
| 1. Standard essay | 1. Short essays |
| 2. Role-playing essay | 2. Design |
| 3. Structured essay | 3. Advice on design |
| 4. Home-experiment based | 4. Description of processes |
| 5. Interpretation of data | 5. Interpretation of data |
| 6. Project | 6. Hypotheses |
| 7. A set of notes | 7. Definitions |
| 8. Design | 8. Accounts of experiments |
| 9. Research report | 9. 'Sketch', 'plot a graph', etc. |
| | 10. Calculations |
| | 11. Notes |
| | 12. Critical review |

**203**

13. Historical commentary

14. Maths 'in a setting'

Nicola Durbridge added descriptive notes on some of her twenty-three varieties:

(a) *A 'structured essay'* (3) is one where the content or approach is unusually restricted, e.g., by giving a list of questions to be answered or of points to be included.

(b) *A 'role-playing essay'* (2) is one where the student is asked to project himself into a 'real-life' situation or to adopt a fictitious role in order to answer the question.

(c) *A 'standard essay'* (1) is any other type, regardless of the skills that may be involved in writing a 'good' answer. 'Bare' questions form the bulk of the list closely followed by those stating a point of view or containing a quotation followed by the command 'Discuss'. In descending order, and with slight variants, the following are the most common other commands: 'evaluate' or 'assess'; 'explain'; 'critically consider'; 'compare' and 'contrast'; 'analyse'.

(d) *'Research report'* (9). All of these are linked to projects; they may either form a separate assignment or occasionally be the final part of a double or triple assignment, and be the only part which is officially assessed.

To further illustrate her classifications, she took a single topic (in Urban Development) and tried to show as many different ways as possible of assessing it. As she admits, the attempt is somewhat artificial. Nevertheless, we can learn something useful from it.

*Standard essay.* ' "Land values are both the product and the determinant of the pattern of urban development" Discuss.'

*Structured essay.* 'Identify and discuss some of the determinants of urban land values and their impact on urban development. In your answer you should:

(a) define the following terms:
  (i) Property rights in land
  (ii) Zoning
  (iii) Site value rating

(b) explain the influence of these terms on determining land values

(c) select (i) one activity of public authorities
  and (ii) one market factor
  which affect land values and explain how each might influence urban development.'

*Role-playing essay.* 'You have inherited your late uncle's urban estate under his will and are considering whether it would be more profitable to sell the property quickly or 'sit and speculate'. Describe some of the factors as discussed in Unit 14 you would consider in making your decision.'

*Design.* 'As a town planner you are involved with the design and siting of a new small shopping precinct. You favour a site which involves the demolition of an old street in the city centre. Consider the possible effects on land value and accessibility of such redevelopment and present an argument for such a siting.'

*Project (or research report).* 'Assemble a file of items, e.g., newspaper cuttings, results of an interview with local planners and businessmen which you might conduct yourself, relating to a piece of proposed or completed redevelopment and its possible effects on property and land values. Include your assessment of the problems as you learn more about them.'

*Interpretation of data.* 'You own a house in a developing suburban area but are considering selling your property and moving closer to the city centre. Given the following demographic data: . . . what are some of the economic and social factors which you'd consider in coming to a decision?'

*Notes.* 'Select some of the main economic factors which affect the pattern of changing land values. List both the limitations and potentialities of these factors for predicting future urban development. Your answer may be in note form.'

Now let us look at items of the kind found in 'multi-task' assignments. (These were assignments with several shorter exercises rather than one long one.) Nicola Durbridge illustrated eight types:

*Hypotheses.* 'Suggest the relationships between nearby house prices and (a) the development of a new shopping precinct in a suburban area (b) a road widening scheme in the same area.'

*Critical review.* 'Give a reasoned critique of Henry George's thesis that a tax on property rights in land is a remedy for the problems caused by increasing rents. State whether or not you agree with his conclusions and give your reasons for the view you put forward.'

*Sketch/plot a graph, etc.* 'The map reproduced below shows X town with some of its major facilities: e.g.

the main roads traversing it
the railway line
the siting of the parks
the canal

The two lines A–B and C–D cross the city.

Plot two graphs for A–B and C–D to represent the likely office development land values and their fluctuations across the town.'

*Definitions.* 'Define the following terms:

**205**

Property rights in land     Betterment
Zoning     Access
Imputed rent     Accessibility.'
Externalities

*Design.* 'Develop a game for two or more people that will model the principles and factors involved in the decentralization of warehouse and factories.'

*Calculations.* 'Given the formula:

$$M = \sum^{\text{all } i} \frac{Qi}{Ti}$$

and the two sets of values: (a) ... (b) ...

Where $M$ = Market potential for Firm $X$ sited in the city centre
     $Qi$ = Potential market in area $i$ and
     $Ti$ = Transport cost between the firm's location and area $i$.

1. Measure the market potentials for (a) and (b) and compare their relative values.
2. The two measures of accessibility described in the text are not often used to explain land values. Why are such calculations less than satisfactory?'

*Description of processes.* 'Define the term 'Externalities' as used by an economist. Select a land use with both positive and negative externalities and describe the influence of these activities upon each other and upon urban land values.'

*Interpretation of data.* 'Using the figures in the text and their interpretation as an example, consider the maps reproduced below of 'X' town in 1910, 1940 and 1960 and explain the possible causes for the changes in the pattern of land values over the period.'

We may or may not disagree with how Nicola Durbridge has classified some of the above items. What does seem indisputable, however, is the *variety* among the items. Whatever we call them, it is clearly possible to set very different tasks on the same subject-area.

As I have said several times in this chapter (and in others), how you assess (and how you teach) must depend on what kind of learning you are interested in. Now it is pretty obvious that, say, arts teachers and teachers of the sciences are interested in very different learning objectives. Consequently, one would hope to find that they tend to favour very different assessment methods. So it is not surprising that when Nicola Durbridge examined all the tutor-marked assessment items set by Open University faculties in the year of her investigation, she found very obvious differences between arts-based and science-based faculties.

In the arts and social science faculties, between 60 and 70 per cent of assessment items were 'standard essays'. Social sciences made significant use of 'practical' assessments, which arts did not. The 'standard essay' was not used at all in the science or technology faculties. Both science and technology used 'short essays', however. The most frequently used items in science (accounting for about 60 per cent in all) were 'accounts of experiments', 'calculations' or 'description of processes'. In technology, about 60 per cent of assessment items were 'short essay', 'description of processes', or 'design'.

SITUATIONAL EXERCISES

As I suggested earlier, some intellectual, practical, or social skills can only truly be assessed by having the assessor present while the student performs some activity in which they are involved. This will be necessary when there is no assessable product resulting from his actions (e.g., a dramatic performance) or when it is difficult to tell from the product whether or not it was produced using acceptable methods (e.g., carrying out an experimental procedure).

If your objectives are concerned with *how* a student does or makes something, or with how he interacts with other people, then there may be no valid substitute for watching him do it. For such assessment, it is useful to produce a checklist of points you will be looking for in his performance. This will be especially useful if *someone else* has to do some of the assessment and advise you on what he has seen. Fig. 5.1 shows a checklist for use in observing a medical student interviewing a patient (from Maddison, 1977); the examiner is asked to mark each of 22 aspects of the student's performance out of a given possible total. (Overall, 10 per cent of the marks are for knowledge, 12.5 per cent for interpretation, 45 per cent for problem-solving, and 32.5 per cent for affective skills.) The examiner is also asked to use a 10-point scale in rating the student as a potential family physician.

In some cases, it may be possible to assess 'performance' skills by listening to an audio-tape recording (or viewing a video-tape) of a practical activity that you cannot observe 'in the flesh'. (Such recordings can be valuable to students' *self*-assessment, as in 'micro-teaching' and related activities.) But such an alternative might prove cumbersome and expensive, and still not allow for a very true (i.e., valid) assessment of the student's abilities.

**207**

**DIAGNOSTIC INTERVIEW RATING FORM**

Candidate's name .................................... Number .....................

Examiners.................................. Case no..................... LDI .......

| TO WHAT EXTENT DOES HE | Possible marks | Know-ledge | Inter-pretation | Problem Solving | Affective behaviour |
|---|---|---|---|---|---|
| 1. Show interest, consideration and empathy? | 5 | | | | |
| 2. Exhibit confidence? | 4 | | | | |
| 3. Build up confidence in the patient? | 3.5 | | | | |
| 4. Communicate effectively — does he listen carefully and use appropriate questioning? | 6 | | | | |
| 5. Elicit the presenting complaint and establish why the patient has come? | 2 | | | | |
| 6. Elicit the patient's other complaints and establish their chronological sequence and does he follow up important leads? | 5 | | | | |
| 7. Carry out relevant systematic interrogation? | 4 | | | | |
| 8. Elicit relevant past history? | 3 | | | | |
| 9. Elicit relevant personal and social history? | 2 | | | | |
| 10. Elicit the relevant family history? | 2 | | | | |
| 11. Interpret the historical data correctly? | 2 | | | | |
| 12. Draw logical diagnostic impressions after the history? | 5 | | | | |
| 13. Carry out appropriate physical examination? | 3 | | | | |
| 14. Give a lucid explanation to the patient of his diagnostic impressions and further diagnostic work-up? | 7 | | | | |
| 15. Interpret the examination findings correctly? | 3 | | | | |
| 16. Draw logical diagnostic conclusions from the physical findings? | 8 | | | | |
| 17. Select appropriate investigations? | 2.5 | | | | |
| 18. Interpret the investigations selected correctly? | 2 | | | | |
| 19. Make the correct diagnosis? | 8 | | | | |
| 20. Explore relevant differential diagnoses? | 6 | | | | |
| 21. Give a lucid explanation to the patient of his diagnostic impressions? | 7 | | | | |
| 22. Exhibit knowledge of the pathological processes exhibited by the patient? | 10 | | | | |
| Possible Marks | 100 | 10 | 12.5 | 45 | 32.5 |
| Candidate Category Marks | | | | | |
| Candidate Adjusted % Marks | | | | | |
| (Office use only) | | | | | |

What is your personal impression of the candidate as a family physician? Encircle appropriate number.

| Poor | Not very good | Average | Good | Very Good |
|---|---|---|---|---|
| 1  2 | 3  4 | 5  6 | 7  8 | 9  10 |

COMMENTS

**Fig. 5.1** Diagnostic interview rating form. (Reproduced by permission of WONCA and the Royal Australian College of General Practitioners)

Even a product like a project report may give very little indication of the intellectual skills and the scholarly attitudes that went into its making. Such interesting aspects as how the student repeatedly redefined his problem, or how he coped with disappointments in his early investigations, or how he struggled to do justice to ideas that he was not initially in sympathy with; these may all be hidden from the reader behind the bland 'whiggishness' (see page 67) of academic-type reportage. The teacher may, of course, have been able to assess such process-aspects in occasional discussions with the student prior to the completion of the project. If not, the student may need to be interviewed if an attempt to bring them to light again seems at all worthwhile.

With on-campus courses, a limited amount of assessment of 'performance' skills (or process abilities) can be carried out as part of the teaching. With distance education it is more difficult, and calls for special arrangements to be made. In either case, it is very expensive in staff time if it is to play a major role in the assessment strategy. The only alternative, unfortunately, would be to shift the assessment emphasis away from the practical and even more heavily towards theory. This shift would conceivably be disastrous in some areas, e.g., nursing, drama, design, counselling, and so on.

### Validity and reliability

As we have seen, for many important educational objectives some assessment methods are likely to be more valid than others. That is to say, they are likely to give a *truer* picture of the qualities we are looking for in a student. Thus, essays allow a more valid assessment of his ability to structure an argument than do multiple-choice questions. Likewise, situational tests allow a more valid assessment of his ability to carry on a conversation in a foreign language than would an essay or short-answer question.

However, it must be admitted that many of the more educationally relevant methods of assessment run us into problems of *reliability*. That is, unlike the objective test (where every marker would award the same score), we cannot rely on different teachers giving the same mark to a piece of writing or to the process skills they have observed. Even before the beginning of this century (Edgeworth, 1890), researchers were demonstrating that a group of assessors (all apparently well qualified) may award a wide range of marks to the same essay. Worse than that, they may not even agree as to whether that essay is better or worse than another essay.

A recent study in the Open University concerned the marking by each of ten tutors of each of eighteen essays from one social sciences course. The study revealed that eight of the essays were each given four out of six possible grades (A, B, C, D, F, R), none was given less than two different grades and, on average, the tutors between them awarded 3.4 different grades per essay. (See Edwards, 1979, for a further study of this kind and an explanation of the ways in which such tutor-differences can arise and, to some extent, be avoided.)

The assessment of essays and reports (not to mention dramatic performances and practical work) is a highly subjective activity. Different assessors will apply different criteria. Some will pay special attention to one aspect of students' work, some to another. So they will differ as to the overall quality they see in a student's product or performance. Even in mathematical exercises, different teachers are liable to view the same piece of work differently. Some will give credit for correct method or the number of correctly worked steps towards the solution, even if the answer is wrong; others will not. Some will take elegance or economy of working into account; others will not. The succession of six possible questions on Sweden's political stability (page 202) illustrates a progressive increase in reliability accompanied by a corresponding decrease in validity.

There are two ways of lessening the problem (without falling back on multiple-choice questions). Firstly, we can give the student considerable guidance as to what kind of answer we are expecting. Secondly, we can give guidance to our fellow-assessors as to what they should look for and reward in the student's response.

As an illustration of the first of these two approaches, students working on a mathematical project might be told (Hirst and Biggs, 1969) how marks will be awarded to their work under the following headings:

● *Exposition* (mathematical accuracy, clarity, literary presentation).
● *Study of literature* (understanding, relating different sources, finding new sources).
● *Originality* (examples cited, examples constructed, new treatments and proofs of standard results . . .).
● *Scope of topic* (conceptual difficulty, technical difficulty, relationships with previous studies, relevance of material covered . . .).

Similar guidance could be given to the tutors who will be marking the project. For either students or tutors, the guidance could be even more prescriptive, indicating the maximum marks to be awarded for each separate aspect. (This approach is illustrated in

**210**

Fig. 5.1.) To do so would probably increase the reliability of the assessment. Students' work would probably differ less and tutors would probably agree more easily on the mark to give to a particular student's efforts.

Yet to take such explicitness too far, listing so many points for this aspect and so many for that, may be felt stifling by both students and tutors alike. In the end, we may decide to settle for less than maximum reliability in order to leave students some freedom to produce work in their own best way—rather than by numbers—even if there remains a risk that tutors might disagree somewhat as to its value. You must make up your own mind about this. (For a fuller discussion of the issues, see Rowntree, 1977 and 1979*b*.)

Ideally, crucial pieces of student work (e.g., final examination scripts) should be assessed by more than one assessor and their viewpoints compared. But let us hope they do not differ quite as much as these two examiners parodied by Laurie Taylor (1980):

> '. . . Now candidate 666. I found this very jumbled. My notes say "very jumbled—lacks overall coherence—little sign of organization —no evidence of planning—somewhat repetitive phrasing." So I went for nothing more than a compensatable pass, 37 to be exact.'
> 'This is 666?'
> 'Yes.'
> 'Well I must say I've taken a rather more charitable view here. I agree about the lack of organization, but there seemed to be some attempt to be original, some sign of getting away from the standard material. Even a little imagination.'
> 'What have you got then?'
> 'Pardon?'
> 'What mark have you got?'
> 'Emm . . . well I've put down 86—although with a question mark after it—so obviously I'm prepared to move a bit.'
> 'Quite a gap. But at least we both seem to agree on a pass.'

Perhaps my main message so far is that you should remain open as to possible assessment methods. No one method will serve all objectives. You should be finding out about all the kinds possible and asking yourself whether each could be relevant to your educational intentions. In the end you will find a *mixture* of assessment methods works best. If for no other reason, on any lengthy course you will need to ring the changes to avoid boring the student with 'One damn essay after another'. But, more positively, the outcome is likely to be a more accurate and more rounded

**211**

picture of the student's abilities than could be obtained by the use of any one method by itself.

This still leaves some tricky questions to be decided concerning which assessment methods to use for which parts of the course and in what proportions each should be used. There are no easy answers. You will have to be guided both by the nature of your subject matter and by the conditions in which you work. For instance, the total number of students involved may be the decisive factor. With small numbers, objective tests may just not be worth the effort involved in setting them. With very large numbers, it may be impossible to arrange for the marking of essays. With distance students, situational exercises may be difficult to arrange.

### *Learning about assessment methods*

Whatever you decide on, make sure you discuss your assessment strategy with your students. Indeed, you may need to do more than this. You may need to teach them how to work with certain assessment techniques so as to best reveal their knowledge and skills. Thus, for example, in some courses it may be extremely valuable (and educational) to allow students *two* attempts at producing certain assignments. The first attempt you will discuss with them and make suggestions as to how they might improve it; and the second attempt is the one you mark. (See Prescott and Jarvis, 1978.)

Again, a 'mock examination' can be useful in some courses, or at least an in-class discussion of sample questions and how they might be answered. Many students, for example, have never really been led to discriminate among those abundant key-commands with which we pepper our question-papers, e.g., discuss, evaluate, critically compare, analyse, describe, interpret, enumerate. (And, as a result, they may tend to treat all such commands as if they meant simply 'Tell all you know about the subject'.) Such discussions can be seen as an extension of the 'learning to use the media' that I recommend in Chapter 4.

### Case study: Assessment for a new course

We can pull together the ideas I have developed in the first half of this chapter by means of a case study which my colleague Roger Harrison and I produced. In it, we consider how we might assess a new on-campus course on *National Energy Policy*. It is intended for second-year degree students, most of whom will be studying Economics, Business Management, or Planning as their main subject. There will be about thirty such students and the course is meant to occupy them about three hours a week for three terms—about 90 hours in all.

As already indicated, it is vital to plan assessment with the whole course in view. Otherwise, the plan may not do justice to the aims of the course. Certain parts of the course (especially the early parts which are relatively easy, both for the student to learn and for you to assess) may be over-emphasized. So let us get an overview of the proposed *Energy* course. We could list the topics to be covered in the form of a syllabus. But perhaps you will see the topics in better perspective if they are shown embodied in the proposed aims and objectives.

*Aims*

The course aims to explain the concept of energy (using practical demonstrations) and the importance of energy in industrial society, to provide practice in carrying out experiments and surveys relating to energy studies, to engender a sense of concern about the way in which reserves of fossil fuels are being depleted at the present time, and to give guidance in the planning of an energy policy.

*Objectives*

The student should be able to:

*By the end of term 1*

1. List the various forms of energy and describe how one form may be converted into another.
2. Explain why energy is important in modern industrial society.
3. Distinguish between energy and power.
4. Perform simple calculations concerning energy transformation and power.
5. Decide appropriate methods to determine the power of an energy transforming device.
6. Explain what is meant by the conservation of energy and why energy appears to be lost in everyday situations.
7. Explain quantitatively why there are limitations to the proportion of thermal energy which may be transformed into useful work.
8. List the commercial sources of energy currently and prospectively available and estimate the reserves or potential of each.
9. Identify the principal energy flows in a given community (or industry, or factory, etc.).

*By the end of term 2*

10. Identify the deleterious consequences which may result from a given industrial energy transformation proposal.
11. Identify the energy inputs into a given product, using data provided.

**213**

12. Evaluate a technical proposal with regard to energy consumption.

13. Suggest ways of reducing energy consumption in particular contexts, and assess their feasibility.

14. Identify the economic factors relating to the use of energy.

15. Form a judgement as to the weight to be given to economic considerations in evaluating energy proposals.

16. Identify objectives for a national energy policy.

*By the end of term 3*

17. Apply the experience of terms 1 and 2 to real-world situations demanding that the student exercise initiative, selectivity, understanding, judgement, and social skills.

In brief, the first term lays the scientific foundations; the second term brings in the economic and social issues; and the third term requires the student to apply the theories and concepts he has acquired so far. How are we to assess such a course?

To begin with, shall we assess at the end of the course, during the course, or both? Well, the course is certainly one in which the student's final understanding should be greater than can be assessed by adding up all the partial understandings he has attained on the way through. That is, some *integrative* assessment activity seems to be called for. This could be a long essay towards the end of the third term. Or it could be a final examination— perhaps a fairly open one (e.g., questions published in advance, reference works available, etc.).

However, perhaps we need assessment during the course as well? For instance, the third term's objective clearly suggests a *project*. In fact, we can decide that the third term will be devoted to an empirical enquiry related, for example, to objective 9 or 11 (identifying energy flows in a community or energy inputs into a product). The student will negotiate the precise context of his enquiry with his tutor, and will carry it out in a local factory, hospital, or whatever. Such a project will give rise to a report, itself a long 'essay' (with graphs, calculations, etc.). Clearly, this ought to 'count' for purposes of overall assessment since it relates to a vital objective—so vital that a whole term is devoted to it.

At the same time, if the student is concentrating on his project during the third term he cannot be expected also to produce a long essay integrating what he has learned during the course. Nor can his project report be expected to perform this integrative role. So, we had better settle on an examination at the end of the third term. Perhaps it will concentrate on objective 16, giving maximum scope for the pulling together of what has been learned both in terms 1 and 2 and during the term 3 project experience.

So we have decided on a project report towards the end of term 3 and an examination at the end of the course. Is anything more needed? Well, the scientific/experimental background in term 1 is rather vital and we would be unhappy to see students skimp it. In fact, we do not think students could make real sense of the rest of the course without it. So we will assess their attainment of the term 1 objectives at the end of that term. Probably multiple-choice questions will suffice; but, since the test will be marked by tutors (rather than machines), short 'own answer' questions can also be included. While the objectives it will test are vital, we cannot pretend they are very high level. (They will not be tested in the final exam.) It would not be appropriate to let the test contribute too much to the student's overall grade for the course. Let us regard it as a critical, qualifying test. That is, the student has to get a satisfactory score in order to be allowed to continue with the course, but the score will *not* count in deciding his overall grade. (The decision on what is a 'satisfactory' score can be left until we have worked out just what level of proficiency is essential for the rest of the course.)

Now, what about the second term—do we need any assessment there? We do need to help motivate students in their reading on the 'economic/social factors (rather than spending undue effort preparing for the project). So some sort of assessment seems desirable. How about a long essay in the area of objectives 12–15? This, in many ways, can be seen as preparatory to designing an energy policy which is to be tested in the final examination.

So here is the proposal we would put to course team colleagues:

Term 1: Objective/short answer, 'qualifying' test (objectives 1–7).
Term 2: Long essay (objectives 12–15).
Term 3: Project report (largely objectives 8–11). Final exam (largely objective 16).

The only other issue is one of weighting. This is discussed further in the second half of the chapter but, briefly, of the three forms of assessment that are to 'count' towards the student's overall grade for the course, which is to count most and which least? We can see no reason why either the long essay or the project report or the final exam should be given greater importance than either of the other two so let them all count *equally*. That is, the student who does poorly on the exam can still make good by doing particularly well on the other two components. So can the student who does poorly on the project or the long essay. He does not have to 'pass' all three in order to pass the course. But he does have to do well on all three to do well on the course. The criteria by which we are to judge whether students have done well or poorly will have to be argued out with colleagues once the course team has accepted the overall strategy.

So these are our first thoughts on assessment for that course. We would expect them to be modified in discussion with other members of the course team, especially as the coverage and style of the course became more clear. But it is important to throw ideas about assessment into the discussion *before* the course structure does begin to harden. Because, for example, the suggestion that we assess on the basis of a project report in the third term is, indeed, a suggestion also as to the structure of the course.

## How to use assessment results?

This would be quite a good point to recall the definition of assessment introduced earlier:

> Assessment is an attempt to get to know about the student and find out the nature and quality of his learning—his strengths and weaknesses, or his interests and aversions, or his style of learning.

So the result of assessment is *knowledge*: knowledge about the student. How are we to use that knowledge? Briefly, we can use it to report on the student or we can use it to teach him (or we can do both).

### *Teaching through assessment*
In working with students in the classroom, informal assessment is an essential and inevitable component of teaching. For instance, you do not start teaching a student how to use a microscope unless your observations (assessment) tell you he is unable to use it correctly at present. And as soon as your assessments tell you he has mastered the skill, you know you can stop teaching him. Without some attempt to find out (through informal assessment) how your student is responding to your words of wisdom, you may be telling, or lecturing, or haranguing, but I question whether you would be teaching.

More formal assessment exercises (quizzes, essays, laboratory

**216**

reports, etc.) may also provide knowledge about the student that his teacher can use in teaching him. Every so often, as the course progresses, your students will reveal something of their knowledge and skills and attitudes in how they respond to your assessments. Each time they do, new teaching needs and possibilities will appear. Sometimes it will be possible actually to do the teaching, at other times not.

TUTORING IN WRITING

If the students are studying on campus they may be able to meet the person who assessed their work. It may even be assessed in their presence. In such cases, the assessor should be able to launch into teaching, in a sort of mini-tutorial, on the basis of the results before him.

If the marker is dealing with students 'at a distance'—marking tests sent in by students whom he does not meet—it is less easy for him to teach effectively. For one thing, several days may elapse between the student making his response and his getting any feedback from the marker. Thus, he may have lost touch with what his response meant to him at the time he made it; and so he may be incapable of appreciating the tutor's reaction to it. More importantly—and this would be the case even if the tutor were able to send a response within minutes—the tutor is handicapped by being unable to discuss the answers with his student. Telephone conversations may be possible, but even they do not permit the mutual responsiveness tutor and student can enjoy in face-to-face contact with the student's written work in front of them.

Whether he is also meeting his students face-to-face or not, the tutor should make the most of his opportunity to teach through the *comments* and *advice* he sends to students when he returns their scripts. He should direct such comments at what he believes to be the chief strengths and weaknesses of a particular piece of work. Basically, he has to decide his teaching *priorities*. In order to most benefit the student, he may ignore some minor weaknesses in order to help his student remedy the major ones. For example, a particular student's essay may appear to be: poorly organized, missing the point of the question, faulty on some of the references it quotes, and full of spelling mistakes. His tutor might well disregard the first, third and fourth weaknesses in order to concentrate his help on the second, since even the best organized, factually accurate, and immaculately spelled essay is wasted if it is irrelevant.

**217**

So, when the marker becomes tutor, he will try to write down a response that will help the student think again about what he has done. It should guide him as to how he might do such things better another time. Obviously this written response needs to be considerably fuller than would be necessary if the tutor were able to discuss the work with his student face-to-face almost immediately. So it will not be sufficient to cover the script with ticks and crosses and question marks, underlining or circling a word or phrase here and there. More is needed. But how much more?

Suppose the comment represented in Fig. 5.2 were the only thing written on a student's script. How would you feel about its adequacy (in terms of helping him improve his work)?

> This is quite a fair piece and you make a number of points well. But some are rather less well illustrated than others and the argument is sometimes weak or not fully expressed.

**Fig. 5.2** Tutor's comment

The problem here is that the tutor's comment is too general. The student is not told precisely *where* and *how* he has illustrated less well, argued weakly, or expressed less than fully, let alone *what* he might have done to avoid this charge. At the very least, the tutor should have directed the student's attention to specific examples of the faults he found in the script.

However, the above tutor can at least be commended for starting off with some encouragement. Some tutors seem to notice only the faults in a student's work and neglect to mention its positive aspects. If they are not to be seen as bearers of unrelieved gloom, tutors might do well to work to the motto 'first the good news, now the bad news'. But, as you will appreciate, there is something of an art even to conveying the 'bad news', if we want students to learn from it.

Certainly, the tone of the tutor's response is very important. Such comments as these might do more harm than good to the tutor–student relationship:

'This just won't do'
'Style!'
'Disorganized and inchoate'
'Your spelling is atrocious'
'You can't see the difference between facts and opinions'

But guidance can be offered to the student without sounding condescending or threatening. The following responses, collected from the margins of students' work, have the flavour of *dialogue* in which tutors are seeking clarification, evidence, or amplification; or are drawing their students' attention to errors or anomalies; or are trying to stretch their thinking:

'The meaning is not very clear here. I find what it appears to mean very unlikely. Can you quote the figures?'
'Important point but needs broadening out from the specific example—also did any benefits accrue for schools and children?'
'If you had given the electronic structures of neon and sodium it would have helped show the essential difference between them.'
'Your answer is OK as far as it goes but you do not explain why the drop in IE is so large; look again at Figure 7 of the unit and ask yourself what is so special about the electronic structure of neon and how does it differ from that of sodium.'
'Yes it is very difficult to assess the effectiveness of the Labour Party, either nationally or locally in this role. I would have welcomed an example on a local issue known to you.'

(For more examples and discussion, see Grugeon, 1973 and Sewart, 1977.)

Notice that good tutor-commenting may depend more on the ability to ask the student stimulating questions than to provide him with ready-made answers. Here is a particularly handsome example, from a mathematics assignment, where the tutor's comments are largely put as questions leading the student towards answering his problem, which is to determine, given that set (i) $\{\wedge, \vee, \sim\}$ is an adequate set of connectives, whether set (ii) $\{\square, \sim\}$ is an adequate set:

What does $\{\wedge, \vee, \sim\}$ being an adequate set of connectives mean? All connectives can be written in terms of $\{\wedge, \vee, \sim\}$. How do we show that $\{\square, \sim\}$ is an adequate set? By showing all connectives can be written in terms of $\{\square, \sim\}$. Knowing set (i) how do we show set (ii)? In other words, how can we replace set (i) by set (ii)? How do they differ?'

In a recent internal report on tutor commenting in the Open

**219**

University, my colleague Nicola Durbridge mentioned one tutor who reckoned to use her comments on the students' work for the following purposes:

● An opportunity to refer them to passages or sections in the course materials.
● An occasion to illustrate precisely *why* clear expression and precision are important.
● A chance to guide students on the selection of material: i.e., to advise them where he/she had been too detailed, irrelevant or too sketchy, or to reassure if there was a right balance.
● To inform, by providing extra background information.
● To point out and explain the need to refer to or to quote from the text.
● To show them how to *use* and introduce quotations.
● To introduce students to new ideas—through supplementary texts, etc.

As I have made plain, I believe that the student's assessment results should lead to some kind of teaching. However, this does not apply only to the student's responses to own-answer questions. Even with short-answer questions, or objective-type, multiple-choice items, teaching feedback can still be given to the student —feedback that is intended to help him review his work and improve it. At the very least, the student can be told which are the preferred answers. Better still, he can also be told why. For every question he may have gone astray on, he can even be directed to specific teaching material in order to brush up his understanding.

COMPARING STANDARDS
Obviously, teaching based on the assessment results will only be fully under your control if you do it yourself. But what if other instructors, or even student-proctors, are doing the marking? Here, you are very dependent (or rather the students are) on the personal skills of the person who happens to be marking their work. Teachers who teach well face-to-face are not necessarily so proficient at teaching through written comments, where they cannot see the student's reaction to what they have said and so amend it accordingly. Conversely, some people who can write careful, sympathetic, and useful comments may not be so good in a 'tutorial' situation.

If it will be necessary for other people to mark your students' work, what steps might you take to ensure that their comments and advice to students will be as useful as possible? There are various things you could do to help them.

1. Discuss with markers the importance of teaching comments and how they might usefully be made.
2. Show them examples of good and bad commenting on typical student work.
3. Ask each marker to examine a few pieces of student work and record the comments he would want to make to each student to help him improve. (You should do this too, of course.) Then compare notes and seek consensus in discussion as to how best to help such students.
4. Monitor the markers' commenting occasionally. Without threatening them or making them feel you don't trust them, look at returned student scripts now and again, or talk with students about how they feel about the feedback (written or spoken) they are getting. Have 'refresher' discussions with any markers who seem to have lost the art of helpful commenting or who seem to be failing to acquire it (or are too tough or too lenient in their grading, for that matter).

What we have been discussing so far is often called *formative* assessment. That is, we are, in a sense, using assessment to help form the students' learning. Now we go on to look at what is often called *summative* assessment. Here we are using the assessment results to sum up and report on what is known of the student.

### Reporting assessment results

Apart from their use in teaching, assessment results can be used in *reporting* what has been discovered about the student. Reporting to whom? Perhaps to the student himself, to the teacher himself (in the form of a written record), to other teachers, to potential employers, and so on. The need to report emphasizes two questions which are never far away from assessment situations:

1. How do we know what is good and what is not good in a student's performance? (*Standards*)
2. How do we combine the results of many different assessments, over a period of time, to report an overall assessment of the student? (*Conflation?*)

WHERE DO STANDARDS COME FROM?

How do we decide whether a particular student's essay is worth

**221**

60 or 70 per cent? Or whether his laboratory 'practical' is worth C+ or B−? How do we decide whether 40 or 50 per cent should be the boundary between 'pass' and 'fail'? Or whether 'distinction' is to be awarded only to A− students or to those with B+ also?

In fact, it may not be 'we' (or you) who does the deciding. The decisions may be taken by someone else and we (as teachers) implement them either willingly or unwillingly, and with or without protest. But decisions there definitely are. No discipline, from Anthropology to Zoology, imposes absolute, eternal standards of its own. What counts as 'good mathematics' or 'first class history' will change (gradually no doubt) according to what is supported by the currently powerful opinion-leaders among the discipline's practitioners.

Standards are thus decided by those practitioners who are considered to best represent the discipline. If your institution's students are externally assessed, then you may expect to influence, but you will not expect to make the decisions. If you assess your own students, and especially if you are the only local practitioner of your discipline, then you can expect to have a very large say in the setting of standards. Usually, however, you will probably find that standards are decided upon or arrived at, as a kind of professional consensus, after discussion and negotiation with your discipline colleagues and perhaps with external (visiting) assessors from other institutions. In theory, such consensus would be observable among several different assessors looking at a particular student's work and all agreeing on the standard he had reached. And, again in theory, the standard they all agreed the student had reached this year should be the same standard they would all have agreed on if they had assessed his work in a previous year.

Such overall consensus, or at least consent, involves a number of separate decisions and agreements. The assessors must agree (whether tacitly or after vigorous debate) on a number of issues we have already touched on in this chapter. What knowledge, skills and attitudes are to be assessed? What weight shall be given to various kinds of learning, in terms of the number of assessment exercises relating to each? What assessment methods are appropriate? What is to count as a satisfactory performance on each? What instructions are to be given to markers to ensure reasonable reliability? In addition, there will be two other areas of contention that we have not yet touched upon. How are the marks obtained from various assessment exercises (e.g., course work and examinations) to be combined in order to provide an overall indication of the student's level of attainment? (This process is often referred to as conflation and is discussed more fully below.) And, finally, what fraction of the total possible mark must the student achieve in order to be awarded a pass, credit, distinction, etc. (or third class, second class, first class)?

Faced with so many decisions to make, all of them based on judgements that might well differ from assessor to assessor according to the values they bring to teaching and learning, it may seem surprising to some that assessors ever do reach agreement. In practice, diplomacy and persuasion are often unnecessary. Much of the detailed, agonising decision-making is avoided by sticking to the local 'traditions of the discipline' (even if it needs the head of the department to say what these are!). Thus, the same sorts of question are set year after year within the institution—perhaps even in all local institutions teaching comparable courses. The questions are often published and there is generally some forum for public discussion of the appropriate standard of answer. On the whole, practitioners of a discipline do not seem to spend much time fretting about whether they (or their colleagues) have got the standards right. Unless they are developing, say, a new interdisciplinary course, in which 'traditions' of assessment have to be built from scratch, standards soon get taken pretty much for granted. 'The first class mind proclaims itself!' declared one university examiner; and no doubt he and his colleagues would be equally confident about recognizing minds (or work) of third and second class also.

Assessment in which the student's work is measured against some absolute standard (or criterion) is often described as *criterion-referenced*. That is, if the student reaches a certain level, he may deserve, say, a C; something more will be expected for a B; and an even higher standard must be reached to justify an A. Or, if percentage marks are being used, 50 per cent might mean he has achieved half the objectives, 75 per cent that he has achieved three-quarters of them, and so on. Since a student's work is not being measured by comparison with that of his fellow-students, all of them could, theoretically, achieve the highest grade (or, of course, the lowest).

There is another common approach to awarding grades. It is found especially in national public examinations, where the person who assesses a student is not the person who taught him.

**223**

Here it may be decided *in advance* that the top grade (call it A) will be given to, say, the 10 per cent of students who perform best; B to the next-best 20 per cent; C to the middle 40 per cent; and so on, until the unfortunate bottom 10 per cent of students (or whatever magic number is considered appropriate) gets failed outright. In other words, the assessors start out with a pre-determined grade-distribution in mind (based loosely on the statistical 'normal curve of distribution'). In US colleges, teachers who mark in this way are said to be 'grading on the curve'.

Such an approach to assigning marks and grades is often described as *norm-referenced*. How a student's work is graded depends on the norms established by his particular cohort of fellow-students. The grading is relative. How a particular student fares will not depend on how well his performance might compare with some absolute standard. Rather, it depends on how his work compares with that of his fellows. If he is among students who are very able, then he will need to do far more to achieve a certain grade than he would if his fellows were less able.

The norm-referenced approach to standards may be justified for national examinations involving very large numbers of students; because then it is quite likely that the spread of ability among the candidates will not differ greatly from year to year. Even so, there may be a slow drift in ability or achievement, year by year, on account of social, educational, or other changes. Whatever the causes of any such drift, awarding grades in accordance with a predetermined distribution rather than by reference to absolute standards, means that any given grade awarded this year cannot be assumed to represent the same quality of work as that same grade represented in a previous year.

Norm-referenced grading becomes even more dubious when it is applied to smaller groups of students, such as those going through a particular institution year by year. Most teachers are well aware that some years they have a class that seems unusually full of keen students, while in other years a class may seem to contain many passengers. To apply arbitrary proportions in grading such variable classes would be to over-rate the performance of the weaker students in the poor year and to do less than justice to the abler students in a good year. Furthermore, an institution too may be taking in students whose overall ability, intake by intake, is gradually drifting upwards or downwards over the years while the standards they are reported to have achieved on leaving remain unchanged. For example, Miller (1967)

**224**

pointed out that even though the quality of students entering the University of California at Berkeley increased greatly between 1947 and 1960 (as measured by three different pre-entry criteria), the distribution of overall final grades remained precisely the same.

In practice, neither norm-referencing nor criterion-referencing is usually applied alone in complete disregard of the other. The examiners in a particular institution, even though they may be trying to apply absolute standards, will be quite aware of the proportions of the students falling into the different grades. If they have awarded no distinctions, or 'too many' failures, they will become uneasy and may begin questioning whether they have lost their sense of standards. (Less forgiveably, some assessors may feel it unethical to pass every student, even if all appear to have reached the necessary standard. Such teachers may believe a few failures are needed to demonstrate to the world that they are vigilant about standards, or simply to keep students toeing the line.) And even teachers who regularly 'grade on the curve' are likely to stretch their proportions every now and again, if they recognize that serious injustice would otherwise be done to certain students.

Clearly, there are no simple infallible methods of determining the appropriate standard of performance in educational assessment. Previous experience will probably give you some idea as to what sort of standards are appropriate. On the other hand, looking at the distribution of the marks will help you to check that you have chosen appropriate standards. If you find that the average performance is lower than you had hoped, it may mean that your standards are too high or that you have set assessment exercises that are too difficult. Alternatively, it may indicate that you over-estimated the ability of your students and will need to lower your standards or improve your course. In the last resort you will probably be influenced by the likelihood that if you fail a high proportion of the students you run the risk of getting no students at all in future years, while if you give too many top grades and distinctions your certificates may lose credibility in the outside world.

Before leaving the subject of standards, it is worth noting a point that relates it back to the teaching aspects of the assessment. When we use assessment for teaching, rather than for reporting a grade, we also use what might be called a *self*-referenced approach. By this I mean that our teaching judgements in relation to a particular student's work may be based not on comparison with that of other students, or even with absolute standards, but with what that student himself has achieved in the past or with what we believe he is capable of achieving in the future. It should also go without saying that our grading policy should be discussed with our students. If we leave them to guess at our standards, they may end up as mystified and disenchanted as the science student quoted by Beard and Senior (1980, page 74):

> 'I've found that if you do work hard and give in a good essay you get the same mark. It satisfies me more to write a good essay, but you know you get 7 whatever you give in. If you copy out of a textbook you get 7, or if you work hard, put in a lot of reading and express it in your own words, you still get 7. I've decided that it's not worth it.'

CONFLATION—COMBINING ASSESSMENT RESULTS

However you arrive at your standards, they will be embodied in the judgements you make about your students and the grades you award their work. That is where the next problem arises. In all but the briefest of courses, a number of different student activities are likely to be assessed—resulting in a number of different grades. For example, there may be continuous assessment and a terminal examination; there may be multiple-choice tests and essays; there may be prescribed work and an open-ended project—all assessed and graded separately. How are we to combine or conflate the separate results in order to arrive at a student's 'overall result' for the course?

Suppose a student has earned the following separate grades on a year's course:

| | |
|---|---|
| Essay 1 | : C |
| Essay 2 | : A |
| Essay 3 | : A |
| Essay 4 | : A |
| Multiple-choice test | : D |
| Project | : B |
| Final exam | : C |

Now different teachers might well add up or conflate those grades quite differently from one another. Here are several possible ways of deciding what to report as the student's overall result:

● Give him A because it is the grade he gets most frequently.

**226**

- Give him B because it 'averages out' the three grades that were higher and the three that were lower.
- Give him B because a project should be a truer guide to the student's worth than any of the other components.
- Give him C because the final exam is what really shows a student's true worth.

To know whether any of them actually are reasonable, we would need detailed information about how each of the assessment activities related to the aims and objectives of the course. It may also cross your mind that *no* single letter grade could usefully sum up such a diverse performance. That is a criticism we shall look at again later. Meanwhile, let us continue on the assumption (reasonable for most institutions still) that the student's performance on the course has somehow to be summed up and reported with what has been called 'the all-talking, all-singing, all-dancing, uni-dimensional grade'.

Clearly, conflation is not a simple task. It requires a set of rules that have been decided in advance and preferably communicated to the students so that they know how to direct their efforts. For instance, suppose a course has two assessment components, say a project report and a final exam. The assessors may, on the one hand, make it a rule that students must pass in each component separately in order to pass on the course as a whole. On the other hand, they may rule that grades for the two components are averaged, thus allowing a poor performance on one to be compensated for by superior performance on the other. In practice, the first method tends to be unduly harsh on some students, although it may be justified when the outcome is a licence to practice. Generally, at least a limited degree of compensation is desirable. On the other hand, averaging may give students too much freedom to neglect important parts of the course. So it may be necessary to designate certain assessment components as 'critical' (e.g., the oral test in languages or the practicals in science) and insist upon a minimum performance in such components, even though this might be below the minimum pass level for the course as a whole. Thus a conflation rule may need to provide flexibility by allowing students to average their performance to some extent, while not allowing them to fall too low on any one component.

The arithmetical process of adding or averaging assessment results is also more difficult than might appear. To begin with, we need the results expressed as *numbers*. We cannot add up or average letter grades. It may seem obvious (though it's not) that, for example, grades of A, B, and C would give an average of B. Not so easy, however, to average the three grades of A, C, and C. To do this, we need some rule for converting letter grades to numbers; and numbers back to letter grades again. For instance, we might say:

$$A = 10 \qquad \text{Therefore,}$$
$$B = 9 \qquad A+B+C = \frac{10+9+8}{3} \quad \frac{27}{3} = 9$$
$$C = 8$$
$$D = 7$$
$$E = 6 \qquad A+C+C = \frac{10+8+8}{3} = \frac{26}{3} = 8\tfrac{2}{3}$$

Clearly $A+B+C$ gives an average of 9 which is equivalent to a B. But what of $A+C+C$, which gives an average of $8\tfrac{2}{3}$? We might convert the numbers back into grades as follows:

| | | | | |
|---|---|---|---|---|
| $10 = A$ | or | $10 = A$ | or $9-10 = A$ | or $9\tfrac{2}{3},\ 10 = A$ |
| $9\tfrac{2}{3} = A-$ | | $9 < 10 = B$ | $8 < 9 = B$ | $8\tfrac{2}{3}-9\tfrac{1}{3} = B$ |
| $9\tfrac{1}{3} = B+$ | | $8 < 9 = C$ | $7 < 8 = C$ | $7\tfrac{2}{3}-8\tfrac{1}{3} = C$ |
| $9 = B$ | | $7 < 8 = D$ | $6 < 7 = B$ | $6\tfrac{2}{3}-7\tfrac{1}{3} = D$ |
| $8\tfrac{2}{3} = B-$ | | $6 < 7 = E$ | $6 = E$ | $6,\ 6\tfrac{1}{3} = E$ · |
| $8\tfrac{1}{3} = C+$ | | | | |
| $8 = C$ | | ('6 < 7' means 'at least 6 but less than 7') | | |
| $7\tfrac{2}{3} = C-$ | | | | |
| $7\tfrac{1}{3} = D+$ | | | | |
| $7 = D$ | | | | |
| $6\tfrac{2}{3} = D-$ | | | | |
| $6\tfrac{1}{3} = E+$ | | | | |
| $6 = E$ | | | | |

The left-hand conversion scale offers more exactness but brings in the use of pluses and minuses. The second scale 'rounds down' in averaging. Thus, of two students with averages of, say, $8\tfrac{2}{3}$ and $9\tfrac{1}{3}$, the latter would get the same grade (B) as a student with 9 while the former, though equally close to the score of 9, would get only a C. The next scale 'rounds' *up*: the $8\tfrac{2}{3}$ would get a B, like the 9, but $9\tfrac{1}{3}$ would get A. The right-hand scale, however, 'rounds' to the *nearest* grade: thus the students with $8\tfrac{2}{3}$ and $9\tfrac{1}{3}$ would both get the same grade (B) as the student with 9.

I am not saying that one scale is preferable to another. What I do want to stress is that there is no 'natural' way of converting letters to numbers and back again. Rather there are many ways to *decide* among, and they differ in how they will label our students.

Consider the student whose set of seven grades was mentioned earlier (page 226). Suppose the teacher of that course decided on the following conversion scales:

| Grade = Mark | Average mark = Grade |
|---|---|
| A = 10 | 9 − 10 = A |
| B = 8 | 7 < 9 = B |
| C = 6 | 5 < 7 = C |
| D = 4 | 3 < 5 = D |
| E = 2 | 1 < 3 = E |
| F = 0 | < 1 = F |

What would be the student's overall grade for the course if the teacher's conflation rule says it is to be the average of all his grades? The student's seven grades would average out as follows:

C = 6
A = 10
A = 10
A = 10
D = 4
B = 8
C = 6
‾‾
54     Conflated grade $= \dfrac{54}{7} = 7\frac{5}{7} = B$

However, there are yet more complications involved in adding or averaging scores. For instance, it is usually thought necessary to *weight* some assessment components more heavily than others. The teacher of the above course might have decided to weight examination scores three times as heavily as other scores. In effect that would have meant counting the examination score three times in working out a student's overall grade. Would you expect it to make much of a difference to the student's overall grade if we give his exam score three times the weight? Let us try it and see. We will add in two extra C grades (which is what he scored in the examination) and divide by 9, because we will now have nine grades instead of seven.

Here is the result of giving three-fold weight to the exam score:

$$
\text{Essays:} \begin{cases} C = 6 \\ A = 10 \\ A = 10 \\ A = 10 \end{cases}
$$

M/c test:         D = 4
Project:          B = 8

$$
\text{Exam (3 times):} \begin{cases} C = 6 \\ C = 6 \\ C = 6 \end{cases}
$$

$$\overline{66} \qquad \text{Conflated grade} = \frac{66}{9} = 7\tfrac{1}{3} = B$$

As you see, the extra weighting has made no difference to the overall grade. This is usually the case when we have several components (different grades) but only a few final categories to reduce them to (A, B, C, D, E, F). To alter the overall (conflated) result by giving extra weight of one of those components, the weight must be quite large. In the case above, as you can check, the exam grade would have to be given six times the weight of any other grade before the overall grade came down to C.

On the other hand, the teacher might have said 'I intend to give the exam twice as much weight as all the other components taken together.' That is, he could calculate an overall grade for the 'other components' and *then* conflate that with the double-weighted exam grade. Here is the result of that conflation:

| | |
|---|---|
| Essay 1: | C = 6 |
| Essay 2: | A = 10 |
| Essay 3: | A = 10 |
| Essay 4: | A = 10 |
| M/c test: | D = 4 |
| Project: | B = 8 |

$$\overline{48} \qquad \text{Conflated grade} = \frac{48}{6} = 8 = B$$

| | |
|---|---|
| 'Other components': | B = 8 |
| Exam: | C = 6 |
| Exam: | C = 6 |

$$\overline{20} \qquad \text{Conflated grade} = \frac{20}{3} = 6\tfrac{2}{3} = C$$

Because the several components have, in effect, been reduced to two (by adding most of them together) the overall result has been altered by a relatively small change in the weight of one of the components. Clearly, different ways of weighting have quite different consequences.

The only reason for deciding to introduce weighting is that some particular component (like the final exam in the examples above) is thought to be more important than the others (twice as important in that last example).

Now your course may progress in such a way that each assignment builds on or subsumes skills and knowledge that were tested in earlier assignments. If this is the case, you may decide to give much less weight to early assessment exercises than to later ones. If the course is one where the aim is to make the student capable of practising objective C, to what extent are you justified in counting his earlier performances on objectives A and B? There is some justification if they are worthwhile in their own right, especially if they are not tested subsequently. But what if they were learned only so that they could be put together in performing objective C and are therefore, in effect, assessed at the same time as C anyway? You could easily thus find yourself giving extra weight to the least important objectives! Even to give such early, preparatory assignments *equal* weight with the later ones would be to allow students to get quite high marks out of relatively trivial work. Yet to give them no weight at all might encourage students to skimp them and so suffer, later on, from inadequate preparation. One solution, of course, is to make the early assignments critical—so that students are not allowed to continue with the course unless they reach a certain standard (provided students really are incapable if they have not reached that standard)—but not to count them.

Another problem with weights is that they can creep into our calculations without our having decided to weight at all. This can happen if the two or more sets of grades being conflated are very different in their averages or in their variability (spread). The result can be that students are ranked unfairly. Let us see how this happens.

Suppose students sit two examination papers in chemistry and their performances on the two papers are to be given equal weight in reporting their overall performance in chemistry. That is to say, a student's overall score should be no more like his score on paper I than like his score on paper II. It is generally assumed that if both papers are marked out of the same total, say 100 per cent, then papers are weighted equally. Thus, to treble the weight of one paper compared with the other you might expect to mark it out of 300, instead of 100. However, the papers may turn out to have different weights, to exert different amounts of influence on the student's scores, even if they are both marked out of the same total. What is significant is not the total possible, nor even the average score on each paper, but how much spread there is among the scores. The paper on which scores are more spread out will exert the greater weight.

As a simple but dramatic example, suppose four students only (A, B, C, and D) take two papers meant to have equal weight. Here are their scores and ranks on each paper:

| Student | | A | B | C | D | |
| --- | --- | --- | --- | --- | --- | --- |
| Paper I | Score | 10 | 21 | 38 | 50 | (out of 100) |
| | Rank | 4 | 3 | 2 | 1 | |
| Paper II | Score | 100 | 95 | 85 | 80 | (out of 100) |
| | Rank | 1 | 2 | 3 | 4 | |

How might we report each one's overall performance? The 'obvious' method—adding his two scores—give the following totals and rank positions.

| Student | A | B | C | D | |
| --- | --- | --- | --- | --- | --- |
| Total Score | 110 | 116 | 123 | 130 | (out of 200) |
| Rank | 4 | 3 | 2 | 1 | |

Notice, however, that the overall ranking of the students is exactly the same as on paper I, and the reverse of that on paper II. In other words, far from having equal weight, paper II has had no effect at all on the students' relative positions (although it had pulled the percentage scores closer together). This has happened because the spread of scores on paper I is twice that on paper II— the ranges are 40 marks and 20 marks. Consequently, as far as overall ranking is concerned, a student would have done himself most good by scoring high in the paper with least spread of marks (or least harm by scoring low in the paper with least spread).

Various means are suggested for 'correcting' the situation by 'scaling' the marks (e.g., see Forrest, 1974, Lacey, 1960; Thyne, 1974, page 131). Essentially, the trick is to 'stretch' the least scattered distribution so that its range of scores (or, for greater rigour, its standard deviation) matches that of the other. When several distributions are being combined, they may all be mapped onto a common scale of say 0–100. Many teachers will have used the 'nomogram' method for scaling, based on the idea of similar triangles as shown in Fig. 5.3.

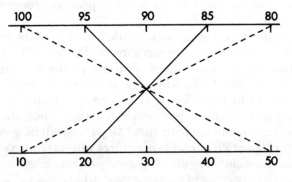

**Fig. 5.3** Nomogram for scaling marks

The maxima on the two scales are connected by two straight lines, as are the minima. A line drawn through the point of intersection from a score on one scale will lead to the corresponding score on the other scale. Thus, if we make scores of 100 and 80 on paper II equivalent to 50 and 10 on paper I, we find that paper II scores of 95 and 85 scale out to 40 and 20 when 'stretched', though the rank-position of those scores is not affected. In fact the nomogram, though quick, is also crude in that it is based entirely on two extreme scores rather than on the scatter near the centre of a distribution, around the mean, where most of the scores are likely to lie. Rigorous scaling is done by standardizing all marks to a common mean and standard deviation. The Appendix to this chapter presents a simple graphical method of accomplishing this.

Having been scaled, the two sets of scores now have comparable spread and can be added in the knowledge that both papers carry equal weight. When we do so, we find the ranking quite transformed:

| Student | A | B | C | D |
|---|---|---|---|---|
| Paper I score | 10 | 21 | 38 | 50 |
| Scaled paper II score | 50 | 40 | 20 | 10 |
| Total | 60 | 61 | 58 | 60 |
| Rank | $2\frac{1}{2}=$ | 1 | 4 | $2\frac{1}{2}=$ |

**233**

The student previously in third place has now come out on top; the student previously second is now fourth; and the two students who each came out best on one of the papers are now sharing the middle rank.

Of course, those figures were loaded to emphasize my point. Nevertheless, whenever there is some difference in spread, and some students are not ranked similarly in the two (or more) distributions, then there will be a tendency for *some* students' rank-positions to be different according to whether or not the scores are scaled before being added together. Thus, the teacher who confidently tells students that 'All papers will be given equal weight' or 'Question one will carry three times as much weight as any other question' may unintentionally be breaking his promise. Marking all papers out of the same total to obtain equal weight, or marking one of the questions out of three times the usual total to obtain three-fold weight, does not in itself guarantee that the required weighting will result. For that to happen, the spread of scores must be the same in each set of marks.

So, in conflating sets of scores, it is advisable to scale or standardize them first. (For technical reasons, to which I do not have space to do justice here, but which are explained in Rowntree, 1977, pages 224–227, this advice can be ignored if you are certain that you and your colleagues are all using criterion-referenced grading.) Otherwise, injustices may creep into the results owing to the presence of arbitrary and unremarked weightings.

### PROFILES—AN ALTERNATIVE TO CONFLATION

Sooner or later the teacher usually has to report his assessments of the student. Perhaps this report goes merely to the student; but more likely it will go also to other teachers or to potential employers. What is the best form for such a report? Some would suggest a conflated grade of the kind I have just been talking about. Or, what amounts to much the same thing, a label such as '2nd class' or 'distinction'. In this final section of the chapter I want to cast doubt on whether the 'all-talking, all-singing, all-dancing, unidimensional grade' (or label) really is a very enlightening outcome of the conflation process.

Assessment results are reported so that someone—students, other teachers, employers—can learn something from them or use them to make decisions. Such decisions often cannot be rationally made on the basis of conflated grades and labels. Thus, a '40 per cent' may warn the student that he needs to improve, but it does not suggest where or how. Similarly, a student may take a Spanish examination consisting of reading, writing, speaking, and responding to native speakers, and he is awarded a criterion-referenced 75 per cent; but has he failed on one of the four aspects and done as well as expected on the other three, or is he about three-quarters proficient in all four, or what?

Again, a student's overall grade may express his combined performance in areas W, X, Y, and Z; but if one employer values W- and Z-type skills while another X- and Y-type skills, neither can place much confidence in the overall grade as a recommendation, especially if the skills he values are not 'critical elements' in achieving a good grade. Consequently, many teachers in recent years have begun playing down conflation, preferring instead to present the decision-maker with separate assessments on the various components, leaving him to weight them according to their importance to him. Such a reporting response is usually called a *profile*.

The crudest form of profile is obtained by quoting the student's scores or ranks on all component dimensions instead of averaging them out into an overall grade. Thus American students will emerge from college clutching a 'transcript', which defines their degree by listing the titles of courses they have taken and the grade obtained in each. For example:

Mervyn Mynde          Class of '81
Degree of Master of Arts (Education)

| | | |
|---|---|---|
| ES608 | Educational concepts and research | A |
| ES611 | Epistemology and education | A |
| ES612 | Moral and social education | B |
| P641 | Ethics and political philosophy | A |
| P653 | Philosophy of science | C |
| P654 | Philosophy of social science | B |
| P672 | Phenomenology and existentialism | C |

Open University students get something similar, except that the results may also be translated for the reader into a degree classification.

A profile could also be issued instead of (or as well as) calculating the student an overall grade in an individual course, for example:

| Physics | Seroja Shah |
|---|---|
| Heat: | 75% |
| Light: | 40% |
| Sound: | 79% |
| Electricity: | 86% |
| Mechanics: | 50% |

Within a course, a profile could be used to show how the student performed on various assessment methods:

| Laboratory work: | 40% |
|---|---|
| Personal project: | 89% |
| Homework: | 70% |
| Final examination: | 57% |

How one interprets such a set of scores (e.g., is 50 per cent for mechanics better than 40 per cent for light?) depends on whether one knows them to have been standardized or not.

Being based on grades or ranks, the profiles we have looked at so far have been rather uncommunicative about what the student can actually *do*. Profiles can, however, be used to spell out more specific talents and abilities observed in the student. The honours graduate of Birmingham School of Architecture (see Hinton, 1973) is given not a classified degree but a profile which takes the form of a sheet with various qualities listed and ticks against those on which he has shown 'special interest' or 'above-average ability'. The sheet might thus indicate, for example, that a particular graduate was good but not outstanding in width of knowledge, reasoning skill, and aptitude for research; showed a subject bias towards technology and social sciences; displayed outstanding practicality in problem-solving (but no special originality or sensitivity); worked best as leader of a team (rather than as a team member or as an individual); was outstanding on drive and determination (but not on concentration or precision); and communicated particularly well orally and visually (but not in writing). Narrative comment could be added on any of these aspects by staff who knew the student's work.

Clearly, the dimensions of a student's work can be laid bare in great detail in a profile. In his profile for a given course, for example, we could indicate the student's performance on all major objectives. Hence a profile for the educational philosophy student mentioned earlier might contain, in addition to his separate course performances, an appraisal of his prowess in such general 'philosophical' process-abilities as these (borrowed from Klug, 1974):

1. Ability to discriminate between essentials and inessentials, to spot the key issue in a complex situation.
2. Ability to see structural similarities in arguments, transfer ideas from familiar to unfamiliar situations.
3. Ability to make critical appraisal and analysis of the arguments of others, to review and comment on the usefulness of particular proposals.
4. Ability, when faced with a problem, to develop one's own solution, to synthesize systematically and constructively.
5. Ability to put across complex ideas in a coherent and understandable way, to explain, communicate, illuminate.

Whatever the span it encompasses, a profile and especially one that includes some narrative analysis, helps humanize the reporting response. Even the simplest of profiles differentiates the student from other students who share the same total but 'add up differently' from him. Thereby, the recipient of the report is being put into a new and more human relationship with the assessors and the assessed. He is no longer encouraged to view the assessors as expert technocrats who will answer the question 'What's this student worth to everybody?'. Rather he is being given a relativistic 'It all depends' answer, one that throws him back on his own criteria. He now knows something of what the assessors know about the many aspects of their student. What does it all add up to for *him*?

But perhaps profile-reporting is still too novel for many of our institutions to embrace. For some years yet we are likely to be reporting conflated assessment data in the form of grades, labels, and classified degrees. In reporting for the benefit of people outside our institutions, we might do well to act upon the suggestions of Sussex University's Working Party on BA Degree Assessment:

> ... prospective employers should be warned ... that the usefulness of the result is limited. First, because the predictive value of a particular class of degree cannot be guaranteed; second, because the actual measurement is extremely rough; third, because the classified degree may be measuring qualities which are not necessarily relevant to the purposes an employer may have in mind. (Sussex, 1969)

## Appendix: Standardizing grades

As we have seen in Chapter 5, combining grades from different sets that differ much in their spread can result in unwanted weightings. To avoid this, the grades in each set can be scaled or standardized. That is, the grades are 'stretched' (up or down) so that each set has the same spread (and average). In fact, the two (or more) sets are given the same *arithmetic mean* and the same *standard deviation*.

The arithmetic mean is what we normally think of as 'the average'. That is, we add together the grade for each student on a given component and divide by the number of students. Thus, if we had just five students whose grades were 30, 33, 37, 38, 42:

$$\text{Mean} = \frac{30+33+37+38+42}{5} = \frac{180}{5} = 36$$

And in mathematical symbols the general formula is:

$$\bar{X} = \frac{\Sigma X}{N}$$

Where $X$ = any grade; $\Sigma X$ = sum of all the $X$s; and $N$ = the number of $X$s (grades, students) and $\bar{X}$ represents the arithmetic mean.

Calculating the standard deviation of a set of grades is rather more complicated. What the standard deviation tries to do is indicate the average amount by which the grades in the set deviate from the mean of the set. The formula here is:

$$\text{SD} = \frac{\Sigma(X-\bar{X})^2}{N}$$

Translated into ordinary language this means: once you have calculated the mean of the set: ($\bar{X}$), subtract it from each of the grades in the set: ($X - \bar{X}$). (This gives you a set of differences or deviations—some positive, some negative.) You are going to have to add them up before calculating the average deviation; but, if you add them as they are, the positives will cancel the negatives and you will end up with zero. So, first, square the deviations, which will make all the negative deviations positive: $(X - \bar{X})^2$. Then add up all the squared deviations: $\Sigma(X - \bar{X})^2$. Then, to find the average of the squared deviations, divide by the number of grades (and therefore of deviations) in the set:

$$\frac{\Sigma(X-\bar{X})^2}{N}$$

But, since you squared earlier, you must now take the square root to get back to figures of the proper magnitude:

$$\sqrt{\frac{\Sigma(X-\bar{X})^2}{N}}$$

We can apply this to our set of five grades for which we have already found the mean = 36:

| $X$ | $X-\bar{X}$ | $(X-\bar{X})^2$ |
|---|---|---|
| 30 | $30-36=-6$ | 36 |
| 33 | $33-36=-3$ | 9 |
| 37 | $37-36=+1$ | 1 |
| 38 | $38-36=+2$ | 4 |
| 42 | $42-36=+6$ | 36 |
| | | $\overline{86}=\Sigma(X-\bar{X})^2$ |

$$SD = \sqrt{\frac{\Sigma(X-\bar{X})^2}{N}}$$
$$= \sqrt{\frac{86}{5}}$$
$$= \sqrt{\frac{17.2}{4.15}}$$

So this set of grades has a mean of 36 marks and a standard deviation of 4.15 marks.

Normally we would not work out $\bar{X}$ and SD for such a small group of grades. Usually we would have, perhaps, $N=30$ or thereabouts. With such numbers, the calculation can become rather tedious. Fortunately, there are short-cuts which give reasonably accurate results. One method, quoted by Paul Diederich (1969) is as follows:

$$SD = \frac{\text{sum of } top\ sixth \text{ of grades} - \text{sum of } bottom\ sixth \text{ of grades}}{\text{half of number of students, i.e., } \dfrac{N}{2}}$$

Thus, if you have 30 students you add up the top five scores, subtract the sum of the bottom five scores and divide by 15. If your $N$ is not an exact multiple of 6, then slightly more work is needed (but not as much as in using the squared deviations formula). If you had say 27 students, one sixth would be $\frac{27}{6} = 4\frac{1}{2}$ scores. Thus, you would add the top four scores plus *half* of the fifth. Similarly with the four bottom scores and half of the fifth from bottom.

Now that you know all you need to know about calculating means and standard deviations(!), let us see how they are applied in scaling two sets of grades to a common $\bar{X}$ and SD. A group of students (again, far smaller than we would normally do this calculation for) get the following marks (out of 30) on continuous assessment (CA) and exam:

| Student | CA | Exam | Total |
|---------|-----|------|-------|
| P | 22 | 21 | 43 |
| Q | 23 | 16 | 39 |
| R | 25 | 9 | 34 |
| S | 27 | 5 | 32 |
| T | 29 | 2 | 31 |

If these results were conflated as they stand, the rank order of the students (as you can see) would be determined by their ranking on the examination. And, in fact, their overall ranking would be the reverse of their ranking on continuous assessment. This is because the spread of the exam marks is greater than that of the continuous assessment marks.

In fact, the means and standard deviations of the grades on the two components are as follows:

| | Mean | SD |
|------|------|------|
| CA: | 25.2 | 2.56 |
| Exam: | 10.06 | 7.00 |

There is more than one way of scaling the two sets of grades to a common mean and standard deviation. The one we shall use is a graphical method explained by MacIntosh and Hale (1976, page 106).

Suppose we decide to stretch the continuous assessment grades so that they are scaled to the same $\bar{X}$ and SD as the exam marks. (We could, of course, do it the other way round. Or we could alter both sets of scores so as to give both of them another common mean and standard deviation. A scale with $\bar{X} = 50$ and $SD = 15$ is commonly chosen.) So a set of marks with $\bar{X} = 25.2$ and $SD = 2.56$

**240**

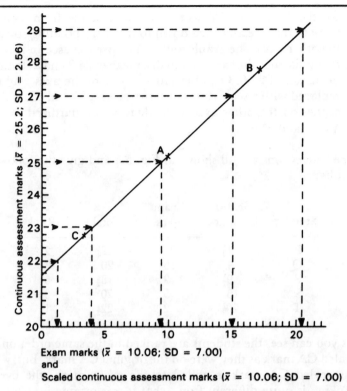

**Fig. 5.4** This graphical method is based on MacIntosh and Hale, 1976, page 106

is to be standardized so as to have $\bar{X} = 10.06$ and $SD = 7.00$. Here is how we do it (as illustrated in the graph in Fig. 5.4):

1. Use one axis of the graph for exam marks and the other for continuous assessment. (Include the mean and standard deviation in your labelling.)
2. Plot three points, A, B, and C as follows:
   A—opposite the exam mean (10.06) and the CA mean (25.2).
   B—opposite the exam mean plus one standard deviation $(10.06 + 7.00 = 17.06)$ and the CA mean plus one standard deviation $(25.2 + 2.56 = 27.76)$.
   C—opposite the exam mean minus one standard deviation $(10.06 - 7.00 = 3.06)$ and the CA mean minus one standard deviation $(25.2 - 2.56 = 22.64)$.
3. Join the points with a straight line.

4. Read off the scaled CA scores by reading across from each CA score to the line and then down to the corresponding score on the other axis. The graph could, of course, be used in reverse: to standardize the exam scores to a mean of 25.2 and a standard deviation of 2.56. Or, alternatively, one of the axes could be replaced with a scale running between, say, 35 and 65, and the grades on the other axis could then be standardized to, say, $\bar{X} = 50$ and $SD = 15$.

The conversions are all shown in Fig. 5.4 and give the following results:

| Student | Scaled CA mark | Exam mark | Total | Rank |
|---------|------------|------|-------|------|
| P | $1\frac{1}{4}$ | 21 | $22\frac{1}{4}$ | 2 |
| Q | 4 | 16 | 20 | 3= |
| R | $9\frac{1}{2}$ | 9 | $18\frac{1}{2}$ | 5 |
| S | 15 | 5 | 20 | 3= |
| T | $20\frac{1}{2}$ | 2 | $22\frac{1}{2}$ | 1 |

As you can see, the students are ranked in the same order on the scaled CA mark as they were on the original CA mark. But, when the scaled CA mark is added to the exam mark, the overall ranking is quite different from what it was originally. (But it is the same as would have been achieved by scaling the exam marks to the same mean and standard deviation as the CA mark; or by scaling both to a different mean and standard deviation.)

# 6. Evaluating your course

For many teachers, especially in North America, 'evaluation' is simply the word they would normally use for 'student assessment'. For others, especially in the UK, it implies something wider. As I use the term, in talking of evaluating courses, it refers to any means by which we observe and appraise *the context, the effects, and the effectiveness* of the teaching and learning we have set in motion.

Notice that I have distinguished between 'effects' and 'effectiveness'. For me, 'effectiveness' implies concern with the extent to which the course has been successful in achieving certain *pre-specified* ends. This will usually be an important concern in evaluation. But it is not the only one; we can also be concerned with course 'effects' or outcomes that were not anticipated (and may not even have been desirable). If the evaluation is to be worthwhile, we cannot afford to overlook the unexpected. For example, the evaluation of a course, during which all students had improved satisfactorily in relation to the objectives, could hardly be much use if the evaluator were unaware that the students were complaining of being overworked and were warning all their friends against taking the course! As a more positive, but equally thought-provoking example, while the students may appear quite happy, they may be happily pursuing, and attaining, objectives quite different from those expected by the course developers. (I am here recalling an in-service course for nurses on how to *understand* research, which several of the students seemed determined to use as a course on how to *do* research.)

## Why evaluate?

The mention of 'worthwhile', 'much use', and 'thought-provoking' raises the question of what evaluation is *for*. What is the point of doing it? (There are other questions naturally. When should it be done? Who should do it? What should be evaluated? How should it be done?) But, for the moment, let us consider the purpose of evaluation.

In practice, teachers and others carry out evaluation for a variety of reasons. Sometimes their main purpose is to be able to prove that they *have* done it—lest it be done 'on their behalf' (possibly to their disadvantage) by someone else. However, apart from such political aspects, the main purpose of course evaluation

**243**

is to understand the course so as to be able to *make informed decisions* about it. For the teacher, the chief such decision may be how to sustain, develop and improve the course, and perhaps his own expertise as a teacher.

People other than the teachers, administrators and students, for instance, may also use evaluation in making decisions. Even before the course is put on, administrators will be asking whether there is a sufficient demand for the course, what its 'competitors' are, and whether the costs of putting it on will be justified, and so on. Such 'market research' and budgeting questions are, in essence, evaluative. Once the course is running, administrators will have further questions. Is it attracting students as expected? Are they 'surviving'? Do they attain a standard adequate to satisfy subsequent teachers or employers? Are the costs in line with the budget? Students, too, will be interested in survival-rates, not to mention workload, and other costs (financial or otherwise) that might be involved in taking that particular course.

I mention such questions here simply to remind us that the teacher is not the only one wishing to make decisions related to the course. Hence, he is not the only one with an interest in evaluation. However, different parties may have rather different interests—because the decisions they wish to make are different and require different evaluative questions to be asked. Therefore, an evaluation strategy planned by one of the interested parties cannot necessarily be relied upon to give the others just what information they need.

Since this book is aimed at teachers, from now on I shall discuss evaluation from the teacher's viewpoint. That is to say, I shall emphasize its contribution to understanding a course with a view to sustaining and improving it. To begin with, what aspects of the course should be evaluated? We might be interested in appraising, for instance:

● The planning process by which the course was produced.
● The proposed aims, objectives, and content of the course.
● The proposed teaching strategy.
● The materials and facilities that might be used by students.
● The institutional setting within which students will be experiencing our course.

## Preliminary evaluation

All of these aspects might be evaluated before the students ever begin studying the course. We might call them, collectively with other such aspects, the 'context' of the course. Evaluations of such contextual aspects should provide data to help sustain and improve the course. Such *a priori* or preliminary evaluation usually involves *critical commenting* by people whose views we know we can respect, e.g., certain subject-experts, teachers, students, and others.

It may seem odd to select the first aspect mentioned above—the course planning process itself—for critical commenting. However, if one is planning alone, it should be obvious that one can easily get obsessive about certain topics, and budget far too much time for them, while leaving critical gaps in the syllabus elsewhere. Here, a 'critical friend' commenting on our proposals as we develop them can help us reconsider our priorities. Even more so, in a course-team situation, such a 'critical friend'—one who is with the group yet not of it—can gently draw its attention to the stresses and contradictions among its interests that are not being acknowledged. Thus, one group or individual within a team may be merrily masterminding other people's contributions on the assumption that they have all acquiesced when actually they have simply given up protesting and are seething with suppressed rage and frustration. Only the 'critical friend', with no personal stake in the course to be lost, can dare to confront colleagues with the tensions he sees among the way they feel about one another, and quietly insist that they discuss the implications. This role of 'critical friend' is one that educational technologists or educational development staff often fill.

If one is planning a course as a member of a team, the proposed aims, objectives, and content may well have been arrived at as a result of considerable (evaluative) debate. However, it can sometimes happen that members of a team pay more attention to preserving their own patches of course territory than to probing too seriously at those of their team-mates: 'You let me do what I want to do in my section and I'll let you do what you want to do in yours'. Hence it can be valuable (and perhaps even more so if one is planning alone) to have an outside 'expert' look over one's plans. Some courses, especially inter- or multidisciplinary courses, might need several such experts.

## *Academic credibility*

Such an evaluator would need to be an expert in the *subject-matter*. He (or she) would be advising on the academic worthwhileness, relevance, up-to-dateness, accuracy, etc., of what you propose. He might also be a teacher and therefore able to comment on the likely teaching effectiveness. But that would be a bonus. Your subject-matter expert might be a researcher or a lawyer or a business executive, for example, depending on the nature of your subject-matter. Potential students (if you can identify them) might be consulted also. Does the course, as proposed, sound attractive; if not, why not? What can they do to help improve on what is proposed? (See pages 38–39.)

You may provide external subject-matters expert with a simple checklist on which to base their comments. The points you would like them to consider will vary from one course to another (and even from section to section within a course) but might *include* something like the following:

● Are the aims and objectives sufficiently explicit?
● Do the aims seem relevant to the needs of the target students?
● Do the objectives support the aims?
● Are there any additional aims and objectives we should include?
● Is the content up-to-date?
● Is it accurate?
● Are there any important omissions?
● Do there seem to be any faults of emphasis?

Your subject-expert should be able to offer some opinion on such matters, given your lists of aims and objectives and your description of target students and your content outline and/or concept diagrams. Ideally, the expert would be able to meet with the team to discuss and refine his suggestions—or at least clarify problematical areas in discussion with a single member, if necessary by telephone. If, of course, you are planning to use pre-prepared learning materials in your course, then your expert would be able to evaluate them too for their subject-matter acceptability. For example, you could ask him if the material fulfils the following demands:

● Factually accurate?
● Up-to-date?
● Adequately supported by evidence?

- Careful to avoid oversimplification or overgeneralization?
- True to the nature of the subject/discipline etc.?
- Balanced, and at pains to present opposing points of view where appropriate?

If you are planning to use existing materials (e.g., textbooks, films, or audio-tapes) as a crucial part of your course, these might well be made available to your expert at the time you first contact him. This contact, however, is likely to be made some time before you have produced any learning materials that you plan to develop yourself. (Naturally, you will be loath to invest too much time in developing your own materials without having had some comments on the general plan.) Thus, if you do later go ahead to produce learning materials of your own, you may wish to return to your external subject-matter expert for his further comments on the course content as then made manifest.

## CONTENT ANALYSIS

As I have already suggested, the evaluation of what I have called 'academic credibility' and 'likely educational effectiveness' are two different tasks. Some advisors may be able to perform both. Where this is possible, it may be particularly valuable. But there is no reason why you should not look to different evaluators for subject-matter and for educational appraisals. I will return in a moment to the appraisal of 'likely educational effectiveness'. First, let us consider the possible need for what is often called *content analysis* (Berelson, 1952; Carney, 1972).

In origin, content analysis is a quantitative approach, defined by Berelson (1952) as 'a research technique for the objective, systematic and quantitative description of the manifest content of communication'. The 'communication' involved may be spoken or written, nonverbal or pictorial. In fact, the technique has been used chiefly in the detection of political bias in textual material. It has been little used in educational situations, except perhaps in the analysis of sexism or racism in textbooks and the like. However, the term content analysis is often used more generally to cover qualitative approaches (more akin to literary criticism or linguistic analysis) to the evaluation of the sub-stantive content and rhetorical structure of a piece of communication.

In applying such an approach to texts in, say, the social sciences, one may discover, for example, that an author seems bent on persuading students towards some predestined conclusion. In consequence, he may be found to indulge (consciously or otherwise) in such devices as: ignoring contrary evidence or travestying (so as to deride) the counter-arguments of opponents; using slack and evasive phrases like 'in most cases', 'many experts believe', and 'can be interpreted as' in such a way as to imply more than is actually stated; arguing . from analogies that are emotively attractive enough to mask their logical weakness; covertly but crucially re-defining key terms as the argument unfolds so as to suit the conclusion desired; and so on. I am not, of course, saying that such regrettable practices are peculiar to writers in the social sciences. That just happens to be the area with which I am most familiar and where I and others have found no paucity of examples, not least in my own corner of it—education. Indeed, it would be foolish to pretend that my own writing has always been free of the canker, and it is certainly an aspect for which one should scrutinize one's early drafts as rigorously and routinely as one assesses their accuracy and readability.

What is at issue in evaluating the quality of an academic argument—whether presented in print or in a lecture—is not whether the author's conclusions are right or wrong. Maybe he is right; but if he is presenting a one-sided view of a problem, without recognition of alternative views (except perhaps to parody them), or even with deliberate attempts to distract attention from alternative views, then we may say his teaching style is definitely wrong, and bad for students. They are all too likely to assimilate the message that such practices constitute acceptable scholarship.

Unfortunately, even when students appear unaware of an author's rhetorical deviousness, they may be equally unaware that they are being denied a discussion of alternative schemes of explanation. As my colleague Michael Macdonald-Ross (1979) has remarked:

> . . . the evidence we have collected shows that most students are not aware of bias in their social science courses, nor are they aware of the full range of views that might be brought to bear on a particular subject. For example, the first unit of our foundation course in Social Science (D101) is on *unemployment*. This unit treats the issue entirely from the point of view of Keynesian economics without indicating at any place that quite different kinds of analysis are possible and, indeed, widely discussed today. When asked 'Did you detect any bias in this unit? If so, of what kind?', only *one* out of 128 respondents

managed to identify the Keynesian slant. The bias is, incidentally, not repaired later in the course.

## THE ANALYSIS OF TEXT—AN EXAMPLE

The kind of content analysis that uncovers such bias and/or rhetorical sleight-of-mind is a somewhat neglected area of evaluation. In consequence, much 'educational effectiveness testing' concerns itself, at some expense, with material whose

---

1. I may claim that the contents of the preceding chapters
2. are natural science. . . . Now, however, we leave the record
3. of facts elicited by observations and experiments on
4. the aggressive behaviour of animals and turn to the
5. question of whether they can teach us something
6. applicable to man and useful in circumventing the
7. dangers arising from his aggressive drives.

8. There are people who see in this question an insult to
9. human dignity. All too willingly man sees himself as
10. the centre of the universe, as something not belonging
11. to the rest of nature but standing apart as a different
12. and higher being. Many people cling to this error and
13. remain deaf to the wisest command ever given by a sage,
14. the famous 'know thyself' inscribed in the temple of
15. Delphi. What keeps people from listening to it? . . .

16. I think I know a simple method of reconciling people
17. to the fact that they are part of nature and have
18. themselves originated by natural evolution . . . : one need
19. only show them the beauty and greatness of the universe,
20. and the awe-inspiring laws that govern it. Surely
21. nobody who knows enough about the phylogenetic evolution
22. of organisms can feel any inner resistance to the
23. knowledge that he himself owes his existence to the
24. greatest of all natural phenomena . . .

25. Anyone who understands this cannot possibly be repelled
26. by Darwin's recognition of the fact that we have a
27. common origin with animals, nor by Freud's realization
28. that we are still driven by the same instincts as our
29. prehuman ancestors.

---

**Fig. 6.1** On the virtue of scientific humility. Line numbers added for easy reference. (From *On Aggression* by Konrad Lorenz, Methuen University Paperbacks, 1967)

intellectual probity has been rather naively taken for granted. Since most of the remainder of this chapter is concerned with such testing, I think it is worth pausing here to give you the flavour of content analysis with an extended example from the work of my colleague Oswald Hanfling (1978). This example seems particularly apposite because it is drawn from a publication in which he is introducing *students* to the analysis of argument—a venture that is itself much a part of the 'learning to use the media' that I advocate in Chapters 4 and 5.

Oswald Hanfling is asking students to look with him at just four paragraphs (see Fig. 6.1) from the book *On Aggression* by the ethologist Konrad Lorenz (1967), a book that might easily be required reading in a college course. He suggests students should look out for various ploys which he has already discussed and has labelled:

> Question-begging words
> You-can't-win wording
> Persuader words
> Crafty conflation
> You-won't-believe-this challenge

The central argument of *On Aggression* is that studies of animal behaviour can improve our understanding of human behaviour, especially where aggression is concerned. In the first 11 chapters, Lorenz describes aggressive and other behaviour in animals. In the twelfth chapter, from which the passage in Fig. 6.1 is taken, the argument turns to the human condition. Having examined the passage themselves, students can compare their analysis with Oswald Hanfling's which (in rather abbreviated form) follows below:

> . . . question-beggers: 'The fact that . . .' in line 17 is a pretty straightforward case—though you might wonder whether just *one* fact is at issue in that sentence. In line 23 the author describes as 'knowledge' the statement that he wants us to believe. 'Darwin's recognition of the fact that . . .', and 'Freud's realization that . . .' (lines 26–27) both imply, in a question-begging way, that what Darwin and Freud said is true. (In Darwin's case, admittedly, it might be argued that his theory is so well established that one may speak of it as 'recognition'. The same could hardly be claimed for Freud, however.)
> The fifth kind of question-begger is in line 12. . . . It is the word 'error'. If I propose to discuss why some people 'cling to an error',

then I take it as established that their view is *false* (just as in referring to my own view as 'knowledge' or 'fact', I take for granted that my view is *true*).

You-can't-win wordings are to be found in lines 21 and 25: 'Nobody who knows enough . . .'; 'Anyone who understands . . .'. If you will not accept what is said there, that shows that you don't know enough, that you don't understand. Perhaps . . . also . . . lines 19–20, with their implication that anyone who doesn't agree can't have seen the beauty and greatness of the universe.

The persuader-words occur in lines 20 and 25 . . . 'surely' and 'cannot possibly'.

Now for the crafty conflations (cc). They occur in lines 10–11, 12–13 and 17–18. . . . In lines 10–11 three (at least) different notions about man are run together: that he is 'the centre of the universe', that he is 'different' and that he is 'higher'. . . . Now I for one would want to say that man is, in certain ways, 'different'. . . . Many readers, I imagine, would want to say both that man is 'different' and that he is 'higher', but not that he is 'the centre of the universe'. All these descriptions, to be sure, are vague and need going into; but even so, it seems clear that *different* ideas are here conflated. The reader is being offered a package-deal of goods of mixed quality; he should be allowed to choose for himself.

The next crafty conflation turns on the word 'and' in line 12 . . . 'this error' is being conflated with 'remaining deaf' etc. According to what it says here, thinking that man is 'a different and higher being' ('clinging to this error') comes to much the same as refusing to heed the inscription at Delphi. Now again we may ask exactly what that inscription is supposed to mean. But it would be very odd to take its meaning to be, more or less, equivalent to the views of Lorenz (not to mention those of Darwin and Freud!).

About lines 17–18 I questioned whether just *one* fact was at issue there. 'They [human beings] are part of nature' and 'they . . . have . . . originated by natural evolution'—the author runs these together as 'the fact'. Most people nowadays would accept, I think, that human beings have developed by natural evolution . . . however, it is clear that the author intends ['part of nature'] to mean something rather *un*acceptable to most people . . . that man is not 'a different and higher being' compared to the rest of the animals (lines 11–12). . . .

For examples of the you-won't-believe-this [y-w-b-t] challenge we might mention first the heading of the whole passage and the sentence 'There . . .' (lines 8–9). The heading challenges us to be humble enough to accept what follows; and this is coupled with a 'science-has-shown' approach. . . . We ought not to stick out against it, even if (lines 8–9) we see in it 'an insult to human dignity', because this would be going, apparently, against [scientific

**251**

findings]. But . . . the y-w-b-t challenge really runs through the whole passage. 'All too willingly', 'cling to this error', . . . 're- conciling people to the fact', 'inner resistance', 'don't be repelled'— all these phrases are typical of the y-w-b-t practitioner; all of them *challenge* the reader to believe something rather than giving him good grounds for believing it.

Such micro-evaluation—probing the intellectual coherence of a piece of teaching—could be applied not merely to texts but also to lectures, discussions, tutorials, and other media involving the processes of human interaction. However, we may feel that we do not have the time to apply it even to the texts used by our students. Though if we wonder also whether we have the requisite skills, there is a wealth of literature (e.g., Stebbing, 1948; Thouless, 1970; Wilson, 1974) replete with examples from which we and, more crucially perhaps, *our students* might learn.

Where we have produced our own texts, we should certainly find the time to examine their rhetoric with a stern eye and/or get critical friends to do it for us. Most of us would prefer to have early drafts of our material gnawed at in private by critics who are basically friendly rather than risk sending it out unmodified to be savaged by whatever wolves prowl beyond out doors! Internal criticism can be painful but productive; external criticism can be death-dealing.

### Likely effectiveness

Now, what about the likely educational effectiveness of the course you are proposing? Here we shall be looking. for example, at the intended teaching strategy and at the facilities available and (again, but from a different viewpoint) at any materials that are involved. Again, we can call on experts for opinions. We can seek reactions from people teaching with similar aims and objectives or content elsewhere. If we are intending to experiment with new kinds of teaching methods (e.g., Keller Plan or simulation games or project work) we may go to someone with experience of such methods (even if not in precisely our subject). Discussion with such people can often alert us to potential problems (or potential developments) that we have overlooked. For instance, if our students are from a department that is unsympathetic or even hostile to the approach we propose, we may find that we have some confusions and anxieties to cope with.

Where our course is being validated by some external body

(e.g., the CNAA in the UK) it will probably impose such an evaluation on us anyway. But if we are wise, we will have anticipated its evaluation questions. Is there enough space in the laboratories? Is the necessary equipment available? Is the number and arrangement of available rooms conducive to the small-group exercises proposed? Are the library facilities adequate? Is the postal service capable of delivering learning materials to 'distance students' regularly and on time? If a course is being planned to cater for 2000 students a year for five years (as happens in the Open University), can we be sure that the publishers will be keeping in print the textbooks we wish to use as required reading? (However good a text may be, students will not learn from it if it is not available to them.)

Many and various are the questions. You and your colleagues (perhaps with a critical friend from outside the team) will need to think up your own. And, as so often in course planning, such questions cannot all be disposed of by the time students start work on the course; if we are alert (and evaluating) they will continue to assert themselves (though less massively, we hope) throughout the life of the course.

Evaluating the likely effectiveness of learning materials (as opposed to general teaching strategies and facilities) is a more complex matter. In the end, the proof of the pudding is in the eating—or in whether it stays down (and nourishes) once the students have eaten it. But our evaluation can go some way towards this happy digestive consummation.

To begin with we can read (or view or listen to) materials ourselves. And we can speculate, on the basis of our experience of how students responded to such materials in the past, as to how our *intended* students will respond in the future. This we will do, for instance, in making a choice among textbooks. Also, if we are producing our own learning materials (texts, tapes, films, etc.), each member of the team can evaluate his colleagues' productions. And, of course, outside experts (teachers of the subject-matter concerned) can also be consulted. Again, some form of checklist may be valuable in this evaluation. (See Eraut *et al.*, 1975*b*, for a useful review of such checklists.) Here, as an example, is one I devised for use with self-instructional texts (Rowntree, 1979*c*) but similar questions could be asked of films, audio-tapes, conventional textbooks, and so on.

*Educational effectiveness checklist*

1. Does the structure of the lesson seem sensible and coherent, with introductions or previews, and summaries or reviews used where appropriate, and means available for allowing students with different needs to use the lesson in different ways?

2. Are adequate steps taken to motivate the students and make clear to them what they are to do with the material and to get out of it?

3. Is the lesson pitched at the right level of difficulty—challenging without being inaccessible—and matched to assumed prerequisite skills and understandings of students?

4. Is the tone that of a rigorous, but friendly, tutor, lively and interesting, light of touch, and with humour used where appropriate?

5. Is the language plain and straightforward (e.g., what is the reading ease score?): are the words and sentences as short as the subject matter allows, with technical terms used only when essential and then adequately defined and explained?

6. Are analogies, examples (and nonexamples), case studies, and illustrations used where appropriate to develop understanding?

7. Are questions, exercises, and activities properly integrated into the text to encourage students in self-assessment and practice of relevant skills?

8. Are nonprint media (e.g., practical work, discussion with other students, listening to audio-tapes) effectively built in where more appropriate than print?

9. Is the form of presentation (layout of the lesson, typestyle, headings, use of underlining, etc.) conducive to effective learning?

10. Is the student given sufficient information and practice of a kind likely to help him towards achieving the objectives of the lesson?

11. Are any assessment items related to aims and objectives of the lesson, clear in what they demand of the student, and likely to result in answers that can be marked with reasonable consensus of agreement among different markers?

12. Is the likely student workload (in terms of study time) reasonable for the topic of the lesson?

However, what we are speculating about here is *likely* educational effectiveness. Some people are better than others at predicting where and why students are likely to have difficulties or success with a sequence of learning material. Some are better than others at suggesting how weaknesses in material might be overcome. Nevertheless, such speculation does remain guesswork, even in people who are brilliantly intuitive and usually correct. That is, we cannot know for certain how such materials actually work with students until they are being used on the course itself. The only way we can approach this knowledge in advance is to work with *other* students in *developmental testing*.

## Developmental testing

Developmental testing involves us in trying out learning materials (or teaching strategies) with students in the hope of developing or improving those materials (or strategies) for the benefit of *future students*. Such materials (or strategies) may be a self-instructional text, a Keller Plan module, a simulation game, a film, or whatever. The students on whom we try out the material, or strategy, should be as similar as possible to those who will be taking the course. (There will be more about this later.)

### *Tutorial tryouts*

One method of developmental testing is what I have called the *tutorial tryout*. Here we may be working with just one student at a time, if we are testing, say, a self-instructional lesson or unit. On the other hand, if we are testing materials or a strategy that can or must (e.g., a film or a simulation game) involve a group, then several students will be needed at a time. Either way, we may need to repeat the tryout with more than one such individual or group.

Now, how might such a tutorial tryout work? Suppose you are evaluating the second draft of a self-instructional lesson that has already been vetted by your 'experts'. Sit down with your student and check (with a test if necessary) that he is competent to begin on the lesson. That is, has he already acquired whatever prior or prerequisite abilities will be expected of a student? He may have acquired these by helping evaluate earlier lessons in a series. It may also be worth testing the student on the ideas in the lesson itself. It is just possible that he is (somehow) already so familiar with them that his response to the lesson may not imply much about those of the students it is eventually intended for. In any case, his *prior* perceptions of the ideas in the lesson may help you understand how he reacts to them in the lesson itself.

Make sure your student understands the nature of your collaboration—that the lesson is under trial, not him. Admit that you expect there to be weaknesses in the lesson and that you hope, with his help, to eradicate them before it goes into wider circulation. Obviously, the more lessons a particular student tries out with you, the more relaxed he will be—and the less likely to allow your presence to influence his approach to learning.

You will then observe how he works through your lesson. How does he get started on it? What sequence does he follow? How does he respond to the exercises and activities you have included within it? Where does he seem to be having difficulty? If you have to give him oral help, make a note of what you say because you may decide to write it into a later version of the lesson. You will also want to note any comments the student makes about the difficulty, relevance, interest, or effectiveness of various parts of the lesson. And how long is it taking him to work through the various sections?

When the student has finished you will test him again to ascertain what he has learned. Discussing his answers with him should lead you into looking again at your lesson. Which parts has the student learned most from? And from which parts has he learned least? Can he suggest why this might be? How does his present understanding compare with what he already knew about the topic? What changes would he like to see in the lesson?

How such a discussion might go, and the kinds of improvement that might be suggested, will vary according to what sort of learning experience is being tried out. (For more detailed discussion of the testing of self-teaching materials, see Lewis and Jones, 1980, Nathenson and Henderson, 1980, and Rowntree, 1979*c*.) Once you have corrected any glaring errors revealed by your first student, you can try the lesson out with one or two more. Take particular note of any reactions they have in *common*.

Such a tutorial tryout—observing individual students at work on one's material—can give the teacher a great deal of useful information, not just about the particular lesson being tested but about lesson writing in general. Admittedly, such knowledge often arrives rather painfully: 'How can he possibly not be learning from such carefully written materials?' However, the situation I have described will not give you all the information you need. It is too time-consuming to repeat more than a few times per lesson. It

**256**

is also, in an important sense, rather artificial. That is, your eventual students will not have you sitting alongside them while they work through your materials. So, having revised your material in the light of a tutorial tryout, you may then evaluate it more naturally in what we can call a *field trial*.

### Field trials

With a field trial you can use larger numbers, say 20 or 30 students, and must try to have them work through your materials in circumstances as similar as possible to those in which your eventual students will work. The problem is, since this probably precludes your being with them, how do you find out how they are using your materials and what they get out of them? To some extent you can do this by:

1. Requiring them to tackle an 'end-of-lesson test' and hand in their results, both before and after working through the lesson.
2. Asking them to fill in a 'log sheet' and/or questionnaire. (Figs. 6.2, 6.3, and 6.4) after completing the lesson, commenting for each section on, for example:
   (a) How long it took to work through.
   (b) How easy/interesting it was.
   (c) What they liked and disliked about it.
   (The answers to (a), (b), and (c) may be illuminating in their own right, but are perhaps even more so when compared with responses to other lessons or sections thereof.)
3. Interviewing some of the students afterwards to discuss their general attitudes to the lesson and how they think it might be improved.

Such procedures could be used in evaluating many kinds of educational material, for example, textbooks, films, audio-tapes, practical exercises. None of the procedures mentioned above makes the situation of field trial students markedly different from what will be the 'regular' working conditions. However, they do fail to collect one useful kind of information that is richly available in the face-to-face tutorial tryouts. That is, field trials may give us little information about *how* the student tackles the material. Even if it is realistic to have all students working together in one room (and it may not be) we cannot follow the moment-by-moment progress of each.

The nearest we can get is to ask the students themselves to record their reactions as they work. This does, of course, make

## TESTER'S LOG SHEET

1. YOUR NAME    C.B. Russell

2. TITLE OF COURSE UNIT    KANT, Units 17, 18

| SECTION | STARTED AT | FINISHED AT | TOTAL TIME | YOUR COMMENT ON THE SECTION AS A WHOLE |
|---------|-----------|-------------|------------|----------------------------------------|
| 1.1 – 2.8 | 4.20 | 5.0 | .40 | Clear & well presented |
| (pp. 1–20) | 6.40 | 7.30 | .50 | Since I have no experience of philosophy, I am glad that you are introducing it gradually |
| | 7.30 | 9.30 | 2. | The difficulties started |
| 3.1 – 3.6 | 11.15 | 1.00 | 1.45 | when you asked me to read long passages from Kant. |
| (pp. 21–57) | 2.30 | 3.45 | 1.15 | I did not feel properly |
| | 6.30 | 8.00 | 1.30 | prepared for this. |
| | 2. | 3.20 | 1.20 | I became saturated, and |
| 4.1 – 6.2 | 4.50 | 6.30 | 1.40 | lost the thread of your commentary. I was not |
| (pp. 57–97) | 9. | 9.45 | .45 | sure what the Exercises required me to do. |
| | 9.30 | 11.15 | 1.45 | My problem was whether to confine myself to the |
| Assessment | 1.30 | 3.40 | 2.10 | Autonomy of the Will, or |
| Exercise | 7.00 | 9.00 | 2. | to try a broader approach. |
| (p. 98) | 10.00 | 1.20 | 3.20 | The latter seemed to give me a better chance of showing what I know. |
| **TOTAL TIME** (INCL. ASSESSMENT) | | | 21.40 | |

**Fig. 6.2** Tester's log sheet

## END OF UNIT QUESTIONNAIRE (Part One)

1. Name:

   J. Brodie

2. Unit title/No.

   No. 19

3. What did you particularly like about this unit?

   The examples discussed are basically interesting but ↴

4. What did you particularly dislike? Most of my time and effort was spent struggling with the sociological terms & the writing style of sociologists. The overall themes & concepts are difficult to master because of the language barrier.

5. Were there any sections, concepts or words that you found particularly difficult, or not well explained? If there were, please give details.

   The terms were copiously explained but with definitions that were hard to recall during later reading. Repeated re-reading & refreshing of memory was necessary during difficult & complex passages, e.g. first paragraph of section 3.1

6. Can you suggest what might have helped you in these cases?

   Use the same definitions in self-assessment questions as are printed in text: 'action', 'role', 'norms', etc.

7. Do you have any other comments about this unit?

   As with other sociologically-based units, my difficulties stem from the terminology. Other disciplines' approaches to the same topics (crime, unemployment, immigration, etc.) seem to overcome this difficulty & get their message across using more familiar, or at least more clearly defined terms.

Fig. 6.3   End of unit questionnaire

## END OF UNIT QUESTIONNAIRE (Part Two)

1. NAME...*K. Mitchell*...... 2. Course Unit...*Unit 12*.....

Put a tick in the appropriate box for each of the questions below:

3 How much of the subject matter of the unit was already familiar to you?
- [ ] All of it
- [ ] Most of it
- [ ] About half
- [ ] A small amount
- [✓] None at all

4 To what extent did you enjoy working through the unit?
- [ ] I liked it very much
- [✓] I quite liked it (*espec. 1.1.- 2.8*)
- [ ] I felt indifferent to it
- [ ] I rather disliked it
- [ ] I disliked it very much

5 How difficult did you find the <u>course unit</u>?
- [✓] Very difficult (*espec. 4.1.-5.2*)
- [ ] Fairly difficult
- [ ] Neither too difficult nor
- [ ] Fairly easy      too easy
- [ ] Very easy

6 How difficult did you find the <u>assignment exercise</u> which followed the unit?
- [ ] Very difficult
- [✓] Fairly difficult
- [ ] Neither too difficult nor
- [ ] Fairly easy      too easy
- [ ] Very easy

7 Do you think the unit gave you enough <u>practice</u> in using the ideas it contained?
- [ ] Too much practice
- [✓] Neither too much nor too little practice
- [ ] Too little practice

8 In view of the amount of time the unit required of you, do you feel you learned as much as you might have expected from it?
- [ ] I learned a great deal
- [✓] I learned a reasonable amount
- [ ] I learned too little

9 If this course unit were considered typical material from the course for which you have applied, how would your experience of it affect your desire to take this course?

My desire to take the course would be:
- [ ] Very much increased
- [✓] Somewhat increased
- [ ] Unaffected
- [ ] Somewhat decreased
- [ ] Very much decreased

10 Are you willing to test further units?
- [✓] Yes
- [ ] No

11 Please give overleaf any other general comments that you would like the author (or illustrator) to take into account when revising this course unit for publication.

**Fig. 6.4** End of unit questionnaire

their situation different from that of the students for whom the material is intended. It could mean they get more or get less from the material than will the ultimate students. This depends on whether writing down their reactions focuses their attention or acts as a distraction. Nevertheless, for the sake of getting more detailed information, you may be prepared to accept that your trial students may experience the materials rather differently than will your eventual students—who will not be writing down reactions.

The simplest way of getting moment-by-moment reactions is to invite students to write their comments in the margins of the text as they read, or, perhaps, in a separate notebook with nontext materials. Below are some comments of the kind I have had from students. And they are quite similar to the comments one may get from some 'experts'. As you will see, many of them are quite likely to persuade one to take another (evaluative) look at the material one has produced.

- I can't see what the writer is getting at here.
- Haven't we had this already on page 12?
- Now I begin to understand.
- This paragraph is contradicting itself.
- This whole section is pompous and patronizing.
- I've lost the drift of the argument.
- What is this supposed to be an example of?
- Too long-winded.
- We need photographs to appreciate this distinction.
- What has this paragraph got to do with the topic?
- I am getting quite intrigued now.
- Too many technical terms all at once.
- Beautifully clear and logical.
- So dull, I'm beginning to wonder whether I can go on.
- I think we should be shown a worked example before being expected to tackle this exercise.
- This section is too easy—there's nothing to think about.
- I don't see how this follows—have you jumped a step in the argument?.
- Isn't it time for a summary of what we've covered so far?
- Why can't it all be as humorous and light-hearted as this?
- How is this different from the everyday meaning of the word?
- I'm thoroughly confused now.

As well as, or instead of, inviting free commenting, one can include special 'field trial questions' in the material. That is, in addition to whatever exercises and activities your eventual students will see, you can write special questions that will be in the field trial version only. These can invite students to give you information about their use of the materials.

For example, at the beginning of a self-instructional lesson, say after the author's statement of aims and objectives, you might print the following:

| In the space below, say what is your reaction to the author's aims and objectives. (e.g., Are they clear to you? Do they seem relevant? etc.). |
| --- |
|  |

At the beginning of each section within a lesson you may have a box as follows:

| Time started | |
| --- | --- |

And a 'Time finished' box at the end.

After each major exercise (especially one that relates to a main objective) you may ask a set of questions such as these:

1. Write down your answer to Exercise X in the space below.
2. How long did the exercise take you?
3. Was it clear what you were supposed to do?
4. How easy was it?
5. Did you consider it a worthwhile exercise?
6. How similar did you think your answer was to the author's?
7. What was your reaction to the author's discussion of answers?
8. If you were not satisfied with your answer:
   (a) What did you do about it?
   (b) How do you account for your getting it wrong?
9. If you didn't tackle Exercise X, please say why not.

Thus, when you get back the printed lesson at the end of the field trial, you will get not only the student's written answers to the key exercises but also his comments on those exercises.

After each section of the lesson you may include such questions as:

1. How long did this section take you?
2. Without referring back, summarize the author's main points in not more than 100 words.
3. How difficult was the section?
4. How interesting was it?
5. Did it seem clearly related to the aims and objectives of the lesson?
6. How useful or relevant were the diagrams, cartoons, tables, etc?
7. Can you suggest any ways of improving the section?
8. Do you have any other comments about the section?

With all such 'field trial questions', *leave sufficient space* on the page for the students to write in their answers.

When the students have completed their work on the lesson they will return their copies to you and you will analyse their reactions along with their test results. Thus you will form an overall picture of how they reacted to the lesson, how long they took over it, and what they learned from it. You may then be able to meet with some of them to discuss common reactions and suggestions for improvement. Key questions to ask in such a discussion (or in a questionnaire if you cannot get together with your field trial students) are:

1. What did you like most about the lesson?
2. What did you dislike most about the lesson?
3. What changes would you like to see made in the lessons?

You can then put the finishing touches to your material and have it produced in the final version for the students it was always intended for. (See Nathenson and Henderson, 1980, for detailed advice on field-trial evaluation.)

### *Limitations*

However much you learn from the developmental testing, and however much you improve the materials, the 'real' students will usually surprise you with their responses. Even if the physical and organizational context in which they tackle the work appears the same, it is likely that the *psychological* context will differ. In other words, your 'real' students will be motivated differently. While your developmental testers are *testing*, whether for love, money, or interest in the subject, your 'real' students will be *studying* in earnest, *needing* to learn in order to survive and prosper within the

**263**

course, and conscious of demands being made on them by the system that are quite different from those made on the developmental testers. Hence they may use the materials differently—for better or for worse.

Perhaps there is only one way of ensuring complete identity between developmental testing students and those who will be taking the course 'for real'. That is to regard the first running of the course as an experimental, developmental testing run. This may mean admitting a smaller number of students than will be the case subsequently and demanding of those students that they provide feedback of the kind described above. (See Cowan, 1978, for an example.) Hence, the course can be revised prior to admitting the next intake of students. This principle has been followed by the Open University in its practice of 'developmental testing for credit' (see Henderson et al., 1980). Of course, many institutions would claim that their first mounting of a new course is inevitably regarded as a trial run. But sometimes the implications of this may not be discussed with the students, and little in the way of an evaluation strategy may be evident. Very often, costs, time, and the plain difficulty of finding suitable 'guinea pig' students, militates against much in the way of developmental testing.

In any case, and especially when the course is not much dependent on pre-prepared materials, there is a definite limit to the improvements that can be made before the course is officially under way. From then, the emphasis must be on understanding what is going on within the course so that it can be improved for the students taking it or, in some cases, at least for the next intake of students. This process can be called 'continuous monitoring'.

## Continuous Monitoring

Essentially, this is a matter of 'keeping an eye on things'. But it needs to be a pretty active and imaginative eye. Not only does it need to be alert to the faintest signs that things are going adrift, or that good things are emerging and should be enhanced, it also has to see into the future and prepare for evaluation of aspects that have not yet materialized.

A course can usefully be seen as a voyage. In fact, it may be that the word originates in nautical usage, e.g., 'setting a course for Cape Horn'. However clear the ultimate destination at the outset, hundreds of corrections and decisions must be made along the way, both to ensure that the agreed destination, which may itself change, does get reached and to make the voyaging itself a positive, or at least not a negative, experience. Normally the captain will keep a daily record of all significant happenings—to ship, crew, passengers, cargo, etc.—and of decisions they have led him to make. This is the ship's *log*.

### A course log-book

By analogy, it can be a very useful evaluation practice to keep a *log-book* for a course. This is especially the case when a course is new, on its 'maiden voyage', you might say. Such a log-book can be used to record the main things you have noticed in the running of the course and the main in-course corrections you have made. Committing oneself to writing down, say at no more than weekly intervals, the emerging strengths and weaknesses and puzzling features of the course—and what you are doing about them—both prompts you to be more systematic and objective in your evaluation and produces an archive that you or your colleagues may refer to in future course development. It will surely be a rare week in which you will write 'nothing to report'. For an extract from what is, in effect, the start of a course log-book, see Fig. 6.5.

---

34 students have signed up—too many really—but I can't turn any away. Despite the publicity being aimed at Arts and Social Sciences, I've got three mathematicians and two engineers. Not sure I'll be able to offer them much. We'll see.

*Session 1:   Introduction*
29 students turned up. Spent first half getting acquainted by discussing individual study interests/problems in pairs and then small groups. This technique new to most students and got us off to a lively start. Built on this in second half to elicit expectations for the course. Only one surprise here—a strong interest in how to learn in discussion groups, which one student (to general approval) said were usually 'a dead loss'. Asked them to keep a diary of how they spend their study time over the week before we meet again.

*Session 2:   Organizing time*
25 turned up. Still got both engineers but the mathematicians (whom I didn't have enough time to talk with specially last week) not here. (I'd better contact them and see whether I or anyone else can do anything for them.)
    First got students to write individual answers to a questionnaire

**Fig. 6.5**   The beginning of a tutor's notes (log-book) about a course of ten two-hour sessions on study skills

about study habits; then compare answers in pairs. Pairs joined in fours to suggest ways of overcoming problems identified. Some dissatisfaction expressed over this exercise—'too negative'. (Maybe I didn't intervene enough.) Then got onto comparing study diaries (which all but three had more or less completed). This produced intense discussion. Students were amazed at their variety of approaches to organizing time. Some claimed to have now seen ways of doing things better. Others expressed relief that they weren't as eccentric as they'd thought in their methods!

Asked students to bring some of their lecture or reading notes next time.

*Session 3: Taking notes v. making notes*
26 turned up. Began with general buzz-session on the purposes of note-taking and different ways of doing it. The expected variety failed to materialize. Most seem very assiduous (too assiduous?) Showed them the television programme—got them to make notes (so did I). Each then showed them to a neighbour and explained. Then, in fours, decided on best composite notes and why.

I gave short demonstration of various note-making techniques and discussed handout. Played radio tape. Students took notes. *But* I didn't allow enough time to discuss these properly. Students rightly complained this could have been best bit of session. Promised to see if we could do some more of this next week.

*Session 4: Learning from discussion*
Began by discussing with students the fact that three lecturers (!) have asked if they could 'sit in' on the group. . . .

**Fig. 6.5** *(continued)*

Now what might go in the course log-book? Clearly, you will wish to include the results of student *assessment*. Any exercises and tests and assignments completed during the course will provide you with indicators as to which parts of the course are teaching well and which leave something to be desired. Your analysis of students' work may also be backed up by interviews and discussions (or questionnaires), enabling you to enquire into how they tackled an assignment, what difficulties they encountered, how they felt about what they produced, and so on. However, I have said enough about assessment in Chapter 5. And, in addition, I want to emphasize that, while evaluation *includes* assessment, it takes in much more besides. For instance, assessment tends to concentrate on the *products* of learning, usually physical products in the form of essays, calculations, drawings, etc. But evaluation is also concerned with the *processes* of learning (see Hamilton *et al.*, 1977). So it is useful to look at what else is included.

Continuous monitoring can be thought of as happening in two different ways. The first we might label with such adjectives as casual, accidental, reactive, opportunistic. Essentially, this results from things we 'just happen to notice' during the course. Thus we may notice, or have it brought to our attention, that other teachers are complaining that the amount of work we are giving our students is leaving them insufficient time to cope with assignments set on other courses. Again, we may be surprised to notice, while observing practical work, that some students are circumventing safety precautions in operating certain equipment.

The second way evaluation occurs is as a result of planned attempts to find out what is going on in the course. We might describe this as planned, structured, formal, pro-active, and so on. Thus we may plan to have students respond to questionnaires at intervals during the course or to have an evaluation discussion session at the end. And the teachers may meet regularly, to discuss 'the voyage' to date.

### Casual evaluation
The first type of evaluation is, as you will recognize, part of the everyday business of teaching. In fact, it must surely be part of what 'teaching' means. That is, unless we are appraising what is happening in the situation in which we are operating, we cannot be responsive to it and may therefore be telling or showing, but not teaching. Nevertheless, some teachers are better at it than others. In school, some teachers are often reckoned by their peers to have 'eyes in the back of their heads'. That is, they have an awareness, a 'classroom sense', that enables them to be working with a student in one corner of the room and yet be instantly alert to a 'situation' that is about to erupt behind them in the opposite corner!

Teachers in post-secondary education may or may not be in such close touch with their students. Many are, however, especially in small-group teaching, and they may find themselves responding, moment by moment, to the subtle signals of group interaction.

Unfortunately, even teachers who are proficient at responding to (often unconscious) evaluation within a session, may not (largely because it *is* unconscious) subsequently find time to reflect on whether their responses have any implications for

**267**

changing the course. Here the log-book can help by requiring us to think back over our evaluation experiences, and perhaps thereby become more alert to them in future.

Naturally, when teachers are not with the students while they are learning—as in Keller Plan or distance education schemes— there is no opportunity for moment-by-moment evaluation. If we seek knowledge of how such students learned, we must hope to reconstruct it by jogging their memories with forms and question- naires of the kind we discussed under field trials (pages 257–263). But the casual, 'happen to notice' type of evaluation may occur whether or not we have regular contact with the student. Listed below is a mixed sample of the kinds of thing one might notice during a course and that might lead one to wonder what was going on and what ought to be done about it:

● Class attendance is falling off.

● Students are becoming increasingly late with their assign- ments.

● Other teachers are complaining about our students.

● One of our set books has gone out of print.

● An educational journal has published a heavy critique of the Marxist/sexist/Christian bias of our course.

● Students are dropping out of the course.

● Students are almost all choosing one option and ignoring all others.

● Our colleagues on the course feel they don't know where it's going any more.

● Students' practical/clinical work shows no sign that it has been informed by their theoretical studies.

● A major advance is reported in the knowledge underlying one of the main topics in our course.

● Adverse weather conditions ruin an important field trip.

● Organizations with whom our students are out on 'sandwich courses' begin complaining that they are too 'theory-bound'.

● Work done by students on previous runs of the course is being heavily plagiarized by present students.

● Records of student progress through a Keller Plan course reveal that one unit is occupying students for much longer than it should need to.

● Our course is being regarded as too liberal (maybe even 'not really higher education') by the powers-that-be in our institution.

All this begins to sound like the 'chance' cards in a course development version of *Monopoly*. But the above list is just a tiny sample of the myriad things that might come to our attention and demand action. It also gives some indication of the sources from which information may reach us about the context, effects, and effectiveness of our course. The main sources must be the students themselves, together with any other teachers who are collaborating with us in presenting the course. We must, in addition, be alert for reactions from teachers of other courses with whom our students are working, other organizations with whom the course puts them in contact; and, some time after our students have completed the course, they may feed back further reactions, and so may their then teachers or employers (or workmates). John Cowan (1978), for instance, reports the reactions of a second year teacher to the students who have been through John Cowan's first year experimental course: 'These students are a menace in my class', commented one traditional lecturer. 'Why?', the writer enquired. 'They keep questioning my basic assumptions and suggesting other points I should consider.' 'And are the questions unreasonable?' 'No, no—they are quite valid. But it takes up far too much time discussing them.'

To encourage people other than ourselves to 'notice' things we might establish a course 'suggestion box' or, better still, a notice board (in the manner of a Chinese wall newspaper) on which students and others can publicly record their observations about the courses.

### Deliberate evaluation

Deliberate evaluation differs from casual evaluation in that we are actively seeking specific kinds of information. Rather than simply being on the look out for anything that might be grist to our mill, we may seek answers to certain questions such as the following. Can the written guides to the course be improved in any way? Are women and men feeling differently about the course content? Are students using the cassette-tapes that accompany the course? Do they feel we have allowed enough time for this activity and that? Do other teachers on our course feel that its main purposes are being achieved?

For instance, when you are not teaching all the students on the course yourself, it is essential to obtain regular reports from the *other* teachers. In the Open University, the central course team thus keeps in touch with the regional tutors who assess students' assignment work and provide evaluative reports on the course,

| *Tutor No.* | *Comments* |
|---|---|
| 104286 | Unit 10 reading, Deutsch in particular, seemed to cause students some difficulty, in spite of the summary in Unit 10. The article is good, however, and I found that a tutorial session cleared most of the problems. New tutors might be alerted in advance next year. |
| 369826 | Some of my students are critical of what they describe as the 'jumping about' nature of the course, i.e., a tendency to spend too little time on one topic area before switching to a distantly related theme. I think they would prefer more discrete blocks of emphasis on a particular social science. |
| 264828 | This is the best block to date. |
| 261358 | My own criticism is directed at Unit 10 which I consider to be far too vague and pitched at far too high a level of generalization. It appears to be out of keeping with the course so far. Perhaps a more interesting exercise would be to look at some situation in more detail. This would enable the incorporation of section 4, the controls of politics on communication, to be brought out in an integrated way rather than as a postscript. |
| 150011 | Unit 07 seems excessively technical containing matter not of obvious interest to social science students. This is my reaction with which students appeared to agree (out of politeness?). Unit 09 again seems too technical and more appropriate to a course in physical transport rather than social science aspects. Also appears totally to fail to integrate with earlier Units concerned with natural resources—so that there is no discussion of relative efficiency of fuel usage of different transport modes nor of fossil fuel constraints on transport technology and usage. These are topics most likely to interest D101 students I feel. Also are D101 students likely to be so interested in location of Turkish Railways? |
| 001044 | 07: written work by students showed that they had not grasped the significance of the concept of 'deep structure', despite the SAQ and CMA questions. Suggest that SAQ4 (p. 39) be broken down so as to draw out separately the elements of the definition given on p. 72. Unit 10 looks deceptively short and coming at the end tended to be rushed. I think that the Unit would come better after 08. The spatial factor is less demanding in comprehension because more concrete. |

**Fig. 6.6** Some tutor-comments on units 7–10

based largely on their experience of how students are coping with it. (See Fig. 6.6 for tutor-comments on one block of a course.) Even with on-campus Keller Plan courses, student proctors may see more of other students' work than do the staff-members who devised the course. They should be encouraged to make regular contributions to the course log-book and to attend discussions of the course.

DISCUSSIONS AND INTERVIEWS
Deliberate evaluation can often be conducted in group discussion with tutors and/or students—provided you can bring them together for the purpose. With an on-campus course, all contributing teachers should be able to get together fairly frequently, perhaps weekly during especially busy passages of the course, to discuss 'happenings'. With a Keller Plan course, any advanced students acting as proctors will have much to contribute to these meetings; they may also be feeling certain anxieties about their role, and these may be dispelled in the discussion.

---

*Theoretical instruction*
Relevance of content to course objectives, and whether the latter were clear.
Adequacy of time allowed, including time for personal study.
Suitability of teaching methods.
Availability of personal guidance.

*Clinical experience*
Coverage of all necessary skills.
Relation of theory to practice.
Adequacy of preparation for clinical practice.
Opportunity to practice skills thoroughly under supervision.

*Assessments*
Amount of preparation and information given on the assessment programme.
Conduct of the various assessments.
Availability of counselling and help where assessments show up difficulties.

*General evaluation of course (so far)*
The course member's judgement of his or her achievement of course objectives.
Suggestions for improvement from course members.

---

**Fig. 6.7** An agenda for evaluation discussions. (From Bridge, 1978)

A checklist of issues or questions can provide a useful agenda for an evaluation discussion, whether with staff or students. Fig. 6.7 shows a checklist, prepared by Will Bridge (1978), for discussion on in-service courses for nurses.

Checklists are also valuable where part of your deliberate evaluation consists of observing teachers and students at work or of interviewing people individually. Lacking a checklist, different observers or interviewers might concentrate on quite different issues, which could result in many insights for the individuals without necessarily producing information that needs to be known about all the people interviewed.

USING QUESTIONNAIRES

However, it can often be difficult to interview many participants in the course, or to get them together for evaluation discussions, especially with distance courses where the students may be numbered in hundreds, anyway. But even with a Keller Plan course on-campus, students may not be easy to assemble and, even. if they are, the fastest and slowest may prove to be far apart in their progress through the modules. Though that last eventuality should be apparent in the course records, and may need to be discussed in individual interviews with the students concerned. We may also have doubts about whether evaluation meetings are an effective use of students' time—unless we can convince ourselves that the discussion itself will be a worthwhile learning experience for them (as is often the case).

As an alternative to discussions and interviews, or perhaps as a supplement, our thoughts may turn to *questionnaires*. Perhaps we can more effectively collect information from our course participants by asking them to let us have written answers to our questions. Indeed, even where students and teachers can come together occasionally for evaluation discussions, it may be useful for all to have completed a questionnaire beforehand. Many who are reluctant to commit themselves to a strong opinion in public will do so readily in a questionnaire, especially if it allows anonymity.

Now the design of questionnaires is an art in itself. One or two examples have been shown in this book and a word or two about questionnaire design would be appropriate now. Space is not available here to go into details but there are many good books on the subject (e.g., Oppenheim, 1968) and most people in post-secondary education will have access to advice from someone in their institution, e.g., a social sciences colleague who has experience in this area.

The questions used in questionnaires normally fall into three basic categories:

1. A question, together with several alternative answers expressing different ways of rating some aspect of the course. The student is asked to choose whichever one he agrees with, for example:

> 'How clear do you feel about what the project will be demanding of you?
> (a) Very clear
> (b) Fairly clear
> (c) Rather unclear
> (d) Very unclear
> (e) I've not thought much about it yet.'

An alternative form is to pose the question as a statement with which the student is asked to indicate the extent of his agreement or disagreement, for example:

> 'Would you agree that the demands likely to be made on you by the project are now clear to you?
> (a) Very much yes
> (b) Yes
> (c) Haven't thought about it yet
> (d) No
> (e) Very much no.'

2. A question inviting the student to look at several answers and choose *one or more than one* that apply to him, for example:

> 'For course unit 12, which of the following aspects do you believe might have been improved in some way?
> (a) Aims and objectives
> (b) Study guide
> (c) The case study
> (d) Answers to exercises
> (e) Exercises
> (f) Diagrams
> (g) End-of-module test.'

3. Open-ended questions, inviting the student to make a free response, writing down his comments, for example, as a follow-up question to the last one mentioned above one might ask:

> 'What do you believe should be done to improve those aspects you have mentioned?'

**273**

Clearly, what you ask questions *about* will vary from course to course. It will also vary according to the point within the course at which your questionnaire is to be completed, and according to the use you want to make of the answers. One thing is worth pointing out, however: if it is at all likely that you might want to analyse the responses in order to compare, say, the attitudes of men and women, students with varying degrees of previous educational experience, students with different professional interests, and so on, make sure you ask for the necessary data in your questionnaire. It can be very frustrating, for example, to know that 50 per cent of your students are women and *suspect* that they may have responded differently when there is nothing on the questionnaire to indicate the sex of the person who completed it.

Of course, if students' names were on the questionnaires, any background information can readily be obtained. But one loses something in abandoning the principle of anonymity. In general, it is better for students to leave their names off questionnaires. Otherwise we can never be quite sure that we have not been told—whether out of self-interest or simple politeness—what they think we would like to hear rather than the truth as they see it.

As I mentioned earlier, questionnaire design is an art in itself. Even professional survey researchers are liable to produce inadequate questions from time to time. I am sure we have all experienced confusion in trying to answer questionnaires in which some items are ambiguous or just plain obscure. This can result in questions being ignored or, if people do answer them, in results that the evaluator cannot really rely on because different people have put different interpretations on the question.

The best way of ensuring that your questionnaire is as clear and unambiguous as possible is to try it out on a few people in draft form. That is, developmentally test it through tutorial tryout. Ask a few people to answer your questions and to discuss their answers with you. If you cannot obtain appropriate students to test it on, friends, spouses, and colleagues may well oblige by pointing out its difficulties or ambiguities.

This is a reminder that using questionnaires can be a costly business. And not just in staff time. Here are some of the chief costs that could be incurred:

- Time spent in preparing questions.
- Time spent in testing/revising questions.

- Cost of typing and reprographing, or printing questionnaires.
- Cost of stamps and envelopes if questionnaire is to be mailed.
- Cost of retrieval (e.g., reply-paid envelopes).
- Cost of recording to whom questionnaire is sent and which of them reply.
- Cost of following up those who do not reply.
- Staff time in analysing the data.

In an on-campus course, some of these costs will be avoidable. Questionnaires need not be elaborately produced, and they can be simply handed out to students. And, if students are together in one place to answer the questionnaire, there need be no non-responders to follow up. However, the major costs of staff time in preparing the questionnaire and analysing the results are not avoidable. Clearly, it will be necessary to think about the relationship between the value of the information we are likely to get and the cost of getting it. We shall probably decide that questionnaires are for occasional use only, e.g., at mid-term and end of term or end of course, or after some discrete and important learning experience like an individual project or an industrial attachment in a sandwich course.

RECORDING AND INTERPRETING DATA

How do we record and interpret the data collected by questionnaires? The simplest way, especially if you are dealing with only thirty or so students is to keep a spare copy of the questionnaire and record in its answer spaces the total number of students responding with each answer. See Fig. 6.8 for an example.

Students' answers to open-ended questions can be typed out and attached on a separate sheet. Fig. 6.9 shows a set of students' responses to the two questions 'What has been the best thing about this course so far?' and 'What has been the worst thing?' Open-ended responses can, of course, be analysed further in order to group them according to type of comment or to identify them as 'fors' and 'againsts', and so on. This record can then be discussed with tutors and with students if possible.

Discussion of the evaluation responses can be a valuable teaching device. And it often reveals issues that the questionnaire glossed over or did not touch upon at all. For instance a questionnaire on a course I have recently run indicated that students saw no difficulty with the course assignment they were

**275**

A. *Course of objectives* Please tick the appropriate box alongside each of the course objectives listed below, so as to show whether you agree or disagree (strongly or not) that you achieved each one to a satisfactory degree (satisfactory to you, that is).

DID THE COURSE HELP YOU TO

| | Very much No | No | Yes | Very much Yes |
|---|---|---|---|---|
| 1. Acquire factual knowledge? | 2 | 4 | 14 | 14 |
| 2. Learn principles, concepts, generalizations, theories, etc? | 3 | 4 | 16 | 11 |
| 3. Apply principles to problems/issues? | 4 | 9 | 13 | 8 |
| 4. Understand yourself — your own feelings, attitudes, values, etc? | 9 | 14 | 8 | 3 |
| 5. Understand how the professionals think and feel about the subject? | 3 | 13 | 14 | 4 |
| 6. Develop skill in communication? | 1 | 12 | 15 | 6 |
| 7. Develop critical, independent ideas? | 10 | 11 | 8 | 5 |
| 8. Pursue your own intellectual interests? | 8 | 12 | 10 | 4 |

B. *Teaching evaluation* Please tick the appropriate box alongside each of the following questions, to show how positively or negatively you feel about each.

| | Very much No | No | Yes | Very much Yes |
|---|---|---|---|---|
| 1. Were the aims and objectives of the course made sufficiently clear? | 5 | 7 | 10 | 12 |
| 2. Did the teacher seem to have planned the course carefully enough? | 3 | 7 | 14 | 10 |
| 3. Did the teacher show reasonable flexibility in adapting his plans to the needs/interests of students? | 8 | 13 | 10 | 3 |
| 4. Did the teacher show adequate concern for how individual students were coping with the demands of the course? | 6 | 7 | 12 | 9 |
| 5. Was the time in class used productively? | 4 | 4 | 15 | 11 |
| 6. Was the text material pitched at an appropriate level? | 4 | 12 | 10 | 8 |
| 7. Was the teacher's assessment policy fair? | 2 | 10 | 13 | 9 |
| 8. Are you satisfied with what you got out of the course? | 5 | 6 | 13 | 10 |
| 9. Given that you were one of several students, could the teacher possibly have done anything he did not do to help you get more out of the course? | 7 | 22 | 3 | 2 |

C. *General* Please write overleaf any comments you have on your answers to the above questions, or any other comments about the course that you feel may help the teacher to improve it.

**Fig. 6.8** The number of students (out of 34) ticking each of the various possible answers on an evaluation questionnaire

What has been the *best* thing . . .

What has been the *worst* thing . . .

about this course (on curriculum development) so far?

(In the list below, answers alongside each other are from the same student.)

| *Best* | *Worst* |
|---|---|
| ● The course is tailor-made for my career-plans and an excellent practical exercise forcing me to analyse books I've really only glanced at before. | ● I can see I won't have all the time I'd like to devote to it. Very demanding for such a short course—but don't change this! |
| ● Having the class assignment very well outlined (clear). | ● Getting the assigned readings completed on time. |
| ● The material is presented in an honest and open manner. And the book is interesting and most suitable for the course. | ● Sharing ideas with other students goes on too long. (Some don't have too much relevant experience to draw on.) |
| ● I like the concern and interest of the teacher. I'm enjoying the assignment and appreciate the guidance he's giving. | ● I would prefer more lecturing and exercises from the teacher rather than student discussions. |
| ● Freedom to produce assignment related to one's interests. Tutorial aid is therefore very helpful. | ● Timing of group work—seems to lose track of items/proceedings prior to return to total group discussion. |
| ● I like the structure of the course, i.e., using the assignment as a basis for discussing curriculum development. And the small group discussions are very worthwhile. | ● Not enough practical work done within the class itself. We could do short exercises using examples of curriculum projects and producing our own samples. |
| ● The co-operative nature of the course—between the instructor and individual students, and between students and students. | ● The time constraint: six hours a week, 7–10 pm! It would be better if there was more time and the evenings started earlier. |
| ● What I really like with this course is that we can work for *our own* objectives and reach them. In other words, we have freedom—within limits, of course. | ● Something I don't like is a piece of theory from the book—behavioural objectives. It just isn't for me. Also, I would like to have, besides the book, more exercises in curriculum development within the talk in class. |

**Fig. 6.9** Some students' answers to two questions

shortly due to attempt. In discussion, however, a chance remark from one student revealed that none had yet paid it really close attention and that, in fact, one aspect of it was unworkable! Naturally, a copy (with a report of any subsequent discussion) should go in the course log-book.

Again, rather than looking at how students have responded to several aspects of a given unit, we may record their responses to one aspect of several units, e.g., their interest or difficulty. This we may do with a chart or a table. For example, Fig. 6.10, based on work by my colleague David Hawkridge, shows the figures relating to a course in which the 200 who started had been asked, module by module, to say how difficult they found it, and if they were satisfied with what they felt they had learned from it. The responses in the body of the table have been converted to percentages of those responding for each module. The response rate for each module (based on 200 students) is shown as a percentage at the foot of the table.

What can we see in such a table as Fig. 6.10? Clearly the difficulty rating varies from module to module. $1+5=6$ per cent thought the first module was very difficult or quite difficult, compared with $32+34$ per cent$=66$ per cent saying the same of the eighth module. In fact the difficulty rating or interesting rating for a single module on its own would mean little or nothing. It is in comparisons between modules that we can find illumination. Should some modules be made easier? We cannot tell from these figures alone.

| Rating of difficulty | Modules | | | | | | | |
|---|---|---|---|---|---|---|---|---|
| | 1 | 2 | 3 | 4 | 5 | 6 | 7 | 8 |
| | % | % | % | % | % | % | % | % |
| Very difficult | 1 | 8 | 1 | 0 | 12 | 6 | 24 | 32 |
| Quite difficult | 5 | 22 | 8 | 4 | 30 | 16 | 21 | 34 |
| Just right | 71 | 37 | 44 | 21 | 31 | 58 | 30 | 22 |
| Quite easy | 13 | 21 | 18 | 32 | 20 | 17 | 21 | 8 |
| Very easy | 10 | 12 | 29 | 43 | 7 | 3 | 4 | 4 |
| Number of responses | 140 | 128 | 116 | 110 | 96 | 82 | 78 | 60 |
| % responses | 70 | 64 | 58 | 55 | 48 | 41 | 39 | 30 |

**Fig. 6.10** Students' responses to difficulty rating in a course

We might also notice that the response-rate fell from 70 to 30 per cent over the course. Does this mean that considerable numbers of students have dropped out of the course? Or have they simply stopped completing the questionnaire? Either way, we are left with the question of whether the responses of those who did not respond would have altered the picture shown in the table. Were those people significantly different from those who did respond? For instance, most of the students who found the lessons difficult may have dropped out or been too busy coping with their work to spend time completing a depressing questionnaire about it. The only way to find out is by 'forcing' the nonresponders to respond (if we know who they are) by face-to-face interviews or telephone conversations.

If we have the data with which to do it, we can further analyse, say, the difficulty rating with a cross-tabulation or cross-break. (It is, of course, in this sense that one might hear about a group of students being broken down by age and sex.) That is, we may, for instance, see whether students who carried out the practical work for each module responded differently from those who did not. Thus, in Fig. 6.11, we see that students who did complete the practical work usually rated the modules less difficult than those who did not complete it. But the differences are small and, for module 7, the opposite is true. However, the figures reveal nothing about causation. We cannot jump to the conclusion that doing the practical work will help make a module seem less difficult. Rather it may be *because* they found a module less difficult that students tackled the practical work.

| | Modules | | | | | | | |
|---|---|---|---|---|---|---|---|---|
| | 1 % | 2 % | 3 % | 4 % | 5 % | 6 % | 7 % | 8 % |
| Students *tackling* the practical work and responding 'very difficult' or 'quite difficult' | 42 | 30 | 8 | 2 | 39 | 18 | 49 | 2 |
| Students *not* tackling the practical work and responding 'very difficult' or 'quite difficult' | 68 | 30 | 12 | 7 | 46 | 25 | 40 | 10 |

**Fig. 6.11** Analysis of difficulty rating with cross-tabulation

As we have seen, such figures conceal more than they reveal. Some people are highly impressed (if not overwhelmed) by them. But the variety of human learning is lost within them. They do not tell us what different students may mean by 'difficulty', for example, let alone whether all those who think a module is difficult would favour its being made easier and, if so, how (and, if not, why not). And it is quite conceivable that some of the modules rated as among the most difficult are also rated among the most interesting.

Open-ended comments may be similarly contradictory. Barbara Falk (1967) records the following comments made by four different students about the same series of history lectures;

> 'Made a fascinating period of history very flat.'
> 'Congratulations on an exceedingly workmanlike job of teaching as opposed to purely lecturing.'
> 'Gives students impression that they are back in the schoolroom. By this I mean over-simplification, over-clarification.'
> 'These lectures were the best I've had this year.'

Such a mixed batch of responses may depress those teachers who feel they ought to be pleasing all of the students all of the time, while cheering up those who doubt they are reaching any of them any of the time. But if such ambiguous or contradictory data is to help inform any teacher's *decisions*, it usually needs to be explored further in discussions with the students, either in groups or individually, face-to-face or by telephone.

### Evaluating ourselves

One thing I have glossed over so far is any suggestion that we should be evaluating our own teaching. I have talked about evaluating our own teaching *material* and *methods* but that is a (slightly) less threatening matter. Most of us find it hard to look objectively at our strengths and weaknesses in face-to-face teaching. Yet most of us admit to our nearest and dearest that we are not the master-performers we would wish to be. Some of us have a better grip on the subject-matter than others; some are better at finding ways of helping students get to grips with it. But, all too often, we have never seriously considered which aspects of teaching we are best at. One may be a brilliant lecturer but too effusive to be of much help in small group work. One may be a poor planner but endlessly and subtly inventive in responding to student's here-and-now needs. And so on.

**280**

Evaluating some of our teaching sessions can help us gain some understanding of ourselves. This may or may not help us improve on our weaknesses. But, if it is done communally within a team of teachers, it might enable the group as a whole to allow each person maximum opportunity to exercise his strengths and compensate for his weaknesses with the cooperation of others who are strong in complementary areas.

INDIVIDUALS
One can begin by evaluating one's own teaching, perhaps using a checklist like that in Fig. 6.12. In some institutions it may be easy to record your session on audio-tape or even—if you don't mind the presence of a technician—on video-tape. Even greater objectivity might be obtained by inviting a trusted colleague to sit in on your teaching and offer an evaluation subsequently, perhaps based on a similar checklist. You could offer to do the same for him. Many people might prefer the first such peer-evaluation to be performed by a friend from a department other than their own. Again, you may wish the students to evaluate a particular teaching session. Much has been written on this subject (see Flood-Page, 1974). It is not difficult to formulate a student questionnaire around questions similar to those in the checklist. (See also part B of Fig. 6.8.)

This is not to suggest that every session one takes should be

- Was the venue suitable (e.g., in accessibility, seating etc.)?
- Was the teaching session carefully planned?
- Did the plan prove appropriate?
- Were the objectives clear to the students?
- Was the content sensibly ordered?
- Was it appropriate in amount for the time available?
- Were appropriate media/methods used?
- Were media/methods used successfully?
- Was the 'social climate' conducive to successful learning?
- Did students participate appropriately?
- Are you satisfied with what was learned?
- Do you believe students will be satisfied with what they learned?
- Were appropriate assessment techniques used?
- How might you operate such a session differently another time?

**Fig. 6.12** Self-evaluation checklist

**281**

evaluated in this way. It should be enough to select certain 'critical sessions', e.g., those you know are going to be difficult for you and/or the students, those in which you try a new technique for the first time, those marking a transition from one phase of the course to another.

DEPARTMENTS

If a *group* of colleagues within a department or other teaching unit are interested in evaluation, they may find that student approaches and attitudes previously thought to have been peculiar to a single course are actually reflections of a kind of departmental 'learning climate'. Paul Ramsden (1979) has used questionnaires to ascertain that students in different departments of his university see the context of teaching and learning in quite contrasting ways. For example, two departments were described as follows:

> *Applied Science.* The process of learning is seen in a very formal way. Lectures and classes are more important than individual study as a means of learning; staff are somewhat aloof and they are un-prepared to tackle topics at a level appropriate to students' current understanding. But there are close and cooperative relationships between students with reference to their work, and the students think that their lecturers are prepared to take their suggestions into account when they are planning courses. The goals and standards set are perfectly clear; students 'know where they are going'; the vocational relevance of the courses is high. But the workload students have to deal with is greater than in any of the other departments; 75% of the students think that there is too much work to get through.

> *Arts (1).* In this department the courses are thought to bear little or no relationship to students' future careers. The workload is not too high, but students would like more time to spend on their own interests. The goals of the students' work are unambiguous, but students find it hard to know how closely they are reaching them; in this respect, the context here is similar to the natural science department. Relationships with staff are informal (although less so than in social science), and the lecturers are very willing to give help with study problems. Students have a lot of choice over the methods and content of their studies. Of all the departments, this one most requires students to learn by means of individual study; only 4% of the students think that you can learn nearly everything you need to know from the classes and lectures, without doing much further reading (in contrast to the applied science department, where 61% of students agree with this statement).

**282**

These 'departmental evaluations', being composite pictures, may appear to contain some inconsistencies that could usefully be clarified in discussion with students. Nevertheless, they do indicate striking differences along the dimensions explored by the questionnaire:

Staff commitment to teaching
Helpfulness of staff relationships with students
Social climate
Clarity of goals and standards
Vocational relevance
Formality of teaching methods
Freedom in learning
Workload

In fact, each of the departments appears to have its own distinctive 'educational ethos' or 'learning climate'. Students' expectations, attitudes, and approaches to learning will be very dependent on which department they happen to be working in. Consequently, for example, a teacher introducing certain innovations into his course would find them received very differently according to whether his students were from, say, Applied Science or from Arts (1). In short, we may be unable to benefit fully from the evaluation of an individual course unless we appreciate the wider (departmental or even institutional) context within which our students feel themselves to be operating.

## Using evaluation data

It is time we reminded ourselves of the ultimate questions in evaluation: 'So what? How are we to use the data so gained?' I have suggested that the aim is to understand the course, so as to sustain it, develop it, and, where possible, improve it. Evaluation can enable us to develop and improve:

1. The existing course for present students.
2. Future runs of the same course for subsequent students.
3. Future courses for perhaps quite different students.

The third improvement mentioned above is made possible, of course, by an improvement in ourselves as planners and implementers of teaching. In his book *Zen and the Art of Motor Cycle Maintenance*, Robert Pirsig (1972) suggested that 'the motor cycle you are working on is yourself'. So we might postulate a similar identity and parallel growth between a teacher and the what and how of his teaching. As a college teacher himself, Pirsig would no doubt agree.

The distinction between improvement types 1 and 2 above is marked in the terminology *formative evaluation* and *summative evaluation*. Formative evaluation goes to improve the *existing* course while summative evaluation, being formulated only at the end of a course—summing up its strengths and weaknesses—can normally improve *subsequent* versions of the course only. However, there is perhaps one form of summative evaluation that can contribute educationally to the course being evaluated. This may occur when we involve students in evaluating the course in its closing phases. There is much to be said for this practice, both for social and for pedagogic reasons. It can both deepen the learning achieved during the course and also, especially when the course has been lengthy, teach our students much about managing boundaries between one phase of their lives and the next. Among many other intriguing thoughts about the dynamics of teaching and learning on a course, John Broadbent (1977) suggests that 'the function of evaluation is not so much to chalk up marks for either student or tutor, as to give them both the chance to set the past in a realistic light and so release themselves into the future'. Summative evaluation may address such questions as:

- Did the course attract enough students?
- Were they sufficiently qualified?
- Did enough of them last the course?
- Was the standard high enough?
- Was the course cost-effective?
- Were the students satisfied?
- Were the teachers satisfied?
- Were other (which?) 'interested parties' satisfied?
- What needs to be changed?

One big danger in responding to evaluation data lies in being so bowled over by the sheer volume of diverse information that one sees only those items that confirm what one wants to do to the course anyway. This can be guarded against to some extent by keeping the log-book systematically and by having regular discussions with other evaluators who may see things differently from oneself.

Yet another danger lies in being over-impressed by certain feedback because it happens to have been given in a particularly energetic way. A course team member may come to a meeting saying 'I've just returned from summer school and the tutors/students there had some great ideas for improving Unit Three!' Which may be all very well, but first one must check whether Unit Three needs improving and, even if it does, whether another group of tutors/students might not have come up with different but equally valid suggestions. A third danger, closely related to the last, is of responding too fast or too drastically to evaluation data. Major changes are best made slowly over a cycle of several courses. A change from, say, lecture-based teaching to Keller Plan might be best done gradually with one being phased out while the other is being phased in, allowing the best aspects of the old to protect against the teething troubles of the new.

To conclude, let me give two examples of the kinds of improvement that might be based on evaluation findings. The first is a set of recommendations compiled for a course by my colleague David Hawkridge:

| *Evaluation findings* | *Recommendations for course changes* |
|---|---|
| 1. 40% of students consider workload on Lessons 3 and 4 to be at least 50% greater than for other lessons. | Remove the exercise on p. 64. Eliminate items (c) and (f) from the reading list. |
| 2. 30% of students report that local resources are not available for carrying out the mini-project in Lesson 7. | Replace the mini-project with an essay so that no students are placed at this kind of disadvantage. |
| 3. 52% of students do not find the tapes for Lesson 3 to be useful. | Change the third assignment so that it is based on both the printed material and tapes, or eliminate tapes, or revise tapes so that they are more useful. |
| 4. Students (12%) want additional material on the mathematical aspects of Lesson 9. | Recommend appropriate remedial text if available, *or* prepare suitable material. |
| 5. Academic colleagues (5) want inclusion of alternative material to counter allegations of bias in Lesson 9. | Do not alter materials. Include a summary of their allegations. Add an alternative text to list of recommended books. |

**285**

6. 70% of students want fewer assignments.

Replace the project with an essay (see 2 above) and replace essay C with a quiz-type test, self-marked.

7. Less than 30% of students tackled either of the two integrative, 'course-as-a-whole' questions in the examination; and marks on those two questions averaged 20% below those gained on the questions of more limited scope.

Make the tackling of one integrative question compulsory in the examination; re-write final section of last lesson so as to give students practice in reviewing course to establish overarching principles and general insights.

Many such examples of how evaluation through student feedback has led to significant changes in course materials and teaching methods are given in Nathenson and Henderson (1980). The second example is an extended extract from a lengthy report by Will Bridge (1977) of the evaluation of a self-paced university course in particle mechanics:

The outstanding problems in the initial trial in 1972/3 had been the hurried and crowded nature of the test sessions, the students' slow overall progress which resulted from this, and the lack of a steady routine for them to keep to. To tackle the first problem, it was decided to use a larger classroom (seating approximately 50 students), and to try using fast students on the course to test their colleagues on those units the fast students had passed. The problem of slow progress was tackled by fixing deadlines for passing each of a minimum number of eight units throughout the course. A course-work mark scheme was arranged so that students were given one mark (equivalent to just less than one percent in the final grading) for being a 'tester', and one mark for each test passed before a deadline.

Another change was made to the course for 1974. The units were re-arranged in a branching pattern, so that after a student had covered two introductory units, he was given some freedom as to which units he studied. This change was partly because the needs of the electrical engineers differed somewhat from those of the physical scientists, and partly because it was thought that different students might choose different sequences through the course.

With these changes the course was re-run in 1974. The staffing continued at the same level, but was supplemented by between two and four student testers employed at any one period. There were a number of improvements. A majority of the students completed at least the core of eight units, and there was no drop-off in attendance over the two terms. This time I was the evaluator. I interviewed one third of the students, and looked for the reasons for these improvements. Overall, it seemed that the guidance the deadline provided did help students, particularly the weaker ones, to work steadily. They were also influenced by the (small) credit given for this.

It emerged from two questionnaires that, although throughout the year the student testers were found to be approachable and adequately knowledgeable, early on in the year they had not been sure about exactly what to do. For example, they did not know whether or not to accept correct answers which were not got by the same means as the answers provided by the model solutions, and they were not sure whether or not verbal explanations of written answers could be accepted. Some of the testers learnt by experience what to do, and in consequence became more acceptable.

The branching pattern was popular, although many chose the same sequence as the previous linear one.

However, there were still problems. Complaints about the workload continued, now coming also from weaker students who had previously dropped out. Also, students were still not convinced that they thoroughly understood units they had passed, some thinking the test questions not deep enough, and others thinking that tests did not cover all of each unit.


The evaluation and improvement continued year by year. Some intended improvements turned out to have the opposite effect, e.g., giving students extra credit for passing units regularly may have been responsible for the cheating that took place on some tests. After the fourth running of the course, Will Bridge was able to say 'although no major improvements are planned at the moment, I can't believe that there won't be any!'

Reading Will Bridge's report again prompts two final points worth making about evaluation. The first is that I may have been unduly stressing the first running of the course. But it would be dangerous to think that because you have evaluated and improved during the first run, everything thereafter will go like clockwork. The subject-matter may change; the students will be different; new tutors may join the course and want some scope to do things their way. All such factors and many others will interact to make the course a different experience each time it runs. In terms of our earlier metaphor, your ship will never make the same voyage twice. Hence by 'continuous' monitoring, I mean monitoring throughout the life—or do I mean lives?—of the course.

The second final point that the article suggests is this: when you have evaluated and improved your course, why not write up your experiences as a case study? Many educational journals are interested in such papers. (A few are mentioned in the references section at the end of this book.) At the very least it would be another item for your publication list. And, at best, you could think of yourself contributing not just to the improvement of your present and future courses, and to your own professional development, but also to those of other teachers (perhaps in quite different subjects) whose ideas and enthusiasm about evaluation may be stimulated by the traveller's tales you bring back from your own voyages.

# References

Abercrombie, M. L. J. (1969) *The Anatomy of Judgement*, Hutchinson, London (first published 1960).

Abercrombie, M. L. J. (1974) *Aims and Techniques of Group Teaching*, Society for Research into Higher Education, London.

Adamson, H. and Mercer, F. V. (1970) 'A new approach to undergraduate biology. II. Kits and the open laboratory for internal students', *Journal of Biological Education*, vol. 4, pp. 167–76.

Allen, P. S. (1978) 'Developing a remedial Keller Plan course', *Studies in Higher Education*, vol. 3, no. 2.

Baume, A. D. and Jones, B. (1974) *Education by Objectives*, North East London Polytechnic, London.

Beard, R. (1979) *Teaching and Learning in Higher Education*, 3rd edn, Penguin, London.

Beard, R., Bligh, D., and Harding, A. (1978) *Research into Teaching Methods in Higher Education*, 4th edn, Society for Research into Higher Education, Guildford.

Beard, R. and Senior, I. (1980) *Motivating Students*, Routledge and Kegan Paul, London.

Beaty, E. (1978) 'The student study contract'. Paper presented at 4th International Conference on Higher Education, University of Lancaster.

Becker, H. S., Geer, B., and Hughes, E. C. (1968) *Making the Grade: The Academic Side of College Life*, Wiley, New York.

Bennet, R. (ed.) (1974) *First Class Answers in History*, Weidenfeld and Nicholson, London.

Berelson, B. R. (1952) *Content Analysis in Communication Research*, Free Press, Glencoe, Illinois.

Bishop, A. (1971) 'Mathematics' in *Disciplines of the Curriculum*, R. Whitfield (ed.), McGraw-Hill, Maidenhead, (1971).

Black, P. J. (1969) 'University examinations', *Physics Education*, vol. 3, no. 2.

Bligh, D. (1972) *What's the Use of Lectures?*, Penguin, London.

Bligh, D., Ebrahim, G. J., Jaques, D., and Warren Piper, D. (1975) *Teaching Students*, Exeter University Teaching Services.

Bloom, B. S. (ed.) (1956) *Taxonomy of Educational Objectives: Cognitive Domain*, McKay, New York.

Brew, A. and McCormick, B. (1979) 'Student learning and an independent study course' in special issue of *Higher Education*, vol. 8, 1979, pp. 429–41.

Brickell, H. M. (1969) 'Appraising the effects of innovations in local schools' in *Educational Evaluation: New Roles, New Means*, R. W. Tyler (ed.), (68th Yearbook of the National Society for the Study of Education) University of Chicago Press.

Bridge, W. (1977) 'Changes in a self-paced course' in *Individual Study in Undergraduate Science*, W. Bridge and L. Elton (eds), Heinemann, London.

Bridge, W. (1978) *Course Evaluation Package*, Joint Board of Clinical Nursing Studies, London.

Bridge, W. and Elton, L. (eds) (1977) *Individual Study in Undergraduate Science*, Heinemann, London.

Broadbent, J. (1977) 'The management of teaching' in *New Universities Quarterly*, Autumn 1977, pp. 421–57.

Brown, G. (1978) *Lecturing and Explaining*, Methuen, London.

Bruner, J. S. (1964) 'Some theorems on instruction illustrated with reference to mathematics' in *Theories of Learning and Instruction*, R. Hilgard (ed.), The 63rd Yearbook of the National Society for the Study of Education, University of Chicago Press.

Buzan, T. (1973) *Use your Head*, BBC Publications, London.

Cantor, N. (1972) *Dynamics of Learning*, Agathon, New York, (first published 1946).

Carney, T. F. (1972) *Content Analysis: A Technique for Systematic Interence from Communications*, Batsford, London.

Carroll, J. B. (1974) 'Words, meanings and concepts', *Harvard Educational Review*, vol. 34, pp. 178–202.

Carver, R. P. (1972) 'Speed readers don't read—they skim' in *Psychology Today*, August, 1972.

Cashdan, A. (1971) *Learning Styles*, Unit 1 of Course E281 (Personality Growth and Learning) Open University Press, Milton Keynes, p. 10.

Clarke, J. and Leedham, J. (eds) (1976) *Aspects of Educational Technology X*, Kogan Page, London.

Coffey, J. (1978) *Development of an Open Learning System in Higher Education*, Council for Educational Technology, London.

Cole, H. P. (1972) *Process Education*, Educational Technology Publications, Englewood Cliffs, New Jersey.

Cornwall, M. G. (1976) 'Student-directed project-centred study: an approach to the truly individual curriculum' in *Aspects of Educational Technology X*, J. Clarke and J. Leedham (eds), Kegan Page, London, 1976.

Cowan, J. (1978) 'Freedom in the selection of course content: A case study of a course without a syllabus', *Studies in Higher Education*, vol. 3, no. 2.

Cowell, B. (1972) 'Who's for exams', letter in *The Times Higher Education Supplement*, 16 June, 1972.

Crick, M. (1980) 'Course teams: myth and actuality' in *Distance Education*, vol. 1, no. 2, pp. 127–41.

Dahlgren, L. O. (1978) 'Qualitative differences in conceptions of basic principles in Economics'. Paper presented at the 4th International Conference on Higher Education, University of Lancaster.

Dahlgren, L. O. and Marton, F. (1978) 'Students' conceptions of subject-matter: an aspect of learning and teaching in higher education', *Studies in Higher Education*, vol. 3, no. 1.

Daly, D. W. and Dunn, W. R. (1976) 'An alternative approach to learning in undergraduate mathematics' in *Aspects of Educational Technology X*, J. Clarke and J. Leedham (eds), Kogan Page, London, 1976.

Diederich, P. (1969) *Short-Cut Statistics for the Teacher*, Educational Testing Service, Princeton, New Jersey.

Dixon, J. (1972) *Growth through English*, Oxford University Press, London.

Duchastel, P. (1976) ' "TAD 292—Art and Environment" and its challenge to educational technology', *Programmed Learning and Educational Technology*, vol. 113, no. 4, pp. 61–66.

Ebel, R. L. (1973) Encyclopedia of Educational Research, Macmillan, London.

Economic History Review (1963) vol. 16, August, pp. 119–46.

Edwards, D. (1979) 'A study of the reliability of tutor-marked assignments in the Open University' in *Assessment in Higher Education*, vol. 5, no. 1, December, pp. 16–44.

Eggleston, J. (1971) 'Biology' in *Disciples of the Curriculum*, R. Whitfield (ed.), McGraw-Hill, Maidenhead.

Elkan, W. (1974) 'Bringing economics back to earth', *The Times Higher Education Supplement*, 13 December 1974, p. 13.

Entwistle, N. and Hounsell, D. (eds) (1975) *How Students Learn*, University of Lancaster Institute for Post-Compulsory Education, Lancaster.

Eraut, M., Goad, L., and Smith, G. (1975*b*) *The Analysis of Curriculum Materials*, University of Sussex.

Eraut, M., Mackenzie, N., and Papps, I. (1975*a*) 'The mythology of educational development: reflections on a three-year study of economics teaching', *British Journal of Educational Technology*, vol. 6, no. 3, October, pp. 20–34.

Falk, B. (1967) 'The use of student evaluation' in *The Australian University*, vol. 5, no. 2, pp. 109–21.

Farnes, N. (1976) 'Student-centred learning', *British Journal of Educational Technology*, vol. 7, no. 1, pp. 61–65.

Fitts, P. M. and Jones, R. E. (1947) 'Plot error experiences in operating aircraft controls and psychological aspects of instrument display', reprinted in *Selected Papers in Human Factors and the Design and Use of Control Systems*, H. W. Sinaiko (ed.), Dover, New York, 1961.

Flanagan, J. C. (1954) 'The critical incident technique', *Psychological Bulletin*, vol. 51, pp. 327–58.

Flood-Page, C. (1974) *Student Evaluation of Teaching: The American Experience*, Society for Research into Higher Education, London.

Forrest, G. M. (1974) 'The presentation of results', in *Techniques and Problems of Assessment*, H. E. Macintosh (ed.), Arnold, London, pp. 197–207.

Fritts, H. C. (1966) 'Growth-rings of trees: their correlation with climate', *Science*, 25 November 1966, 154, pp. 973–9.

Gagné, R. M. (1965) *The Conditions of Learning* (2nd edn 1970), Holt, Rinehart and Winston, New York.

Gibbs, G. (1976) *Learning to Study: A Guide to Running Group Sessions*, IET, Open University, Milton Keynes.

Gibbs, G., Morgan, A., and Taylor, L. (1980a) *Understanding Why Students Don't Learn*, IET, Open University, Milton Keynes.

Gibbs, G., Morgan, A., and Taylor, L. (1980b) *An Example of the Quality of Students' Understanding: Initial Conceptions of Psychology*, IET, Open University, Milton Keynes.

Gilbert, T. F. (1962) 'Mathetics: the technology of education', *Journal of Mathetics*, vol. 1; reprinted as supplement to *Recall*, Longman, London 1970.

Goldschmid, B. and Goldschmid, M. L. (1976) 'Peer teaching in higher education: a review', *Higher Education*, vol. 5, pp. 9–33.

Goodyear, M. (1976) *On Student Motivation*, IET, Open University, Milton Keynes.

Green, B. (1979) 'Flexistudy—further education college-based distance learning with face-to-face tutorials', *Aspects of Educational Technology XIII*, G. T. Page and Q. Whitlock (eds.), Kogan Page, London, pp. 94–6.

Gribble, J. H. (1970) 'Pandora's box: the affective domain of educational objectives', *Journal of Curriculum Studies*, pp. 11–24.

Grugeon, D. (ed.) (1973) *Teaching by Correspondence*, Open University, Milton Keynes.

Hamilton, D., Jenkins, D., King, C., Macdonald, B., and Parlett, M. (1977) *Beyond the Numbers Game: A Reader in Educational Evaluation*, Macmillan, London.

Hanfling, O. (1978) *Uses and Abuses of Argument*, Units 2B and 9 of Course A101, Open University, Milton Keynes.

Harris, N. D. C. (1979) *Preparing Educational Materials*, Croom Helm, London.

Harrison, R. and Hopkins, R. (1967) 'The design of cross-cultural training: an alternative to the university model', *Journal of Applied Behavioural Science*, vol. 3, no. 4, pp. 431–60.

HE (1979) Special issue of *Higher Education*, vol. 8, devoted to papers on 'Student learning in its natural setting'.

Henderson, E. S. *et al.* (1980) *Developmental Testing for Credit: An Account of Open University Experience 1976–1979*, IET, Open University, Milton Keynes.

Henry, J. (1978) *The Project Report*, vol. 1, IET, Open University, Milton Keynes.

Hill, W. F. (1969) *Learning Thru Discussion*, Sage, Beverly Hills, California.

Hills, P. J. (1976) *The Self-teaching Process in Higher Education*, Croom Helm, London.

Hinton, D. (1973) 'A team work graduate profile to replace the grading sieve', *The Times Higher Education Supplement*, 20 April.

Hirst, K. and Biggs, N. (1969) 'Undergraduate projects in mathematics', *Educational Studies in Mathematics*, vol. 1, no. 3, pp. 255–8.

Hirst, P. H. (1968) 'The contribution of philosophy to the study of the curriculum' in *Changing the Curriculum*, J. F. Kerr (ed.), University of London Press, London.

Hirst, P. H. and Peters, R. S. (1970) *The Logic of Education*, Routledge and Kegan Paul, London.

Hogg, D. R. (1967) 'The use of programmed learning with second year university students' in *Aspects of Educational Technology I*, D. Unwin and J. Leedham (eds), Methuen, London.

Holderness, G. (1973) 'Those anecdotes can be relevant', Letter to Open University newspaper *Sesame*, vol. 2, no. 4, May.

Hooper, R. (1977) *National Development Programme in Computer Assisted Learning: Final Report of the Director*, Council for Educational Technology, London.

Horowitz, M. J. (1964) *Educating Tomorrow's Doctors*, Meredith, New York.

Hudson, L. (1970) *Frames of Mind*, Penguin, London.

Hughes, E. C., Becker, H. S., and Geer, B. (1958) 'Student culture and academic effort', *Harvard Educational Review*, vol. 28, Winter, 1958, pp. 70–80.

Husbands, C. T. (1976) 'Ideological bias in the marking of examinations: a method for testing its presence and implications' in *Research in Education*, no. 15, pp. 17–38.

Jones, R. T. (1969) 'Multi-form assessment: a York experiment', *Cambridge Review*, 15 November, 1969, pp. 43–47.

Kaye, A. R. and Rumble, G. (eds) (1981) *Distance Teaching for Higher and Adult Education*, Croom Helm, London.

Keller, F. S. (1968) 'Goodbye, teacher . . .', *Journal of Applied Behavioural Analysis*, vol. 1, no. 1, pp. 79–89.

Keller, F. S. and Sherman, J. G. (1974) *The Keller Plan Handbook*, W. A. Benjamin, London.

Kemmis, S., Atkin, R., and Wright, E. (1977) How do Students Learn?, *Working Papers on Computer-Assisted Learning*, Occasional Paper no. 5, Centre for Applied Research in Education, University of East Anglia, Norwich.

Klug, B. (1974) *Pro Profiles*, NUS Publications, London.

Lacey, O. L. (1960) 'How fair are your grades', *Bulletin of American Association of University Professors*, vol. 46, pp. 281–3.

Laurillard, D. (1979) 'The processes of student learning' in special issue of *Higher Education*, vol. 8, 1979, pp. 395–409.

Lewis, B. N. (1973) 'Educational technology at the Open University: an approach to the problem of quality', in *British Journal of Educational Technology*, vol. 4, no. 3, October, pp. 188–204.

Lewis, R. and Jones, G. (eds) (1980) *How to Write a Distance Learning Course: a Self-Study Pack for Authors*, Council for Educational Technology, London.

Lorenz, K. (1967) *On Aggression*, Methuen University Paperbacks, London.

McAleese, R. (ed.) (1978) *Perspectives on Academic Gaming and Simulation 3*, Kogan Page, London.

McClelland, G. and Ogborn, J. (1977) 'The educational design of individual study courses' in *Individual Study in Undergraduate Science*, W. Bridge and L. Elton (eds), Heinemann, London.

Mcdonald, B., Atkin, R., Jenkins, D., and Kemmis, S. (1977) 'The educational evaluation of NDPCAL', *British Journal of Educational Technology*, vol. 8, no. 3, October.

Macdonald-Ross, M. (1973) 'Behavioural objectives—a critical review', *Instructional Science*, vol. 2, pp. 1–52.

Macdonald-Ross, M. (1979) 'Language in texts' in *Review of Research in Education*, L. S. Shulman (ed.), vol. 6, Peacock, Itasca, Illinois.

Macdonald-Ross, M. and Rees, D. T. (1972) 'The design of a university service course', in *Aspects of Educational Technology VI*, K. Austwick and N. D. C. Harris (eds), Pitman, London.

MacIntosh, H. G. and Hale, D. E. (1976) *Assessment and the Secondary School Teacher*, Routledge and Kegan Paul, London.

Mackenzie, N., Eraut, M., and Jones, H. C. (1970) *Teaching and Learning*, UNESCO, Paris.

McLeish, J. (1968) *The Lecture Method*, Cambridge Monograph on Teaching Method, no. 1, Cambridge Institute of Education.

McLuhan, M. (1964) *Understanding Media*, Sphere, London.

Maddison, D. (ed.) (1977) *Working Papers of the Faculty of Medicine*, University of Newcastle, New South Wales, Australia.

Maddox, H. (1963) *How to Study*, Pan, London.

Mager, R. (1961) 'On the sequencing of instructional content' in *Psychological Reports*, vol. 9, pp. 405–13, reprinted in *Contributions to an Educational Technology*, I. K. Davies and J. Hartley (eds), Butterworth, London.

Mann, P. H. (1973) *Books and Students*, National Book League, London.

Mann, P. H. (1976) *Books and Undergraduates*, National Book League, London.

Marton, F. (1975) 'What does it take to learn?' in *How Students Learn*, N. Entwistle and D. Hounsell (eds) (1975), University of Lancaster Institute for Post-Compulsory Education, Lancaster.

Marton, F. and Säljö, R. (1976) 'On qualitative differences in learning. 1. Process and outcome', *British Journal of Psychology*, vol. 46, pp. 4–11.

Mason, J. (1976) 'Life inside the course team', *Teaching at a Distance*, no. 5, March.

Megarry, J. (1978) *Perspectives on Academic Gaming and Simulation*, 1 and 2, Kogan Page, London.

Megarry, J. (1979) 'Developments in simulation and gaming' in *International Yearbook of Educational and Instructional Technology*

*1978/9*, A. Howe and A. J. Romiszowski (eds), Kogan Page, London.

Miller, C. and Parlett, M. (1973) *Up to the Mark: A Research Report in Assessment*, Occasional Paper no. 13, Centre for Research in the Educational Sciences, University of Edinburgh, Edinburgh.

Miller, S. (1967) *Measure, Number and Weight: a Polemical Statement of the College Grading Problem*, Learning Research Center, University of Tennessee.

Morgan, A. S. (1976) 'Learning through projects', *Studies in Higher Education*, vol. 1, no. 1, pp. 63–68.

Morton, J., Bingham, E., and Cowan, J. (1974) 'A free format course based on pre-recorded learning material', *Aspects of Educational Technology VIII*, J. Baggalay, G. H. Jamieson, and H. Marchant (eds), Pitman, London.

Nathenson, M. B. and Henderson, E. S. (1980) *Using Student Feedback to Improve Learning Materials*, Croom Helm, London.

Newey, C. (1975) 'On being a course team chairman', *Teaching at a Distance*, no. 4, November.

Northedge, A. (1976) 'Examining our implicit analogies for learning processes', *Programmed Learning and Educational Technology*, vol. 13, no. 4, pp. 67–78.

Nuffield, (1975) *Course Teams: Four Case Studies and a Commentary*, Nuffield Foundation, London.

Oppenheim, A. (1968) *Questionnaire Design and Attitude Measurement*, Heinemann, London.

Ormell, C. P. (1974) 'Objections to Bloom's Taxonomy' in *Journal of Curriculum Studies*, vol. 6, pp. 3–18.

OU (1979) *Preparing to Study*, Open University Press, Milton Keynes.

Page, E. B. (1958) 'Teacher comments and student performance', in *Journal of Educational Psychology*, vol. 49, pp. 173–81.

Parker, J. C. and Rubin, L. J. (1966) *Process as Content*, Rand McNally, Chicago.

Pask, G. (1976) 'Styles and strategies of learning', *British Journal of Psychology*, vol. 46, pp. 128–48.

Pateman, T. (ed.) (1972) *Counter Course: Handbook for Course Criticism*, Penguin, London.

Perry, W. G. (1970) *Forms of Intellectual and Ethical Development in the College Years*, Holt, Rinehart and Winston, New York.

Phenix, P. H. (1964) *Realms of Meaning*, McGraw-Hill, New York.

**296**

Pirsig, R. (1972) *Zen and the Art of Motor-cycle Maintenance*, Bodley Head, London.

Postlethwaite, S. N., Novak, J., and Murray, H. (1971) *An Audio-tutorial Approach to Learning*, Burgess, Minneapolis.

Postman, N. (1970) 'Curriculum change and technology' in *To Improve Learning*, S. G. Tickton (ed.), Bowker, New York.

Postman, N. and Weingartner, C. (1971) *Teaching as a Subversive Activity*, Penguin, London.

Prescott, B. and Jarvis, B. (1978) 'Continuous teaching and assessment: two stage assignments in a full credit course', *Teaching at a Distance*, no. 12, Summer, pp. 10–25.

Pring, R. (1971) 'Bloom's Taxonomy: a philosophical critique' in *Cambridge Journal of Education 2*, pp. 83–91.

Pronay, N. (1979) 'Towards independence in learning history: the potential of video cassette technology for curricular innovation' in *Studies in Higher Education*, vol. 4, no. 1.

Ramsden, P. (1979) 'Student learning and perceptions of the academic environment' in special issue of *Higher Education*, vol. 8, pp. 411–27.

Reid, R. L. (1965) 'Programmed instruction in University teaching'. Paper presented to the 13th University Congress of the International Association of University Professors and Lecturers, Vienna.

Richards, I. A. (1943) *How to Read a Page*, Routledge and Kegan Paul, London.

Riley, J. (1975) 'Course teams at the Open University' in Nuffield (1975).

Roach, K. and Hammond, R. (1976) 'Zoology by self-instruction', *Studies in Higher Education*, vol. 1, no. 2, pp. 179–96.

Rogers, C. (1961) *On Becoming a Person*, Houghton Mifflin, New York.

Rowntree, D. (1974) *Educational Technology in Curriculum Development*, Harper and Row, London.

Rowntree, D. (1975) 'Two styles of communication and their implications for learning' in *Aspects of Educational Technology VIII*, J. P. Baggalay *et al.* (eds), Pitman, London.

Rowntree, D. (1976) *Learn How to Study*, Macdonald, London.

Rowntree, D. (1977) *Assessing Students: How Shall We Know Them?*, Harper and Row, London.

Rowntree, D. (1979a) 'Writing your lesson' in *How to Develop Self-Instructional Teaching*, D. Rowntree and B. Connors (eds), Open University, Milton Keynes.

Rowntree, D. (1979*b*) 'Assessing your students' in *How to Develop Self-instructional Teaching*, D. Rowntree and B. Connors (eds), Open University, Milton Keynes.

Rowntree, D. (1979*c*) 'Evaluating your lesson' in *How to Develop Self-instructional Teaching*, D. Rowntree and B. Connors (eds), Open University, Milton Keynes.

Rowntree, D. and Connors, B. (eds) (1979) *How to Develop Self-instructional Teaching: A Self-instructional Guide to the Writing of Self-instructional Materials*, Open University, Milton Keynes.

Rushby, N. J. (1979) *An Introduction to Educational Computing*, Croom Helm, London.

Sanders, N. M. (1966) *Classroom Questions: What Kinds?*, Harper and Row, New York.

Schools Council (1973) *Evaluation in Curriculum Development: Twelve Case Studies*, Macmillan, London.

Sewart, D. (ed.) (1977) *Teaching for the Open University*, Open University, Milton Keynes.

Seymour, D. (1968) *Skills Analysis Training*, Pitman, London.

Siann, G. and French, K. (1975) 'Edinburgh students' views on continuous assessment' in *Durham Research Review 7*, Autumn, pp. 1064–70.

Silman, R. (1972) 'Teaching the medical student to become a doctor' in *Counter Course: Handbook for Course Criticism*, T. Pateman (ed.), Penguin, London.

Snyder, B. R. (1971) *The Hidden Curriculum*, Knopf, New York.

Stebbing, S. (1948) *Thinking to Some Purpose*, Penguin, London.

Stones, E. (1969) 'An experiment in the use of programmed learning in a university with an examination of student attitudes and the place of seminar discussion' in *Aspects of Educational Technology 2*, W. R. Dunn and C. Holroyd (eds), Methuen, London.

Stringer, M. (1980) 'Lifting the course team curse' in *Teaching at a Distance*, no. 18, Winter, pp. 13–16.

Stroud, K. A. (1969) 'The development, organization and administration of programmed learning at undergraduate level' in *Aspects of Educational Technology 2*, W. R. Dunn and C. Holroyd (eds), Methuen, London.

Sussex (1969) *Final Report of BA Degree Assessment Working Party*, University of Sussex, Brighton.

TAAD (1979) Three articles: The curse of the course team' by M. Drake plus a 'comment' thereon by N. Costello, and 'Carry on course teams' by A. Blowers, in *Teaching at a Distance*, no. 16, Winter, pp. 50–57.

TAAD (1980) Two articles: 'A one-person course team' by, J. Stanford, and 'Some notes on one-person course teams' by P. Batten in *Teaching at a Distance*, no. 18, Winter, pp. 3–12.

Taylor, L. (1980) in *The Times Higher Education Supplement*, 13 June, p. 34.

Taylor, L., Gibbs, G., and Morgan, A. (1980) *The Orientations of Students Studying the Social Science Foundation Course*, IET, Open University, Milton Keynes.

Taylor, W. (1980) 'Boosting the image of study skills' *The Times Higher Education Supplement*, 3 October, p. 31.

Thomas, E. J. (1972) 'The variation of memory with time information appearing during a lecture', *Studies in Adult Education*, pp. 57–62.

Thouless, R. H. (1970) *Straight and Crooked Thinking*, Pan, London.

Thyne, J. M. (1974) *Principles of Examining*, University of London Press, London.

Travers, R. M. W. (ed.) (1973) *Second Handbook of Research*, Rand McNally, Chicago.

Tribe, M. (1973) 'Designing an introductory programmed course in biology for undergraduates', in *Aspects of Educational Technology VI*, K. Austwick and N. D. C. Harris (eds), Pitman, London.

UTMU (1976) *Improving Teaching in Higher Education*, University Teaching Methods Unit, London University.

Warren Piper, D. J. (1969) 'An approach to designing a course based on the recognition of objectives' in *Conference on Objectives in Higher Education*, University of London Institute of Education.

Webster, O. (1967) *Read Well and Remember*, Pan, London.

Wheeler, K. (1971) 'Geography' in *Disciples of the Curriculum*, R. Whitfield (ed.), McGraw-Hill, Maidenhead.

Whitfield, R. (ed.) (1971) *Disciplines of the Curriculum*, McGraw-Hill, Maidenhead.

Wilson, J. (1974) *Thinking With Concepts*, Cambridge University Press, London.

Yorke, D. M. (1981) *Patterns of Teaching*, Council for Educational Technology, London.

Zoellner, R. (1969) 'Talk-write: a behavioral pedagogy for composition' in *College English*, vol. 30, no. 4, January.

NB: All Harper & Row (London) titles are now published by Paul Chapman Publishing, London

# Index